The
Psychology
of
Democracy

The Psychology of Democracy

FATHALI M. MOGHADDAM

AMERICAN PSYCHOLOGICAL ASSOCIATION

WASHINGTON, DC

Published by
American Psychological Association
750 First Street, NE
Washington, DC 20002-4242
www.apa.org

To order
APA Order Department
P.O. Box 92984
Washington, DC 20090-2984
Tel: (800) 374-2721; Direct: (202) 336-5510
Fax: (202) 336-5502; TDD/TTY: (202) 336-6123
Online: www.apa.org/pubs/books/
E-mail: order@apa.org

In the U.K., Europe, Africa, and the Middle East, copies may be ordered from
American Psychological Association
3 Henrietta Street
Covent Garden, London
WC2E 8LU England

Typeset in Goudy by Circle Graphics, Inc., Columbia, MD

Printer: Maple Press, York, PA
Cover Designer: Berg Design, Albany, NY

The opinions and statements published are the responsibility of the authors, and such opinions and statements do not necessarily represent the policies of the American Psychological Association.

Library of Congress Cataloging-in-Publication Data

Moghaddam, Fathali M.
  The psychology of democracy / Fathali M. Moghaddam.
    pages cm
  Includes bibliographical references and index.
  ISBN 978-1-4338-2087-8 — ISBN 1-4338-2087-0 1. Democracy—Psychological aspects.
2. Democratization—Psychological aspects. I. Title.
  JC423.M6443 2016
  321.801'9—dc23
                                    2015018186

British Library Cataloguing-in-Publication Data
A CIP record is available from the British Library.

Printed in the United States of America
First Edition

http://dx.doi.org/10.1037/14806-000

To Rom Harré:
friend, colleague, mentor.

There never was a democracy yet that did not commit suicide.
—John Adams (1735–1826; Ketchum, n.d.),
second president of the United States

CONTENTS

PREFACE

This book is a result of my lifelong personal involvement in psychological research and practice toward nurturing more open societies. As a psychologist born in a Third World dictatorship, educated in Europe, and with extensive work experiences in North America, I am dedicated to exploring how psychological science can help create more open and democratic societies. I demonstrate in this book that the contribution of psychological research to democratization is foundational. This contribution becomes more significant through a focus on both collective and individual psychological processes. *The Psychology of Democracy* fills a vitally important gap in the research literature and is a companion to my earlier book, *The Psychology of Dictatorship* (2013).

The Psychology of Democracy meets the need for an accessible but critical and in-depth discussion of the role of psychology in democracy for students and researchers in psychology and political science, as well as for lay readers. Few books to date address the psychological characteristics needed to enable a democracy to function (for relevant discussions, see Borgida, Federico, & Sullivan, 2009; Zavedei, 1956). Oppenheimer and Edwards (2012) share my concern with the image of the "irrational citizen" constructed by psychological research, but unlike me, these authors assume that democracy is actually working very well. Other books of relevance (e.g., Bedford & Kwang-Kuo, 2006; Gutmann & Dennis, 1996) are not directly on psychological processes and democracy, or are either "historical" themselves (Kallen, 1924) or dealing with historical trends (e.g., Nye, 1975). A sprinkling of papers relevant to "psychology and democracy" appear in specialized research journals (Bowlby, 1946; Sullivan & Transue, 1999; Warren, 1993), but these narrow publications have limited use for most students and lay readers. Consequently, *The Psychology of Democracy* is the first comprehensive, book-length, *critical* examination of the psychological journey to full or what I call *actualized* democracy.

I have used an accessible style of writing and have explained specialized terms in plain language. My goal has been to stimulate wider discussion, deeper critical thinking, and further research toward helping societies build fuller democracies. Of course, democracy as it is practiced today has many serious shortcomings. Winston Churchill famously quipped that democracy is the worst form of government, except for all those other forms that have been tried. By putting forward actualized democracy, an ideal form of government based on psychological science, I have identified a very worthy goal for citizens, researchers, and governments across the globe to strive toward.

ACKNOWLEDGMENTS

The teachers to whom I wish to acknowledge my deep debt and sincere gratitude, Henry Chambers, Christopher Porteous, Leslie Hearnshaw, and Peter Stringer, are now all deceased, which saves me from considerable embarrassment, because if they could make their voices heard in this mortal world they would no doubt unanimously protest that I seldom followed their wise advice. Despite my intemperate youth, I eventually did learn from these teachers to recognize the significance of the uphill struggle across history to achieve open minds and open societies. From ancient Greece to our 21st century world, progress toward enlightened minds and actualized democracy has been faltering and is as of yet incomplete, including in Western societies where democracy still remains stunted in major ways. Eventually, my former teachers won me over; their tempered sentiments now inspire my life, as I too try to help push the Sisyphean rock uphill toward actualized democracy. Open minds and open societies are monuments carved by such beloved teachers, to whom we aspirers to free thinking are forever indebted.

And thou in this shalt find thy monument
When tyrants' crests and tombs of brass are spent. (Shakespeare, Sonnet 107)

Jonathan Cobb provided extensive and invaluable critical feedback on an earlier draft of this book, and I also received highly constructive feedback from Beth Hatch of American Psychological Association (APA) Books, and several anonymous reviewers. Victoria Heckenlaible and a number of other students also provided comments to help make the writing more accessible. The ideas in this book have also evolved through discussions with colleagues and friends over the years, particularly David Lightfoot, Don Taylor, and Bill Bryson. The initial book project was developed through the support and guidance of Maureen Adams at APA Books, and then brought to fruition by Christopher Kelaher. I particularly thank Christopher for his enthusiasm and encouragement regarding ongoing projects.

The
Psychology
of
Democracy

INTRODUCTION

Progress toward a fully developed democracy has been exceedingly slow and, as yet, is incomplete everywhere. It has taken 2,500 years to move from democracy in Athens to various forms of democracy in Western and non-Western societies today. Athenian democracy only gave political rights to a small number of male citizens, excluding women and slaves. However, Athens held frequent elections, and those with political rights rotated in positions of power and participated in decision making. In contemporary democracies, all adults (felons sometimes excepted) have political rights, but with many years between elections, most people remain unengaged in politics, and those in power can seldom be moved out. As I write, the approval rating for the U.S. Congress has fallen to about 10%, but the vast majority of congressional office holders are likely to be back in power after the next election.

Contemporary democracies have a great deal of room for improvement. This book is part of an effort to bring about this improvement. It explores the psychological processes underlying political behavior with the goal of

http://dx.doi.org/10.1037/14806-001
The Psychology of Democracy, by F. M. Moghaddam

facilitating faster change toward what I call *actualized democracy*: full, informed, equal participation in wide aspects of political, economic, and cultural decision making independent of financial investment and resources.

For several reasons, I strongly believe that democracy is the best form of government and that societies should adopt actualized democracy as their goal. First, democracy provides the greatest freedom of choice and expression to citizens, including the freedom to criticize national leaders, government officials, and government policies. Second, democracy provides the highest level of government transparency. This combination of citizen right to criticize the government and government duty to be transparent ensures the highest level of government efficiency. Third, high efficiency and low corruption are enhanced because democracy gives citizens the opportunity to change government representatives and elect better leaders through regular, genuinely open elections. Fourth, the rule of law and the independence of the judiciary are integral to democracy. Fifth, human rights and the dignity of individuals are upheld better in a democracy. Sixth, democratic nations are less likely to go to war against one another. A world consisting of democratic nation-states would be more peaceful.

Central to actualized democracy is an education system that develops critical thinking skills in the general population and not just a select elite. This education system nurtures and maximizes the blooming of collective talents of all society, as well as the talents of individual citizens. The full and informed participation of all citizens in every important aspect of decision making ensures that political, economic, and cultural policies are transparent and accurately reflect the true interests of every segment of society. No society as yet has qualified as an actualized democracy, although the Scandinavian societies, Holland, and Switzerland have made relatively more progress than others. For a brief time, citizens have come close to the kind of informed, engaged participation central to actualized democracy. An example is the high level of critical engagement among Scottish citizens in the weeks before the September 18, 2014, referendum on Scottish independence from the United Kingdom. To develop an engaged citizenry and make progress toward actualized democracy, attention needs to be given to psychological processes underlying democracy.

PSYCHOLOGY AND DEMOCRACY

The journey from where we are to actualized democracy requires transformations in our psychology—in how we think and act. The *psychology of democracy* concerns the psychological changes we need to experience, the changes in our cognitions and actions that must come about for us to succeed on this journey. My particular approach to psychology begins with the fact that before each of us arrives in this world, society and the larger culture are already here. Individuals develop and take shape within a cultural context. Following Vygotsky (1978), I give considerable importance to collective processes and avoid focusing just on processes within individuals (Harré & Moghaddam, 2012). Thus, a major theme in this text is the power of the context to shape thinking and actions as reflected in the research tradition represented by Milgram (1974), Zimbardo (2007), and many other psychologists (Moghaddam, 2002).

A second major psychological theme is that of the *identity tradition* initiated by Tajfel and Turner (1979). Above all, becoming democratic involves changing the way we see ourselves and how we see our relationships with others, including the leaders of our groups. This transformation involves moving away from *ethnocentrism*, the tendency to view the world only from the perspective of one's own in-group(s) and become more open and accepting toward others. Associated with this change is greater tolerance for ambiguity and less rigid categorical "we are correct and they are wrong" or "we are good and they are evil" thinking. As societies make progress toward actualized democracy, they become more open to new experiences. They also become less unquestioningly obedient and conformist. Leadership style changes from a top-down one to more participatory and collaborative leader–follower relations.

Leadership implies that some individuals enjoy greater power and prestige, and that society is stratified. Psychology plays an important role in stratification. Indeed, debate is ongoing within psychology as to how to explain stratification and inequalities. Some psychologists have argued that individuals with higher intelligence rise to the top in Western and, in particular, American society, and that inequalities in power and resources reflect inequalities in intelligence. However, I argue that although intelligence does play a role in social stratification, the resources one begins with also play a vitally important role. One's position in the social hierarchy is determined largely by the poverty or wealth one is born into. This issue takes us back to a continuous debate in the history of psychology: the role of dispositional versus environmental factors in shaping our behavior.

Psychology is also central to another theme in democracy: justice. Whereas lawyers and judges are interested in formal law (what is on the books), psychologists focus on subjective justice and how people feel, and they think about fairness. In many situations, no objective criteria exist according to which we can judge the justice of a procedure or outcome. For example, should the fine for speeding on a city road be $20 or $200? Should the prison sentence for robbery be lengthier than the prison sentence for injuring a pedestrian while driving under the influence of alcohol? How many times larger than the salary of factory workers should be the salary of the company CEO—10 times larger, 50 times larger, or perhaps 100 times larger? Should term limits exist for all political offices? Should citizens be fined if they fail to vote in national elections? In these situations in which no "correct" answers exist and practices vary across societies, subjective justice takes on even greater importance. However, despite there being no objective criteria to make decisions about fairness and morality in certain contexts, some psychological research and theory (Kohlberg, 1963, 1973) has suggested that people who have reached higher levels of moral development make decisions by applying moral principles.

In some other domains, democracy requires a certain outcome, but the psychological conditions for bringing about the outcome need to be clarified on the basis of research. For example, free speech is integral to democracy: Without free speech, democracy is impaired. However, the successful implementation of free speech requires psychological skills in practicing particular styles of turn-taking, reciprocity, and empathic listening. This book explores how such psychological skills are essential for the successful practice of free speech—particularly true when majority and minority groups with different levels of power are interacting and exercising their free speech rights.

Cultural diversity and the presence of majority and minority groups with different social, religious, linguistic, and other characteristics are common to most major societies today. Psychological research has important implications for how cultural diversity and relations between majority and minority groups can be best managed. I examine how policies such as multiculturalism and assimilation have psychological foundations, and how psychological research helps us assess the validity and viability of these foundations. Also, psychological research has suggested certain areas of behavior, such as tolerance for differences, should be a greater focus for skills training in democracies.

Psychological research also has informed us about how much and in what ways human thinking and action are malleable and can be reshaped toward particular democratic goals. Research on different types of thinking has suggested that, in many instances, human decision making is rapid and implicit, an outcome of long-term evolutionary processes (Kahneman, 2011). Such thinking is often structured by heuristics, hunches, or shortcuts in thinking that enable us to rapidly make decisions. However, although the sheer speed and economy of such rapid thinking can be an advantage in many situations in which fast action is needed, situations exist in which such rapid decision making results in faulty outcomes. One of the issues taken up in this book is the role of heuristics and rapid decision making in voting and other political behavior.

One of the other psychological themes in this book is that of *motivation*, more specifically, the question of whether motivation for self-interest always takes priority over motivation to address group interests. Some psychological research has suggested that individuals engage in *social loafing*, that is, they exert less effort when they have to work as part of a group; but I also discuss psychological research about the conditions in which individuals engage in *social laboring* and make a greater effort when they are working as part of a group. These issues of effort and motivation have to be considered in the larger context, and issues related to how we should measure "progress." For example, should we discuss motivation and effort strictly in relation to material measures, such as gross domestic product? Some countries have started to measure the subjective sense of happiness in society, thus giving psychology a more central place in discussions about "societal progress."

These, then, are the major psychological themes explored in this book as part of the discussion of the psychological foundations of democracy. Becoming democratic involves changing how we think about ourselves and our identities, and changing how we think and act in the political domain in general. Consequently, psychology is at the heart of democratization processes. It is essential to think of such processes as part of an emergence that involves societal and individual level changes.

THE EMERGENCE OF CONTEMPORARY DEMOCRACY

With respect to the opportunity to vote, democracy as we know it today has existed only since the late 1960s. Before that era, in the United States, for example, African Americans and other minorities were largely excluded from political participation, and it was only in the early 20th century that women won the right to vote. Even now, barely 50% of U.S. citizens vote in presidential elections, and voting in local elections routinely falls to below 20% (Sharp, 2012). Almost 6 million American citizens are denied the right to vote because of their past or current felony convictions; Black men are disproportionally and detrimentally affected such that, in some states, about one quarter of all Black men are disenfranchised (Manza & Uggen, 2006).

Taking citizen participation as an important marker, we must question the extent of 21st-century democracy in America and in some other major "democratic" societies. In their study of factors influencing 1,779 important policy issues in the United States, Gilens and Page (2014) concluded that, based on how policy decisions are made, America is an oligarchy rather than a democracy. Important, this conclusion includes policy decisions concerning the allocation of key resources among different interest groups in society. The U.S. president, not Congress, as constitutionally required, has taken the lead in moving the United States to war in numerous engagements in the post-World War II era (Kalb, 2013). Thus, in our nuclear age, when international wars can be especially perilous for humanity, one person has been responsible for leading the United States and many other Western and non-Western countries into war. An example is when, in 2003, President George W. Bush led many nations into the disastrous war in Iraq.

Although the United States and other Western societies typically referred to as democratic have made progress in moving away from dictatorships (see Moghaddam, 2013, for detailed discussion of characteristics of dictatorships), they are still far from becoming fully developed democracies. Increased complexity and size may even weaken contemporary democracies, and rulers may become more removed from the citizens (I. Marsh & Miller, 2012). The countries traditionally described as democratic merely have made relatively more progress than other societies, such as China, Russia, North Korea, Saudi Arabia, and Iran, in moving toward democracy. It is only in a comparative manner that the term *democratic* can be correctly applied to the United States, European Union countries, and other "free world" societies.

All countries categorized by us as democracies or dictatorships for the sake of convenience can be conceived as lying on a continuum with *pure dictatorship* at one end and *pure democracy* at the other (see Figure 1). None of the contemporary democracies, not even the Scandinavian societies, is a fully developed democratic society, just as none of the contemporary dictatorships, not even Iran and North Korea, is a completely dictatorial society. All societies began in the historical past as politically closed and have within them antidemocratic elements that could generate change toward dictatorship (Moghaddam, 2013).

The tradition of categorizing societies simplistically as democratic or dictatorial has had a number of detrimental consequences, among them greater complacency in how we evaluate democracies. Countries in the democratic category are treated as if they are already fully developed democracies, which is far from the truth. India is often described as the world's largest democracy, whereas in-depth studies of Indian society have shown high levels of systematic corruption and discrimination with more than one third of the population deprived of the most rudimentary health, education, and other basic services (Sen & Drèze, 2013). Lack of political representation, grinding poverty, insecurity, corruption, and persecution do not suggest a developed democracy.

Pure Dictatorship  Pure Democracy

Figure 1. The dictatorship–democracy continuum.

Thus, my starting point is that countries we typically refer to as democratic have only made modest progress toward actualized democracy. Unlike critics who see little hope in the future of capitalist democracy (e.g., Zizek, 1991) and who advocate anarchism (R. P. Wolff, 1970), monarchy (Hoppe, 2001), or guardianship in various forms (see discussions in Dahl, 1989), I firmly believe that we can achieve actualized democracy. Furthermore, we must continually be reminded that societal movement has not always been, and will not always be, in a forward direction. All societies are in a state of flux, and there is no inevitability about the direction of future change (Moghaddam, 2013). Although the general trend for most countries has been a gradual move away from pure dictatorship toward increased openness, countries labeled as dictatorships today could grow more democratic, and those labeled democracies today could become more dictatorial. In some cases, the move backward is orchestrated from the top by outside powers, such as in 1973, when the U.S. Central Intelligence Agency backed a coup d'état against the popularly elected President Salvador Allende (1908–1973), which took Chile back to dictatorship.

Underlying transformations in large-scale political systems are psychological processes concerning how people think, feel, and act (Moghaddam, 2002). Political socialization is such that the cognitive styles, relational skills, values, and allegiances needed to function in a political system become integrated within individual identities; they become part of personal and collective identities, "the sort of person" I see myself to be, and the "sort of people" we are.

Although individuals are not passive in the process of socialization, and even in dictatorships people can resist taking on the ruling group's ideology and values, most people, for survival, learn to outwardly conform and obey to a sufficient degree. Behavior is shaped to be functional in specific political systems. Popper (1966) made a useful distinction between societies that are less and more open. *More open societies* are characterized by individual choice, critical thinking, and governments that are transparent, tolerant, and responsive to the people's needs. In *less open societies*, the mechanisms of influencing mass behavior are, to a greater degree, based on brute force and the explicit threat of imprisonment, torture, assassination, and punishments; I examined such mechanisms in an earlier book on the psychology of dictatorship (Moghaddam, 2013). In more open societies, such as capitalist democracies with their enormous and increasing group-based inequalities (Piketty, 2014), the mechanisms of influencing mass behavior are subtler and based more on ideology, and often are transmitted in implicit and indirect ways through the education system and media. Given the present circumstances of more open societies, how can we move toward actualized democracy?

The central question addressed in this book is: What are the psychological processes underlying change toward actualized societies? This question includes the changes in thinking, social skills, and action needed to achieve the "psychological citizen" who is capable of fully participating in and sustaining actualized democracy (Moghaddam, 2008c). Developing or third world societies, such as those involved in the Arab Spring, are confronted by the challenge of socializing "democratic psychological citizens," but so are "democratic" Western societies that currently are characterized by alienated and distrustful populations, including tens of millions of new immigrants. What kinds of psychological characteristics should we be trying to develop within immigrants so that they will move themselves and their adopted societies further toward actualized democracy rather than away from it? This is a vitally important question in the context of 21st-century globalization, which is characterized by its vast movements of people—many of whom originated from dictatorships—across national borders in search of better lives for themselves and especially for their children.

To address these questions and to help arrive at actualized democracy, I introduce a circle model that details the characteristics societies and individuals ultimately must have to become actualized (see Figure 2). Leadership

Figure 2. The democracy circle.

style is at the center of the circle because it affects societal progress at every step of the way. The nine components of this circle are (a) leaders responsive to wishes of citizens, (b) rule of law, (c) leaders removable through popular will, (d) freedom of expression, (e) minority rights, (f) independent judiciary, (g) universal suffrage, (h) meritocracy, and (i) distributive justice. I identified these components after conducting extensive and in-depth reviews of the research literature. Each component is associated with particular psychological processes, and progress to the next segment requires successful psychological changes. The changes are primarily collective, but they also occur at the individual level. These psychological changes, involving styles of thinking, doing, and relating to the self and others, often develop only over longer periods and through collective processes.

QUESTIONING DEMOCRACY

> Politics is the battleground for fights over how to divide nation's economic pie. It is a battle that the 1 percent have been winning. That isn't how it's supposed to be in a democracy. (Stiglitz, 2012, p. 118)

Nobel prize-winning economist Joseph Stiglitz (2012) is among those who have questioned the workings of Western democracies; he has even argued that electoral politics seem to have "failed in Western democracies" (p. x). R. Wolff (2012) went further and argued that we need to develop an alternative bottom-up democracy because capitalism has fatally impaired contemporary democracies by concentrating power in the hands of the few: "In capitalism, the directors are the capitalists; workers are excluded from direction" (p. 90). Although Stiglitz and R. Wolff represent the intellectual force of a critical left-leaning movement, outcry in the early 21st century comes from street-level movements on both sides of the political spectrum. Occupy Wall Street protests the current system from the left and the Tea Party movement rages against the inadequacies of the present American political system and government overreach from the political right. Although the political left and the political right disagree about the solutions, they report feeling strongly that the current state of democracy is not working satisfactorily.

But those firmly on the political left and right are not alone. Many in the political center also are questioning how well democracy is currently working. In a recent talk I gave on psychology and politics to a group of well-educated Americans in Washington, DC, a businessman self-described as "middle of the road" stood up at the end of my talk and seriously asked if it is not time for us to set aside democracy, at least for a while, and adopt "the Chinese system" of government. He justified his question by noting that, 30 years ago, China and India were comparable economically but the Chinese now have pulled ahead: Democratic India has fallen economically behind "dictatorial China." Is the Chinese model not superior? Many Americans echo that businessman's question, seeing too much democracy as a problem (Goidel, 2014).

I have heard exactly the same sentiment from moderate Europeans who feel threatened by what seems to be an inevitable economic decline and a tidal wave of immigrant populations that do not share Europe's democratic values. Some even advocate a solution adopted in ancient Rome: In times of crisis, give a dictator temporary absolute power to steer society out of trouble (Lintott, 1999). The press of corporate globalization also can be associated with these unsettled feelings and enormous new challenges. Pinkney (2005), for example, suggested that

> the extent to which society's problems can or should be resolved through the democratic process [is not clear]. In both affluent and poor countries, globalization constrains democratic solutions, as governments have to bow to the demands of global businesses or risk the loss of investment, employment and goods to other countries. In both, the ability of civil society to perform its textbook role as an intermediary between government and the governed is in question. (p. 36)

The questioning of 21st-century democracies is particularly heated in the European Union, where the economic recession and austerity measures are resulting in severe economic hardship for the majority of people and where many fear that the arrival of tens of millions of immigrants from Asia and Africa is threatening the "European way of life." In reaction is a growth of extreme right-wing political groups, such as the Golden Dawn in Greece and the English Defense League in England ("Briefing: Europe's Populist Insurgents," 2014). During my travels in 2014, I witnessed swastikas painted on walls in rural Greece. Ironically, some of these extreme movements are represented by political parties, such as the Freedom Party in Austria and Jean-Marie Le Pen's National Front in France, that have done well in democratic elections but are at their core hyper-ethnocentric, antiminority rights, and antidemocracy. Under certain conditions, these right-wing movements could help create the political, economic, cultural, and psychological conditions— the springboard that could enable a potential dictator to spring to power (Moghaddam, 2013).

Although globalization is associated with some movements for social justice, through bitter personal experiences in Iran and elsewhere, I am keenly aware that globalization also is associated with the growth of movements that nurture closed, corrupt, and repressive political systems. Globalization is resulting in the growth of extremist nationalist, ethnic, and other movements (Moghaddam, 2008a), among the most dangerous being fundamentalist religious movements. Religious fundamentalists—extremist Muslims, Jews, and Christians, among others—represent a major challenge to democratic values because, to them, the "will of the people" is irrelevant compared to the "truth" set out by God in holy books. Representatives of God on Earth, in the shape of mullahs, rabbis, and priests, insist that only they have the right to interpret the "word of God." As globalization accelerates and ideas about human rights and democratic freedoms spread, an increasingly fierce backlash will come from religious extremists against more open societies (Moghaddam, 2008a). That religious groups may come to power through the ballot box, as the Muslim Brotherhood did in Egypt in 2012, certainly does not guarantee that they support democracy.

The time thus seems ripe for a fresh investigation of democracy, and specifically from the psychological point of view. In this era when global trends are placing greater pressure on national and local populations, political and economic changes across the globe are associated with the serious questioning of democracy (Runciman, 2013) as a political system capable of solving 21st-century challenges. Increasing economic inequalities and the economic and political decline of the middle class in many democracies continue as formidable challenges. Also a challenge is the need to limit the influence of big money in democratic politics (Phillips-Fein, 2009) and the need for stronger government regulation of the financial sector (Barth, Caprio, & Levine, 2012). A focus on actualized democracy as a goal and the psychological changes required to reach this goal help in the broader struggle to meet these challenges.

There seems to be another reason why the subject of the psychology of democracy is especially pertinent now. The rising power on the global stage is China, which is still closer to being a dictatorship than a democracy. The United States is a democratic superpower, but it may have reached the height of its relative military and economic superiority. After this point, U.S. relative superiority will probably decrease as China catches up. The emergence of China and the resurgence of Russia under President Vladimir Putin further highlight the contrast between the varieties of relatively closed and open societies, thus raising questions about why democracy might be the better path to take.

Unfortunately, historical examples exist of societies moving backward from democracy to dictatorship, such as Germany in the 1930s. There is no guarantee it will not happen again, particularly as public participation in the United States, the United Kingdom, and some other major democracies is at historically low levels. Indeed, dictatorship rather than democracy has been the norm in human history (Moghaddam, 2013). As Held (1997) pointed out,

> A uniform commitment to democracy is a very recent phenomenon.
> Moreover, democracy is a remarkably difficult form of government to

create and sustain. The history of twentieth-century Europe alone makes this clear: fascism, Nazism and Stalinism came very close to obliterating democracy altogether. (p. 78)

Similarly, referring to democracy, Moller and Skaaning (2011) noted, "Not until the French Revolution did salient political actors start to use the term to signify something positive" (p. xvi). This important observation raises a number of questions that are central to psychological science and its relation to political behavior in the modern pro-democracy era.

What psychological characteristics are needed in a population for democracy to be sustained? What are the psychological changes required at the individual and societal levels for substantial progress toward full democracy? The goal of this book is to explore these and other related questions about democracy through the framework of psychological science and, in so doing, help to move democracy forward over the next few decades of national and global challenges.

WHAT IS DEMOCRACY?

Democracy comes from the Greek roots of *demos* (the people) and *kratos* (rule), and means "rule by the people." Athens had *direct democracy* in which the eligible voters were small enough in numbers to make decisions by voting. Plato (trans. 1987) wrote about a republic of perhaps 5,000 people. The movement toward democracy in modern societies has involved societies with far larger populations. The U.S. Constitution was ratified when the American population was about 3 million. It has been, in part because of the challenge of what engineers refer to as *scale-up* (i.e., moving from small-scale model to large-scale implementation) that larger societies shifted to *representative democracy*, in which the voters elect representatives to make decisions on their behalf.

The contemporary United States has about 320 million people and India, the world's largest democracy, about 1.3 billion people. Both attempt to be representative democracies. How do 1.3 billion people rule through elected representatives? How many representatives? How are they elected? Do they have term limits, and if so, how long? How do they campaign to be elected? How much money can they spend in election campaigns? Such questions quickly complicate the theory and practice of representative democracy, and, of course, the definition of democracy. Therefore, the following working definition of *democracy* is useful in the context of the 21st-century: rule by leaders who are elected through free and fair elections by a society's full adult population and who are removable through regular popular elections, and with independent legislative and judicial checks, protection for minority rights, and freedom of speech and of movement.

But this definition itself raises a number of questions. First, even this minimalist definition proves to be too idealistic when applied to major contemporary democracies, the United States included. The majority of citizens in contemporary democracies are anything but engaged: So few of them vote in even the most important elections. Many of these citizens do not feel they have anyone representing their views and would rather not vote than give credibility to a candidate. Second, by this definition, there were no democracies before sometime in the 20th century. Before the 20th century, the United States and Western European societies did not give every adult the vote (women and ethnic minorities, and sometimes nonproperty owners, were excluded), nor did they protect minority rights in line with the requirements of democracy as understood in the 21st century. Even contemporary parliamentary democracies, such as the United Kingdom and Canada, do not have a strict separation of powers—the executive is answerable to the legislature, but no strong check on the legislature exists.

Freedom of speech and the ideal of equality of voice enshrined in the dictum "one person, one vote" also have become murky, at least in the U.S. context. In 2010, the U.S. Supreme Court held that corporations and unions could not be prevented from contributing to political campaigns because to do so would constitute a free speech violation (*Citizens United v. Federal Election Commission*, No. 08-205, in Liptak, 2010). Thus, in the 2012 presidential elections, billions of dollars were spent as billionaires exercised what the Supreme Court decided is their First Amendment free speech right: influencing election results through enormous campaign spending (a topic discussed in Chapter 7). Obviously, the vast majority of Americans could not exercise free speech in the same way because they do not have the spending power or access to the dominant mass media.

Underlying definitional debates about democracy are two other issues we need to consider. First, implicit in these discussions is the idea that democracy is superior, an ideal we should strive toward. But if democracy is so wonderful, why is it only applicable to selected and narrow aspects of societies? In some countries, democracy is practiced more broadly. When I lectured at the Universities of Caracas, Venezuela, and Oslo, Norway, I learned that deans and many other university officials are elected for limited terms by faculty and staff. Although the United States is the superpower democracy, officials in American universities are appointed top down, rather than elected. If democracy is superior, why do we not adopt democratic procedures for selecting the top officials in American universities and corporations? What makes sheriffs and judges in some U.S. districts different such that they have to be elected by popular vote? Why are U.S. Supreme Court judges and university presidents, among many other possibilities, not elected by popular vote?

A second issue is the basis on which voters and politicians in contemporary democracies make political decisions: Many voters and politicians make decisions based on inadequate knowledge and, critics say, irrationally. By "irrationally," those critics often mean that decisions are influenced by emotions and feelings, rather than guided only by facts. But are not these same shortcomings relevant in many other domains, from choosing a career, to buying a house, to selecting a marriage partner, and having a child? Surely having a child is among the most important events in one's life, yet we do not ask for tests of knowledge or rationality from would-be parents. Thus, the concern shown by psychologists for people falling "far short on almost every normative criterion" when it comes to democracy (Borgida, Federico, & Sullivan, 2009) is not shown in other domains that are arguably just as important, or even more so.

IDEALIST AND REALIST APPROACHES TO UNDERSTANDING SOCIETY

> Wise men saw that the one and only path to public safety lay in equality of property. (More, 1516/1965, p. 37)

> But when a prince acquires a new state as an addition to his old one, then it is necessary to disarm that [new] state, except those who in acquiring it have sided with you; and even those one must, when time and opportunity serve, render weak and effeminate, and arrange things so that all the arms of the new state are in the hands of your soldiers who live near you in your old state. (Machiavelli, 1532/1950, p. 78)

In discussing the psychology of democracy, it is useful to position this work with respect to two contrasting traditions of examining societies. The first tradition represented by Sir Thomas More's (1478–1535) *Utopia* (More, 1516/1965) is idealist, presented as a goal toward which humans should strive. Sir Thomas More was preceded in this idealist tradition by many other thinkers, including Plato, and also followed by many, including Karl Marx (1818–1883). The second tradition is realist and is epitomized by Machiavelli (1469–1527), who wrote about society as he found it and of leaders and followers as he saw them to be rather than as they ideally should be (Machiavelli, 1532/1950). Whereas More's *Utopia* proposes that private property should be ended and all property equally distributed, Machiavelli saw such schemes as fit only for the realm of dreams. He adopted a hard-nosed approach, giving advice to ensure the subservience of the newly acquired citizens by disarming the additional states a prince captures. Although I present actualized democracy as an ideal toward which societies should strive, I simultaneously adopt a realist approach that most societies are far from arriving at such an ideal, and some societies are moving, at least in some important respects, in the opposite direction and becoming *less* democratic.

Many reasons exist why we in the 21st century could fall into the trap of being overly optimistic and unrealistic about the future prospects of democracy. In discussions about the future of democracy, current developments associated with globalization and the technology revolution are routinely strutted out to argue that everyone in the world is now interconnected, that new technologies have given ordinary people real power, and that we are moving toward a more open and democratic world. This optimistic perspective should be balanced by noting that globalization forces also support an opposite trend: more powerful tools in the hands of those who support closed societies and greater monitoring of everyday lives and control of information. For example, consider the censorship of the Internet in China, Russia, Iran, and other dictatorships. Even within societies that we currently label as democratic, the massive monitoring of social communications and the lack of mass engagement in political life is a cause for concern to those who seek movement toward actualized democracy.

People were not born either apathetic toward, or engaged with, the political events that directly affect their own lives; rather, they became apathetic or engaged through their socialization experiences. By neglecting citizenship training and critical thinking, the education system and the mass media subtly socialize people to become apathetic and disenchanted, to feel that they are powerless and that nothing can be done to change the political system.

Furthermore, it is clear from events during major elections, such as the 2012 U.S. presidential elections and the 2014 midterm elections, that certain American leaders and groups intentionally attempt to suppress voter participation—as evidenced by the unexpected shortening of the voting day in the presidential elections in Florida and some other states in November 2012 (see Hasen, 2012, for a discussion of voter suppression). Voter suppression is just one indicator that democracy that entails mass voter participation is actively discouraged by some sectors of the elite in the United States and other democracies.

A powerful elite motivated to control mass political participation is common to both dictatorships and democracies, although the motivation for it is subtly different. In capitalist democracies, control of mass participation protects inequalities in economic resources. Key indicators have shown that economic inequalities have been increasing in the United States, the

United Kingdom, and other capitalist democracies (Piketty, 2014). Given that people who are rich are the numerical minority and have fewer votes in democratic elections than the rest of the population, the danger always exists that mass political participation will result in a demand by the majority for more equal resource distribution through, for example, higher taxes on the rich.

On the other hand, many individuals could be persuaded that group-based inequalities must be protected and even extended because they too could rise up the social hierarchy and join the elite super-rich, moving from the 99% to the richest 1%. The task of persuading people to accept that every person has a fair—if not equal—opportunity to rise in the social hierarchy falls not just on politicians but also on the educational system and much of the mass media.

Democracy as an ideal, in the sense of people's being fully engaged in decision making about their future, has taken hold in much of the world. But as interpreted by many influential policymakers in the United States from the idea that American democracy is an ideal fit for all humanity, it is not much of a leap to the idea that America should be "exporting" its brand of democracy to other countries, such as Afghanistan and Iraq. Unfortunately, this eagerness to export American democracy neglects the fact that American democracy is itself still in an early stage of development and, indeed, is rather underdeveloped in important respects. For example, citizen participation is far more fully developed in the economic sphere in the form of material consumption than in the political sphere. Some such qualifications seem needed because in other spheres of the economy, such as areas of control over working conditions or shares of corporate wealth, there's close to zero development for most citizens. In America, "choice," "freedom," and other concepts central to democracy are practiced far more widely and fervently in that dimension of the economy—as epitomized by the dominance of consumer choice. Freedom comes to mean *consumer choice*, the availability of an ever-widening range of goods and services offered to consumers. However, this freedom does not increase the shared ability among the entire population to purchase such goods and services.

More specifically, freedom in America often is, in practice, the possibility of spending money through choices; the wider the choices, the greater the freedom is assumed to be. Thus, having 100 varieties of salad dressing is seen as greater freedom than having only five varieties, and having 200 different car models to choose from is seen as greater freedom than having only 10 different models. It is not important that Joe cannot afford to buy a car; the important point is that Joe believes he has the freedom to make money and gain the ability to buy a car and to choose from among the numerous models available on the free market.

PLAN OF THE BOOK

The two chapters that make up Part I of this book examine how cultural and historical factors can lead to distinct types of democracy, and to the psychological characteristics of prodemocracy individuals. The focus of Chapter 1 is the relationship between the cultural–historical context and the kind of democracy that emerges. This relationship is illustrated through case studies of Britain and Switzerland, two nations that have made serious progress toward becoming democratic. But all societies, even those that currently are dictatorships, have cultural characteristics that could, under the appropriate conditions, contribute to democratic growth. This point is illustrated through a discussion of Iran. The main question addressed in Chapter 2 is: What are the psychological characteristics of citizens who actively participate in and support democracy? This question addresses important issues concerning the sorts of people we can count on to defend democracy against threats, particularly the threat of sliding toward dictatorship. The larger context of these introductory discussions is the relationship between globalization and democracy, which is complex and multifaceted (Eichengreen & Leblang, 2006).

The 10 chapters in Part II describe the necessary conditions for actualized democracy, which I collectively refer to as the "democracy circle." I outline the conditions in Chapter 3 and discuss them in greater detail in Chapters 4 to 12. Specifically, Chapters 4 to 12 consider how specific psychological processes help or hinder these components of democracy.

In Part III, Chapter 13 concludes the volume by exploring democratic actualization, which is not an end to societal development but, rather, a point of departure for societies to grow in their different ways. Democratic actualization consists of a minimum set of conditions that need to be met for actualization growth to occur. The democratic actualization of the collective sets the context for the democratic actualization of individuals. It is possible for some exceptional individuals to reach the point of democratic actualization in societies that are under-developed democratically. On the other hand, even in a society that has achieved democratic actualization, some individuals will fail to grow along with the society in which they live.

CONCLUSION

This book maps out the path of psychological progress that societies and individuals need to take to reach democratic actualization. Contemporary societies traditionally labeled as democracies and dictatorships are located on the democracy–dictatorship continuum and have been shown to be some distance from pure democracy and pure dictatorship. Even the Scandinavian countries, probably closest to the pure democracy end of the continuum, have a long way to go to reach pure democracy, just as even North Korea and Iran, probably closest to the pure dictatorship end of the continuum, have not reached the pure dictatorship end.

Although I am critical of the shortcomings of contemporary democracies, and even more so of dictatorships, my analysis is intended to help pro-democracy forces move the world toward more open societies. By understanding the psychological changes that need to take place for societies to progress toward actualized democracy, citizens, practitioners, researchers, and government officials will be able to better plan and implement different educational, training, cultural, and scientific programs that will further this progress.

I

PSYCHOLOGY AND THE CONTEXT OF DEMOCRACY

The two chapters in this section explore the interconnections between two sets of processes or becomings. The first occurs at the collective level, and the second at the individual level of the psychological citizen (Moghaddam, 2008c). The processes I focus on involve becoming democratic, and the questions guiding my exploration are: What identity processes take place when societies and individuals come to see themselves as "the sort of person/people who should and do behave democratically?" And how do societies and individuals come to hold their behavior as appropriately evaluated according to the criteria of democracy?

I begin (in Chapter 1) by examining the concept of contextualized democracy. Our categorization of societies, such as those of North America and the European Union, as "democratic" is of course simplistic and problematic. First, no society has as yet progressed to become a fully developed democracy. Second, the countries that we categorize as democratic are politically different from one another. In examining these differences, I highlight how history and culture affect the divergent paths along which democracies develop.

A transition from dictatorship toward democracy (or the reverse) always takes place within an historical context and upon a cultural foundation.

The different cultural foundations provided by the United States, Germany, Switzerland, Canada, the United Kingdom, and other societies traditionally categorized as democracies have contributed to some key differences in the political systems of these countries. The progress these and other societies have made toward democracy is dependent on past histories as well as present cultures and physical environments (e.g., geographical and geological features; Diamond, 2005). We should expect any future growth in non-Western societies toward democracies to be similarly contextual.

While the first chapter focuses on the collective change related to the concept of contextualized democracy, the second chapter explores identity processes at both collective and individual levels. Becoming democratic involves changes in conceptions of the sorts of people we are collectively and the sorts of persons we are individually. These changes in identity are accompanied by changes in cognition and action, the processes through which we think about issues, the decisions we make, and the actions we carry out.

1

GLOBALIZATION AND NATIONAL IDENTITY

Considering whether to winter on the coast, intolerably wet but offering the possibility of contact with a ship, or to seek some drier inland spot up the Columbia, the captains took the step, rare in the annals of exploration, of taking a vote of the party. Even York, the slave, and Sacagawea, the Indian woman, had their opinions recorded.

—Gary E. Moulton (1983, p. 2)

Among the momentous events in the early history of the United States, one of the boldest and most adventurous was the pioneering expedition in the years 1804–1806 of Meriwether Lewis (1774–1809) and William Clark (1770–1838) across the entire continent—from the Atlantic to the Pacific shores and back again. Commissioned by President Thomas Jefferson (1743–1826) soon after the Louisiana Purchase in 1803 had vastly expanded the size of the infant nation, the Lewis and Clark expedition awakened the American imagination to the North American continent's apparently limitless open spaces and seemingly endless bounty, launched Westward expansion, and stamped its mark on the character of the United States. Afterward, America acquired a distinct destiny: open spaces and seemingly endless bounty that awaited exploration. The quintessential American poet Walt Whitman (1855/1955) wrote, as a poet could have written only in America:

> Alone far in the wilds and mountains I hunt,
> Wandering amazed at my own lightness and glee,

http://dx.doi.org/10.1037/14806-002
The Psychology of Democracy, by F. M. Moghaddam

In the late afternoon choosing a safe spot to pass the night,
Kindling a fire and broiling the fresh-kill'd game,
Falling asleep on the gather'd leaves with my dog and gun by my side.
(pp. 55–56)

One of the most remarkable episodes during the Lewis and Clark expedition was the vote taken by the two leaders when deciding where to wait out the harsh Northwest winter of 1805–1806. The pioneering expedition was in a life-or-death struggle as the small band of men and one Native Indian woman fought to survive in the harsh environment. The vote was truly remarkable, not just because, rather than make the decision top-down themselves as leaders of the expedition, Lewis and Clark based their decision of where to camp on the votes of every expedition member, but because the opinions of a slave and a Native Indian woman accompanying the expedition also were recorded (the votes are recorded in a detailed table, pp. 83–84 of Volume 6 in the Lewis and Clark journals [see Moulton, 1983]. Sacagawea's name is recorded as "Janey," her nickname; see footnote 5, p. 86, Moulton, 1983). The votes of the slave and the Native Indian counted equally with the others, and the decision was made on the basis of majority vote.

How is it that the opinions of a slave and a Native Indian woman were given any credibility at a time when slaves in the existing slave states of the new nation were treated as chattel by Whites and when Native Americans were regarded as savages? What led Lewis and Clark to behave in this extraordinary manner? Psychological research on the power of context on behavior (e.g., Milgram, 1974; Zimbardo, 2007) has suggested that the answer lies in the conditions in which Lewis and Clark, and the rest of the expedition party, found themselves. In the harsh northwestern environment, where the survival of all depended on the contributions and survival of each person, distinctions based on gender, race, class, language, religion, and other group identities were temporarily swept aside.

Psychological research on individuals in different social contexts (Moghaddam, 2002) has suggested that the life-or-death conditions temporarily erased the normative system of American culture as it existed then and resulted in the emergence of a new, alternative normative system that was critical to their survival. Later, similarly harsh conditions would lead to women on the Western frontiers being granted political rights earlier than women in major eastern U.S. cities. In 1869, Wyoming, a frontier territory, became the first to grant women suffrage (McCammon, Campbell, Granberg, & Mowery, 2001). Political development in different regions of America depended on local conditions.

The Lewis and Clark expedition provides a graphic and consequential example of the relationship between context and political behavior

(Moghaddam, 2002). The pioneers were in harsh new conditions that called for dramatically different problem-solving strategies. When the crisis passed, though, and the expedition returned east, social relations among the people in the expedition returned to what were taken to be normal for the civilization of the American East at that time. The slave went back to being a slave and the Native American guide and translator resumed her former life (and died shortly thereafter in 1812). This return to normal social relations illustrates a general point about the contextual conditions for political systems: The characteristics of political systems arise out of the environmental and cultural conditions of society. In this sense, it is accurate to describe democracy as contextualized because each democracy owes parts of its characteristics to the larger historical and environmental context from which it emerges.

This chapter explores contextualized democracy through illustrative examples of how local cultural meanings and symbols shape democracy in particular ways, some unique to their specific culture. Particular attention is given to globalization and national identity, key factors in contextualized democracy. Just as variations in historical, environmental, and other conditions give rise to differences in the socially constructed worlds and in the styles of thinking in different cultures (Shweder, 1991), variations in conditions also give rise to variations in the characteristics of democracies and other political systems (see papers in L. Diamond & Plattner, 2001). The concept of contextualized democracy helps us explore more deeply the situational roots of democratic tendencies and emerging systems. That, in turn, should be useful in considering what policies could enhance democratic tendencies. In addition to looking at differences among democracies, it is essential to discuss the prodemocratic potentials of countries that currently are decidedly undemocratic. Even the harshest dictatorships may have features that could play a role in nurturing prodemocracy developments.

After examining examples of contextualized democracy in the "older" democracies of the West, with a focus on Britain and Switzerland, I consider the situation of Iran as an example of a society in which progress toward democracy has been limited but certain cultural roots exist that could be used to nurture possible forms of democracy. The lesson is not just that context matters in how democracy takes shape but that, even in societies that seem antidemocratic at present, cultural features exist that could serve as the basis for democratic growth. Our challenge is to identify and build on such cultural features. The development of democratic culture and institutions will enable us to develop democratic individuals (a topic addressed in Chapter 2).

CONTEXT AND THE "OLDER" DEMOCRACIES

In this first major part of the chapter, the focus of discussion is the cultural context of two older democracies. By examining the cultural roots of the older democracies, we can better understand how we can identify and build on prodemocracy roots of potential democracies.

Great Britain

> The main reason why Britain is almost the only country in the world without a written constitution is that it has not, for nearly three hundred years, been subject to the kind of fundamental constitutional upheavals which have normally given rise to the creation of constitutions in other countries. (Wright, 2000, p. 33)

Democracy and law in Britain have evolved out of particular historical and cultural contexts that are unique in some key respects unique—or at least unlike the contexts for democracies in other leading Western societies. Part of this uniqueness has been the incremental move toward fuller democracy over many centuries. An essential part of the context in which British democracy began to develop was the Norman invasion of England led by William the Conqueror (1028–1087) in 1066 and the subsequent Norman domination of Anglo-Saxons over the next few centuries. Many among the Anglo-Saxon elite emigrated from England following the invasion, and those who remained lost their lands and offices to the Normans. In addition to attempts at armed rebellion, which mostly occurred in the 11th century and were snuffed out by the Normans, Anglo-Saxons developed defensive narratives that idealized life before the Norman invasion and fed subsequent desires for independence.

A dominant narrative discussed by historian Christopher Hill (see, in particular, Chapter 3 in Hill, 1958/1997) is the myth of the Norman yoke: the idea that, before the Norman invasion, Anglo-Saxons not only had given their allegiance freely to kings and other nobles but that such allegiance was conditional, and the nobility could revoke it if conditions warranted. The Norman invasion ended this freedom of the old Anglo-Saxon world, according to the narrative shared among Anglo-Saxons. The implication of the Norman yoke myth was that if the Anglo-Saxons could throw off their Norman rulers, they could return to the golden pre-Norman age of freedom and justice. Although this narrative had little historical basis and was developed as an undercurrent of Anglo-Saxon resistance to Norman rule, the belief itself contributed to later democratic attempts. (Similar myths have developed in Hong Kong around ideas about democratic freedoms the Hong Kong population supposedly enjoyed under British rule before 1997, when

China resumed sovereignty. During British colonial rule, Hong Kong did not enjoy democracy, but the myths persist.)

From the perspective of believers in the myth of the Norman yoke, the Magna Carta issued by King John of England in 1215 was of little value to Anglo-Saxon masses because it was primarily concerned with the rights and duties of nobles and the king (see Howard, 1997, for a traditional commentary on the Magna Carta; see Linebaugh, 2008, for an alternative commentary that depicts the Magna Carta as having highly progressive implications, particularly for collective ownership). The Anglo-Saxon masses continued to be deprived of basic rights they supposedly once enjoyed. The myth of the Norman yoke became associated with popular revolts in medieval England (Cohn, 2013), the most important of which was the Peasants' Revolt of 1381. The myth also was integral to the narratives associated with the Civil Wars of the 17th century in the British Isles, when politically radical groups, such as the Diggers, attempted to practice communal land ownership (Hill, 1991).

But the Restoration—the period in British history when King Charles II came to the throne—brought the monarchy back to the British Isles, and, on the surface, it may appear that little changed in the political system and formal laws after the "English Revolution" (Zaret, 2000, p. 38). However, on a deeper level, change had come about subtly and almost imperceptibly. The revolution that seemed to yield little political and economic change "produced . . . novel ideas on the political order, ideas that upheld important democratic principles that sprang from experience with using printed texts to constitute and invoke public opinion in contests between rival political factions" (Zaret, 2000, p. 38).

The development of relatively inexpensive printing methods had meant a huge increase by all sides in the numbers of printed political declarations, pamphlets, newspapers, and other such materials (see, in particular, pp. 150–151, Zaret, 2000). The result was an increase in petitions and other means of appealing to public opinion. Undoubtedly, as war tends to accelerate certain types of innovations, the civil war in England speeded up this process. "From the adoption of printing in England until 1640, only a few petitions were printed. But after 1640 all sides quickly grasped the tactical importance of printing for publishing petitions as well as broadsides, declarations, pamphlets, and newspapers" (Zaret, 2000, p. 240). A further motivation for the proliferation of political printed material was that of profit: Printers were eager to increase their market. A broader public opinion meant a larger potential market for printed material and, of course, increased profits.

In this way, a profound but subtle change occurred from the start to the end of 17th-century political life in England. At the start of the 17th century, political debates were restricted to an elite and were kept secret (e.g., it was illegal to report parliamentary debates); however, by the end of that century, the political elite were justifying their political claims by making appeals to public opinion. The changed situation meant that the elite were claiming that public opinion supported their position and simultaneously were trying to shape public opinion through public communications (in line with the dominant and resilient role of elites envisaged by Pareto; see Pareto, 1935).

Another important shift during the 17th century was a new emphasis on liberty of conscience. Oliver Cromwell (1599–1658), the eventual leader of the revolutionaries in England, traditionally has been associated with closed-mindedness and religious intolerance. But an alternative view is that "Cromwell's insistence on liberty of conscience provided a critical foundational point in the development of religious liberty" (Jendrysik, 2002, p. 77).

The American and French Revolutions in 1776 and 1789, respectively, overshadowed the Revolution in the British Isles (1640–1660), so that the overwhelming impression that Britain has not experience major upheaval is reflected in the quote from T. Wright (2000) at the beginning of this section. Because the past 300 years have not seen political revolutions in the British Isles, T. Wright (2000) argued, a written constitution seemed to not be needed. The major violent revolts and civil wars in the British Isles had taken place, and the world had been "turned upside down" already, to use Hill's (1991) phrase, by the end of the 17th century.

A key feature of democratic development in Britain, then, has been its incremental, step-by-step movement. The tone was set by the long struggle of the Anglo-Saxons to gain their rights against the Norman invaders. The roots of British democracy are found in the Charter of Liberties and the Magna Carta that, in 1100 and 1215, respectively, set limits to the power of the king (i.e., King Henry I, c. 1168–1135, and King John, 1166–1216, respectively) and established a tradition of rule of law (Holt, 1992). The Revolution in the British Isles brought more changes in the 17th century, although none was dramatic in the short term. During the 18th and 19th centuries, spurred by the Industrial Revolution, political reforms that brought movement toward democracy in the British Isles progressed incrementally (Conacher, 1971) and culminated in the Great Reform Act of 1832; the Second and Third Reform Acts in 1867 and 1884, respectively; and the Redistribution of Seats Act in 1885. Gradually, further reform acts extended the secret ballot (in 1872) and limited corruption (in 1883) in elections. The most important outcomes of these changes were the empowerment of the middle class and the far greater empowerment of the new class of entrepreneurs. These changes came at the cost of the traditional landed gentry, whose relative influence diminished.

By the beginning of the 20th century, the British Empire was in decline, and a self-critical mood pervaded. Reflecting this mood, the political theorist Leonard Hobhouse (1864–1929) wrote,

> It must be allowed that the principle of self-government is at times aban-doned by those who ordinarily profess it, but as much could be said of every other principle. The errors of democratic Imperialism are an argu-ment against ascribing supreme wisdom to any self-governing people, but clearly are no arguments against leaving people to govern themselves. (Hobhouse, 1904, p. 168)

The role of Britain on the world stage had resulted in the highlighting of certain contradictions between democracy and imperialism. (The same process seems to have been repeated for the United States in the 21st century, as reflected in the case of Edward Snowden, the former National Security Agency contractor who, in 2013, became a whistle-blower who revealed the vast scope of eavesdropping conducted by the U.S. government around the world. Mehta [2013] commented that "Snowden's revelations highlight the moral decline of America. . . . The debate reinstates the most morally prob-lematic aspect of imperialism: rules that apply to the 'civilized' do not apply to outsiders" [p. 11].)

Democracy in the United Kingdom has developed out of a particular historical and cultural context to take on certain unique characteristics recognized by anyone who has witnessed the prime minister's question time in Parliament. The challenge of incrementally implementing democracy continues in Western societies today and is by no means near completion.

Switzerland

> The creation of a multicultural state, and the political integration of different religions and languages without destroying particular cultural identities, is probably the most precious legacy of Switzerland's democracy. (Linder, 1994, p. xvii)

Switzerland is often considered to be a model country (Jones, 2009). A nation of only about 8 million inhabitants, it is surrounded by much larger nations that repeatedly have engaged in destructive warfare. Founded in 1291, when three local leaders made a contract to remain neutral and politically independent, Switzerland since the mid-19th century has managed to maintain neutrality and stay out of wars, including World Wars I and II. Switzerland only joined the United Nations in 2002 and voted that same year to not enter into negotiations to join the European Union. Despite being landlocked and mountainous, and lacking oil, gas, minerals, large areas of arable land, and other major natural resources, the Swiss have achieved one of the highest standards of living in the world with health care and educational systems second to none. But, as Linder (1994) pointed out, the most precious Swiss achievement may be the successful integration of groups with different languages, religions, and cultural traditions. Currently, about 67% of the population speaks German as a first language; 20%, French; 7%, Italian; and 1%, Romansch (the rest are immigrants or visiting workers who speak a variety of first languages). Despite being characterized by linguistic, religious, and cultural diversity, Switzerland has become a cohesive state (Dardanelli & Stojanovic, 2011). Politically, the local *cantons* (regions) within the nation have managed to remain, to a high degree, independent of one another and of the federal authority such that minority ways of life can be preserved, at least symbolically.

Historically, though, Switzerland has been far from an ideal democracy. Women in Switzerland were granted the vote in 1971, decades after women gained voting rights in a number of non-Western countries (e.g., Pakistan, the first Islamic Republic established in 1947). Between 1291 and 1891, Switzerland was by no means an island of peace—far from it—as the country for centuries was characterized by religious conflicts, especially between Catholic and Protestant factions in the 16th and 17th centuries. As in the rest of Europe, the Catholics were more conservative and stood for established traditions, and the Protestants were more progressive and supportive of reforms. A major impetus for reforms was the invasion and occupation of Switzerland by Napoleonic forces in 1798, which brought revolutionary ideas (but not always practices to match). The defeat of Napoleon and the Vienna Congress of 1815 put Switzerland on the road to becoming a more cohesive federal state, but one in which minority groups play an important and independent role.

This historical background led to a Swiss democracy that highly prioritizes the rights of minority groups. Direct democracy means that Swiss citizens use the popular initiative and the referendum to directly influence parliamentary decisions—an important way in which smaller groups (e.g., language, religious, and ethnic minorities) can exert influence. The popular initiative requires gathering signatures of support from at least 100,000 citizens within 18 months. Citizens can put forward a constitutional amendment, which is put to the vote of all citizens and cantons. Citizens also use the referendum to force the federal government to submit particular legislation for approval by all citizens (see Chapter 3 in Linder, 1994, for a discussion of different types of referenda in Switzerland).

Even though Switzerland is small, democratic practices vary considerably across the nation. Referring to the 2,600 Swiss municipalities, Ladner and Fiechter (2012) pointed out that "some of them dispose of a long tradition of direct democratic involvement of citizens into political decision-making, whereas others rely on more representative forms of local democracy" (p. 438). Two points need to be made here. First, direct democracy and representative democracy can be equally effective, but in places where they are combined, they sometimes can interfere with one another and result in less positive outcomes (Stadelmann-Steffen & Freitag, 2011). Second, the diversity of political systems in cantons demonstrates the success small units have had in maintaining some level of independence within the Swiss nation.

Swiss democracy, then, evolved out of the coming together of small units. Each of these units wanted to retain its independence, but, at the same time, recognized that unity was necessary to survive against possible invasion from far larger and more powerful neighbor states. The historical successes of minorities to defend their religions, languages, and ways of life more broadly proved to be instrumental in developing the distinct *double-democracy*, which involves both direct and representative systems and is practiced in Switzerland. Since the beginnings of the nation in the 13th century, the powers of the central authority at the national level have been limited by an insistence that local cantons and ordinary citizens have a direct say in government policies and legislation. Consequently, even after industrialization gained momentum and a modern central government developed in the later 19th century, the direct democracy practices of cantons and citizens put a break on federal power.

Having examined the context from which two older democracies emerged, I turn now to globalization and the context in which potential democracies function in the 21st century (I prefer the term *potential* to *emerging* here because *emerging* seems to imply an inevitability about the growth of democracy, whereas *potential* implies a possibility that such development could happen but might not). This new 21st-century context is different: It entails factors that help and others that hinder democratic growth. The challenge for prodemocracy forces is to identify and enhance factors that nurture democratic growth in societies and individuals (discussed in more detail in Chapter 2).

GLOBALIZATION, CONTEXT, AND POTENTIAL DEMOCRACIES

> Since what you have already heard has covered so many regions of the earth, we shall now pass on and make our way into India to tell you of all its marvels. (Polo, trans. 1958, p. 241)

When Marco Polo (1254–1324) wrote of his travels to distant lands in the 13th century, early forms of globalization already existed. For about 6 centuries, 200 BC to 400 AD, the Roman Empire had forged closer ties across their conquered lands that stretched from England in the West to Egypt in the East. Later, from the 8th to the 10th centuries, the Vikings opened up trade routes everywhere reachable with their aerodynamic longboats.

However, the "globalizations" experienced by the Romans, Vikings, travelers like Marco Polo, and even the 17th- to 19th-century empires of Spain, France, and England are limited and incomparable to 21st-century globalization. The global context in which old democracies function and the potential democracies try to grow has changed dramatically.

Globalization as it is taking place in the 21st century is expansive and new in vitally important ways, and it is having a powerful effect on democracy. However, it is a mistake to assume that globalization necessarily works to enhance democracy and move societies toward democracy where it does not exist.

Additive and Subtractive Globalization

In some respects, globalization serves to strengthen democratic tendencies and, in this sense, is *additive*. For example, globalization involves greater movement of information, goods, services, people, and ideas across national borders. Even in China, Russia, Iran, Cuba, Saudi Arabia, and other countries in which governments attempt to severely clamp down on critical voices, the Internet and new technologies are breaking through some of the government-imposed restrictions and opening windows to the outside world. Greater opportunities to travel also are helping open up societies to the larger world.

However, globalization also can serve a *subtractive* function by weakening democratic tendencies. Two main forces are taking advantage of globalization to advance their own agendas that diminish democracy, limit freedoms, weaken human rights, and generally support a "closed" as opposed to "open" society (as discussed by Popper, 1966). The first group consists of a wide assortment of ideology-driven forces that are prodictatorship. The particular dictatorships they support vary from dictatorships based on Islam or other religious ideologies to political ideologies, such as Marxism. The second group consists of global business organizations primarily concerned with achieving maximum ingroup profits in the global marketplace. The international business community often prefers political stability to instability, even if that involves dictatorships and the suppression of human rights. The international business community is particularly wary of democracy when it involves the danger that the majority of people will vote for increases in taxation on the rich as a way of redistributing wealth in society (Piketty, 2014, proposes a global tax on capital as a way to redistribute wealth).

Divergent and Convergent Forms of Democracy

Associated with accelerated globalization are two different interpretations of democracy with two contrasting interpretations of freedom (see Table 1.1).

TABLE 1.1
Characteristics of Divergent and Convergent Forms of Democracy

| | Interpretation of freedom | |
Form of democracy	Economic freedom	Political freedom
Divergent (i.e., free market)	Unregulated	Unrelated to economic freedom
Convergent (i.e., regulated market)	Regulated	Related to economic freedom

The first, *divergent democracy* (i.e., free market), endorses extreme group-based resource inequalities as compatible with democratic life. In a divergent democracy, the government must not place limits on how much people differ from one another both in economic wealth and in the use of such wealth. The interpretation of democratic freedom is such that any attempt to curtail wealth disparities and create a minimum standard of economic life for everyone is dismissed as "undemocratic" because it restricts the actions of the rich. Consequently, the democratic (i.e., economic) freedom of the have-nots is curtailed. In line with this interpretation, the George W. Bush administration (2000–2008) in the United States abolished the inheritance tax (adroitly renaming it the "death tax") and the U.S. Supreme Court interpreted the First Amendment of the U.S. Constitution to mean that spending money in elections is a form of free speech and thus must not be limited (see *Citizens United v. Federal Election Commission*, No. 08-205, in Liptak, 2010).

Convergent democracy (i.e., regulated market) proposes that freedom in the political sphere must be coupled with genuine freedom in the economic sphere. In both spheres, people must be presented with meaningful choices. Convergent democracy is closer to the interpretation of freedom proposed by Sen (1999) in which freedom from poverty is given importance (among other things). Convergent democracy regulates for a smaller difference between the top and the bottom wealth groups (thus, the term *convergent*), and it requires that the bottom group enjoy real political and economic choices. Only people with real economic resources can have real economic choices, an observation brought to light by caller to a recent radio show featuring a finance guru who was dispensing free advice to the audience about how to manage their incomes and save for their retirement. The caller asked, "How can I manage my income and save for retirement when I have been unemployed and have had no income for the past 2 years, and have had to eat into my small retirement fund?"

Competition between divergent and convergent forms of democracy is occurring at a time when a positive image of democracy is spreading in many parts of the world. The psychological power of democracy is that it has taken hold of the human imagination as a magical solution, as a sacred path to happiness. Democracy has become like romantic love—something the young in particular aspire to, an ideal that many people assume is the right of every human, and a solution to life's problems. Just as many people now feel they have a right to marry for love and that love and happiness go together, the right to live in a democracy and to find happiness through a democracy is assumed by many around the world to be a natural universal human right (e.g., see the research [Doise, 2002] on how attitudes about basic human rights have spread around the world).

Even the most closed communist dictatorships now feel the need to present themselves as somehow democratic: the brutal regimes of North Korea and Laos, respectively, have the official titles of Democratic People's Republic of Korea and People's Democratic Republic of Laos. Additional historical examples of note include totalitarian democracy associated with Stalinism and organic democracy associated with General Francisco Franco's (1892–1975) dictatorship in Spain. "Since the destruction of Axis fascism in World War II, 'democracy' has become an honorific label oratorically affixed to almost every national system in the world" (Gross, 1980, p. 350). Even the ruling dictators in Iran, infamous for their bloody persecution of their own people, force Iranians to regularly participate in so-called elections in which people have to choose between candidates preselected by the regime so that they can put up a "democratic" front.

For genuine democratic citizenship to emerge, though, it is not enough to have truly free elections, a free press, and other formal functioning institutions we associate with the most robust democracies, as important as these institutions are. Also, as shown by the case of China, economic openness does not necessarily lead to increased political openness (Milner & Mukherjee, 2009). Becoming democratic also involves collectives and individuals coming to see themselves as enjoying freedom and choice in their everyday lives, and being able to influence and change their leadership through enforced accountability.

Context, Identity Processes, and Individual Democratic Development

> Village authorities all over the estate espoused their new toughness, and it constituted the firmest inhibition against neighborhood dictators. Zapata and most of his chiefs shared these popular expectations about civilian rule. They had also not lost their sense of who they were— the sons of the pueblo, field hands, sharecroppers, and rancheros. . . . The pretensions they developed were honest, country pretensions. (Womack, 1968, p. 226)

> Social identity will be understood as that *part* of an individual's self-concept which derives from his knowledge of his membership of a social group (or groups) together with the value and emotional significance

attached to that membership. . . . Seen from this intergroup perspective of social identity, social categorization can therefore be considered as a system of orientation which helps create and define the individual's place in society. (Tajfel, 1978, p. 63)

In his exploration of Emiliano Zapata (1879–1919) and the Mexican Revolution, Womack (1968) showed the ways in which identity was at the heart of the changes being attempted and resisted in Mexico during the first decades of the 20th century. The fighting for and against the revolution was ultimately about who they were. As Womack (1968) explained, identity was at the heart of the struggle for change, involving

country people who did not want to move and therefore got into a revolution. . . . Come hell, high water . . . they insisted on staying in the villages and little towns where they had grown up. . . . Other people, powerful entrepreneurs living in the cities, needed to make the villagers move in order to progress themselves. And between the entrepreneurs and the villagers a vivid conflict took shape. (p. ix)

Central to Mexico's becoming more democratic were changes in the conceptions of individuals and groups about "the sort of person I am" and "the sort of group we are." These identity processes involve what Tajfel (1978) referred to above as "social identity" and "social categorization" (p. 63). Identity processes help individuals locate themselves in society, but more than this, in the words of Harré (2003), "a person's appraisal of the social world and its significance is an expression of his or her identity. Of course this is 'identity' in the sense of what sort of person it is who is making the appraisals" (p. xix).

We should not, however, treat the transformation of identity as a purely cognitive change, although cognitive processes are central to it. First, as Tajfel's (1978) discussion of social identity has made clear, emotional attachment is central to identity processes. Individuals come to emotionally invest in ingroups so that they *feel* they belong to particular groups, and emotional ties to groups form a basis for their social identities. In the case of nation-states, emotional ties to the ingroup can lead individuals to make great sacrifices, such as dying to protect and preserve their nations.

A key issue in the 21st-century context is the relationship between democratic identity and *consumer identity*, the extent to which freedom and choice in the marketplace is incorporated into the identities of citizens and their ingroup(s). The United States and some other major democracies have experienced declines in political participation, as reflected by low voter turnout even in national political elections, for example. Only one in three eligible voters participated in the highly important U.S. congressional elections of November 4, 2014—the lowest in more than 7 decades (DelReal, 2014). One interpretation, as noted in the Introduction to the present volume, is that participation and choice in the consumer marketplace is becoming more important and is even replacing participation in the political sphere. Globalization is helping to spread this interpretation of freedom as "consumer choice," and this is a subtractive effect.

Globalization, Sudden Contact, and Identity Threats

A number of transformations associated with globalization give special importance to the consideration of identity development in democracies. Among the consequences of globalization are vast movements of people from different national, religious, ethnic, linguistic, and racial backgrounds across national borders and across continents (Levitt & Jaworsky, 2007). Worldwide, tens of millions of people move across national borders annually, and many more would move if given the opportunity (Besharov, Lopez, & Siegel, 2013). These vast movements of people are motivated by economic, political, and other factors. Collective identity threats often result, wherein one or more groups perceive themselves to be in danger of collective decline and lowered status. In extreme cases, sudden contact—that is, the coming into contact between groups without their preadaptation—can result in *catastrophic evolution*, a swift, sharp, and often fatal decline in the numbers of a particular life form. A historic example of sudden contact between human groups is what happened when Europeans reached the American continent in large numbers around 500 years ago. Thousands of Native American tribes, cultures, and languages were wiped out in a relatively short period. By the end of the 19th century, well more than 90% of the indigenous population of North and South America had been largely killed off (for a more in-depth discussion, see Moghaddam, 2008c).

When sudden contact occurs, minority groups that perceive themselves to be in danger of decline and extinction feel threatened. Collective identity threat is most visible in regions of the world where intergroup relations are undergoing unusual or even unprecedented changes; it causes groups to face the possibility of decline or rise in their status and power. An example is the formation of the European Union, in which the merging of European countries into one large economic, political, and cultural union has created threats for those emotionally wedded to traditional identities of their countries. The result has been the growth of numerous independence political parties that have vowed to get, say, England, France, Germany, or Italy out of the European Union ("Briefing: Europe's Populist Insurgents," 2014). This is a serious and continuous threat to the European Union; to gain support from voters in their home countries, politicians such as U.K. Prime Minister David Cameron have had to adopt increasingly nationalistic, anti-immigrant, anti-E.U. positions.

The sense of collective identity threat associated with globalization has been exaggerated by the growing resource inequalities in capitalist democracies having minority immigrants concentrated in the economically poor sectors of society. Thus, Turks in Germany, North Africans in France, and South Asians in the United Kingdom are economically poor groups that nevertheless pose (perceived) threats to local German, French, and British nationalists because of their non-European cultures, languages, and religions. The situation in the first quarter of the 21st century is reminiscent of events early in the 20th century, when

> critics of the corporation in the United States of the 1930s argued that the concentration of resources within a few giant corporations had delivered the control of industrial life into the hands of a few unaccountable corporations. Yet . . . they had not delivered a system of production and distribution that would ensure national prosperity—as the Depression indicated so clearly. And, on the other hand, the growing autocracy of economic life was not compatible with the values of democracy. (P. Miller & Rose, 1995, p. 436)

This incompatibility between the "growing autocracy of economic life" and the "values of democracy" was because the unelected few were making decisions to shape the lives of the economically powerless masses. Enormous and growing resource inequalities in capitalist democracies in the 21st century have resulted in similar concerns about the concentration of economic and political power in fewer and fewer hands, a trend obviously incompatible "with the values of democracy" (P. Miller & Rose, 1995, p. 436).

In recent years, scholarly attention has been paid to the role of identity in political processes (e.g., Huddy, 2013), social movements (e.g., Brodkin, 2007), and, more specifically, on identity and nation-building (e.g., Balfour & Quiroga, 2007; Neumann, 2010), and identity development within the European Union (e.g., Schmidt, 2009). This work has explored an important challenge in the relationship between diversity and the development of democratic individuals. Mattes (1999) characterized the research literature in this way: "Scholars have been widely skeptical of the prospects of establishing a common national identity and stable democracy under conditions of social diversity" (p. 262). Diversity often is seen to be a stumbling block to social cohesion and democracy. As globalization accelerates and sudden intergroup contact increases, the socialization and education of democratic citizens may become more challenging in some ways.

Thus, sudden intergroup contact is associated with collective identity threats. Globalization is bringing about such sudden contact, but globalization also is associated with increased resource disparities. The concentration of wealth in fewer and fewer hands, and the lack of political engagement by the masses means that the few are making decisions that are shaping the lives of the majority. For progress to be made toward actualized democracy, solutions to this situation have to be found.

Recent Events That Have Influenced the Global Context for Potential Democracies

The collapse of the Soviet Union and the decline of communism have fueled debate about whether the spread of capitalist democracy is inevitable. The (false) argument that we have reached the end of history (Fukuyama, 2006) has gained traction among some politically right-wing groups that are eager to celebrate the defeat of communism and the victory of capitalist democracy. The implication of this argument is that, in political terms at least, change will be limited in the future. Even a focus only on Russia and the Arab States has shown that this expectation is wrong. This illusion that the end of history has been reached also has been demonstrated at the individual level: People have reported that they changed in the past but will change far less in the future (Quoidbach, Gilbert, & Wilson, 2013).

Another factor that has changed the global context for potential democracies was the invasion of Afghanistan (in 2001) and Iraq (in 2003) by the United States and its allies. The invasion of Afghanistan and Iraq was justified by the George W. Bush administration on a number of grounds, one of which was that the West should export democracy to these countries. Although this strategy has been severely criticized (e.g., Beetham, 2009), the invasions did prompt investigations of the possible factors that have prevented democratic development in some parts of the world (L. Diamond, 2010) and of the relationship between culture and democracy (Fish, 2009).

The Arab Spring also made consideration of potential democracy particularly timely. The Arab Spring led to a reassessment of the relationship among religion, culture, and democracy (Stepan & Linz, 2013). The experiences of Egypt and other Arab countries that have overthrown ruling dictators, developed new constitutions, implemented national elections, and struggled to make democracy work—or disappear—in the postrevolution era also suggest the importance of seeing democracy contextualized. In particular, the Egyptian experience and the collapse of the Mohammed Morsi government have highlighted, once again, the tension between Islamic governance and democracy (see Esposito, 1996, for a nuanced discussion of Islam and democracy).

These recent developments add to the complexity of the 21st-century context in which potential democracies function. Next, consider the case of Iran as a potential democracy. Iran is closer to dictatorship than to democracy, but this still leaves open the possibility that features of traditional cultural in Iran could serve as a basis for democratic development. Second, the case of Iran underlines the idea that democratic development can, in some important ways, be different across different cultures. It is simply wrong to try to export democracy from the West to non-Western societies in a wholesale manner.

IRAN

Iran represents the quintessential example of a nation that has experienced a major violent political revolution (1978–1979) that simply moved the country from one form of dictatorship to another. As Arjomand (1988) succinctly put it (as the title of his book), Iran exchanged rule by *The Turban for the Crown*. Indeed, the level of politically motivated killings, imprisonments, torture, rape, and repression has increased rather than decreased since the revolution that overthrew the rule of the shah. The dictatorship imposed by the mullahs soon after the 1979 revolution became increasingly harsh, and the extremist religious ideology used as justification for the regime's continuation would seem to leave no room for openness and democracy. Iran seems to be a case of a fundamentalist religion taking over the political system and suffocating secular freedoms. However, although the tension between religious and secular forces has been continuous in 21st-century Iran, elements of prerevolution Shia Islam can serve as a basis for democratic movements. These elements were highly influential in the revolution that toppled the last shah of Iran (profiled insightfully by Milani, 2011).

Despite the repressive and backward attitudes of the current regime in Iran, four aspects of prerevolution Shia Islam could have served as a foundation for a more open society after the 1979 revolution. If, at that time, Iran had been fortunate enough to have a prodemocracy leader, such as South Africa had in Nelson Mandela after the collapse of apartheid, then the features of prerevolution Shia Islam discussed next could have played a constructive role in transforming Iranian society to become more open. These features initially survived the tension between secular and religious forces in Iran. This tension was evident during the Qajar dynasty in Iran from 1796 to 1921 but became particularly acute after the discovery of oil and the modernization efforts of Reza Shah (1878–1944), who established the Pahlavi dynasty (1926–1978). Religious traditionalists and fundamentalists, in particular, resisted modernization with respect to the role of women because they recognized that changing that role would transform family relations and have profound implications for the rest of society. Milani (2011) pointed out that "in 1963 [Ruhollah] Khomeini had railed against women's right to vote" (p. 407). In a sense, the role of women has become the line in the sand in Iran and other Islamic societies—the determining factor in societal reforms (see the discussion on "The Veiled Solitude," pp. 159–166 in Moghaddam, 2008a).

In the following discussion, I refer to traditional Shia Islam as it was practiced before the political mullahs came to power in Iran after the 1979 revolution. I use the term *political mullahs* to refer to Shia clerics in Iran who have political power but do not necessarily have high standing according to traditional theological criteria. Through their powerful political positions in the dictatorship in Iran, they gave themselves and the clerical members of their political faction lofty religious titles and positions. Unfortunately, since achieving a power monopoly and establishing a dictatorship, the political mullahs have ended the potentially constructive role that religion could have had in establishing a democracy in Iran. Nevertheless, there is value in reviewing the features of traditional Shia Islam that are potentially prodemocratic.

First, in Shia Islam, particularly as it developed in Iran from the 18th century—the end of the Safavi dynasty and the beginning of the Qajar dynasty—each individual practicing Shia Islam was duty bound to select a suitable cleric as a *marja-i-taqlid* (source of imitation). The key point for the purposes of our discussion is that the marja-i-taqlid was freely chosen by each individual practicing Shia Islam; this is a bottom-up rather than top-down process. The practical implication is that an important marja-i-taqlid, selected by millions of people, had strong grassroots support. The cleric selected as marja-i-taqlid would detail how one would live everyday life. For example, from childhood in Iran, I witnessed practicing Shia Muslims consulting with their chosen marja-i-taqlid on a vast variety of questions from "Should I wash my hands both before and after eating meals?" to "Should I enter into a business partnership with a foreigner?" to "How should I manage my jealous second wife?" The important marja-i-taqlid typically publish *risala* (detailed guides) for everyday living and now have websites and chat rooms through which followers can ask questions and obtain detailed guidance about how to live correctly as a Shia Muslim.

Second, practicing Shia Muslims paid religious taxes to a cleric they selected—often the marja-i-taqlid they were following—in addition to secular taxes they paid to the central government. Again, this was a bottom-up process. A marja-i-taqlid with a large following would receive religious taxes from a number of individuals and would use this tax base as a means to extend his influence. For example, he would set up charities, hospitals, and schools. In this way, individual clergy had a financial base directly from the people and independent of the government or an official, central religious authority.

Important clergy also taught and had a following of students. The religious taxes enabled the clergyman to financially support students who attended his classes. This worked like fellowships that students receive at secular Western universities, except with independence from the state and other institutions, including the seminaries in which they held classes. Given the control of academic activities through funding biases within the military–industrial complex in the West, the financial independence of prerevolution Shia teachers is noteworthy.

The direct financial dependence of the clergy on the people meant that lines of communication between the clergy and the people were strong. Although the important ayatollahs in Iran traditionally had strong ties with the rich *bazarees* (merchants who could afford to pay higher religious taxes), the local mullahs developed close ties with ordinary people in their neighborhoods and relied on those people for their income.

The dependence of the Shia clergy on religious taxes paid by the people at will can be described loosely as democratic. It was like voting in the sense that people paid taxes to their selected representatives. This is in contrast to the hierarchical system of some major Christian churches in which funding is centrally controlled by a pope (Catholic Church), an archbishop (Church of England), or another central authority (of course, some Protestant groups have developed greater local independence).

A third feature is the pre-1979 training of the clergy. In major theological training centers, such as Najaf and Karbela in Iraq and Ghom in Iran, the advancement and titles achieved by individuals were by collective consensus rather than through appointment by a single religious or governmental authority. Because no official Shia Muslim church organization existed, no official body or single leader assigned titles. The *talabeh* (students) in seminaries attended classes at a level they believed to be appropriate. However, if they attended classes at an inappropriate level, students and teachers provided corrective feedback and encouraged them to change their classes. In this spirit, students in seminaries were given different titles by fellow students and teachers to signal different stages of their advancement. Years of study might have led the student to acquire the title *Hojjatoleslam*, which indicated solid advancement. After some decades of activity, a few clergy were recognized as *ayatollahs*, meaning they attained *ijtihad* (they were trusted to interpret the Koran, the Muslim holy book still published in classical Arabic). Traditionally, the title *Ayatollah* was attained when other ayatollahs and a large number of practicing Shia Muslims recognized an individual as having achieved this lofty status. A superior kind of reputation among the public led to this recognition.

At present, the public and clergy recognize a supreme ayatollah called the *ayatollah ozma* (Grand Ayatollah). Ali al-Sistani is now the one Shia cleric undeniably recognized as a Grand Ayatollah according to traditional theological criteria—outside of the realm of politics. He was born in 1930 in Marshad, Iran, but resides in Najaf, Iraq. Since the 1979 revolution and the dictatorship established by political mullahs in Iran, the traditional Shia clergy hierarchy has been dismantled in that country. The Supreme Leader of Iran Ali Khamenei has been given the titles of Ayatollah and Grand Ayatollah by political rather than religious authorities. He served as president of Iran in 1981–1989.

Fourth, the attainment of *ijtihad* through religious study gave an individual the right to independently make judgments on religious matters and interpretations of the Koran specifically. As a consequence, Shia Islam developed with a multitude of voices giving independent opinions. Each opinion's sphere of influence depended on the number of practicing Shia Muslims who followed a particular cleric as a marja-i-taqlid.

After 1979, the multivoiced nature of Shia Islam was squashed by the politically installed supreme leader, who demands absolute obedience. Two of the most important ayatollahs, Kazem Shari'atmadari and Hussein Ali Montazeri, were demoted to mere "Mister" in the tumultuous postrevolution period because political mullahs saw them as a danger to their dictatorial regime. This demotion reflects a harsh reality: So far in the postrevolution era, the power of the gun has determined clerical titles, such as Ayatollah and Grand Ayatollah.

To appreciate the democratic potential of the four Shia Muslim traditions described, we must focus on their role in the events leading to the 1979 revolution. The requirement that practicing Shia Muslims select a source of imitation (marja-i-taqlid) meant that recognized religious leaders were already in place when the anti-Shah (which meant anti-American because the Shah was propped up by the United States) mass movement gained momentum in Iran in the 1970s. The practice of Shia Muslims paying religious taxes to a cleric of their choosing meant that lines of communications between clerics and Shia Muslims were direct and effective. The practice of ayatollahs and other titles being attained through consensus meant that religious leaders had broad following among their peers and ordinary practicing Shia Muslims.

The multivoice nature of traditional Shia Islam meant that disagreements and variations in values were tolerated, and numerous religious leaders represented varieties of moderate and radical Islam. The movement could not have been stopped by killing or arresting one or a few leaders because there were multiple leading voices.

These prodemocracy features of Shia Islam, which helped elevate the role of the clergy in the anti-Shah movement, might have served as a foundation for a more democratic Iran. However, the dictatorship established by Khomeini and continued by his successors thwarted these possibilities. In effect, after Khomeini and the mullahs associated with him came to power, they put an end to the prodemocracy tendencies in Shia Islam as traditionally practiced in Iran. In particular, the multivocal feature of traditional Shia Islam was politically quashed, although remnants of this tradition still remain. For example, when the new moon is announced according to the Islamic calendar, different ayatollahs still report their sightings independently, and their sightings are reported in the mass media in Iran.

Although I have discussed potential contextualized democracy in the particular case of Shia Islam as practiced in Iran before the 1979 revolution, the Islamic scholar John Esposito (2011) made the following points in discussing Islam and democracy more broadly:

> With regard to the compatibility of Islamic beliefs and values with democracy, many in the worldwide Muslim community believe that Islam is capable of reinterpretation (ijtihad) and that traditional concepts of consultation (shura), consensus (ijma), and legal principals such as general welfare (maslaha) provide the basis for the development of modern Muslims notions or authentic versions of democracy. (p. 161)

Elements of traditional Islam that exist beyond the four features identified, as reflected by *shura* (the concepts of consultation) and *ijima* (consensus), could serve as support for contextualized democracy in Islamic societies.

CONCLUSION

The first key point illustrated by the cases of Britain, Switzerland, and Iran is that the historical and cultural contexts provide different possibilities and paths for the development and achievement of an actualized democracy. In Britain, changes starting as far back as the Norman invasion of 1066 resulted in the idealization of a hypothetical pre-invasion Anglo-Saxon society in which leaders were elected by consent. A series of popular revolts were partly fueled by the myth of the Norman yoke as was the Revolution in the British Isles (1640–1660). On the surface, these revolutions changed little, but at a deeper level, the will of the people became relevant in the political domain. Incremental change away from dictatorship and toward democracy occurred based on traditions rather than the adoption of a written constitution. In the case of Switzerland, the resolution of small regional units to maintain their independence, while banding for protection from larger, often warring neighbor states, resulted in a double democracy. Representative democracy at the federal level became significantly limited by direct democracy based on the will of cantons.

The second main lesson from the case studies concerns the future of potential democracies. The global context for democratic development has changed dramatically in the 21st century. In some ways, globalization helps democratization; in others, it hinders democratization. A challenge facing prodemocracy movements is to identify and build on elements of traditional culture that could help in democratic development. This challenge is illustrated by the case of Iran, which might have developed toward democracy after the 1978–1979 revolution. Four aspects of traditional Shia Islam could have formed the launching pad for a distinct Iranian democracy. But these open traditions were stamped out when political mullahs took power and reestablished a dictatorship in Iran. These traditional prodemocracy aspects may be revived, though, to help nurture democracy in Iran in the future. The revival of these aspects would be in line with developments in some non-Western societies (Kim, 1997) that have nurtured the psychological characteristics of prodemocracy individuals (a topic discussed in the next chapter).

A brief discussion of temporary dictatorship is warranted. Healthy critical discussions of a number of concepts related to contextualized democracy have focused on culture (see Woo-Cumings, 1994) and economics (see Przeworski & Limongi, 1993). One recurring theme is that authoritarian rule is necessary for a period to achieve economic growth and enlightenment for the masses, an argument used in the current capitalist context of some non-Western countries, but was previously used by Vladimir Lenin in the Soviet Union (Mayer, 1997). In either context, it is a dangerous and destructive path to take because dictatorship, once established, is difficult to throw off, irrespective of whether it has the face of communism, capitalism, or religion. For the majority of people living in those societies, these regimes—the Soviet Union under Joseph Stalin, Iran under the mullahs, and North Korea under the "Dear Leader"—have all been terrible, irrespective of the rhetorical fronts put up by their rulers.

2

CHARACTERISTICS OF THE DEMOCRATIC CITIZEN

The results, as seen and felt in the laboratory, are to this author disturbing. They raise the possibility that human nature, or—more specifically—the kind of character produced in American democratic society, cannot be counted on to insulate its citizens from brutality and inhuman treatment at the direction of malevolent authority. A substantial proportion of people do what they are told to do, irrespective of the content of the act and without limitation of conscience, so long as they perceive that the command comes from a legitimate authority.

—Stanley Milgram (1974, p. 189)

This is how Stanley Milgram (1933–1984) ended his book that reported studies on obedience to authority—in my opinion, the most important experiments in the history of social psychology. Milgram's studies, replicated in various ways over the years (Burger, 2009), demonstrated the power of authority figures to shape behavior. About 60% of American adults (higher percentages in some cross-cultural replications) with normal personality profiles obeyed an authority figure to the point of, they believed, seriously injuring or even killing a stranger in front of them. In his concluding discussion, Milgram (1974) put the spotlight on the "kind of character produced in American democratic society" (p. 189). I have argued that American society is still far from being an actualized democracy. A more fully democratic society would socialize more fully democratic citizens than those produced by American society in Milgram's day—the kind who would be far more likely to disobey than to obey orders that harm others, and to be generally more prosocial. My goal in this chapter is to outline the characteristics of the fully democratic citizen.

http://dx.doi.org/10.1037/14806-003
The Psychology of Democracy, by F. M. Moghaddam

By articulating the ideal characteristics of the democratic citizen, I am putting forward a goal for education systems that train the young and for parents who are socializing the next generation. For an actualized democracy to develop, we need to develop citizens who are capable of functioning correctly in support of such a society. The struggle to develop such citizenry began at least 2,500 years ago with the first great experiments in democratic living in Greece. The early experiments ended when dictatorship returned, but they still hold lessons for us, and I consider these lessons in the next section. My focus in the second part of this chapter is on "becoming democratic" and the psychological characteristics of the democratic individual: a person motivated and psychologically equipped to participate in and support an open society.

THE HISTORIC STRUGGLE

It has always been my nature never to accept advice from any of my friends unless reflection shows it is the best course that reason offers. I cannot abandon the principles which I used to hold in the past simply because this accident has happened to me; they seem to me to be much as they were, and I respect and regard the same principles now as before. So unless we can find better principles on this occasion, you can be quite sure that I shall not agree with you; not even if the power of the people conjures up fresh hordes of bogies to terrify our childish minds, by subjecting us to chains and executions and confiscations of our property. (Plato, trans. 1954, pp. 83–84)

This is how the Greek philosopher Socrates (469 BC–399 BC) responded when his friends suggested he escape the sentence of death, "this accident," brought against him. Across history, Socrates has become symbolic of critical thinkers who make personal sacrifices in support of open societies. Although the open society of the ancient Greek era differs from our ideas about democracy in the 21st century in important ways, it is nevertheless similar in some key respects, such as supporting the development of individuals who may be openly critical of authorities.

Let's reach back about 2,500 years ago to a time when the brief flowering of democracy in the Greek city-states was fading. Emblematic of this decline was the persecution, trial, and death of Socrates, whose main crime was an insistence that all knowledge and assumptions could and should be critically challenged. Some have seen Socrates as antidemocratic because he was critical of the mob mentality and of some majority opinions, but in this, Socrates was upholding one of the foundational principles of democracy: support for minority rights. He insisted on the right to speak out, even when his views went against majority opinion and were unpopular.

Socrates was accused of corrupting the minds of the young. His outspoken skepticism made him an outsider and a target of displaced aggression at a time when many Athenians were unhappy with their declining personal and societal fortunes. Socrates could have saved his own life by recanting or going into exile, which his friends encouraged him to do. However, he chose to die as condemned, and in this way, made a stronger stand for free and open exploration in search of the truth.

Unfortunately, Socrates was killed, Greek democracy was snuffed out, and dictatorship was reimposed. It was not until the Roman republic almost half a millennium later that a kind of democracy, albeit brief and in limited form, came to life again. In the Roman context were individuals who took a stand in favor of a more open society; one of the most articulate examples was Cicero (106 BC–43 BC). An important insight of Cicero's was that the danger of dictatorship does not lie only within the potential individual dictator but within the conditions of the time (Moghaddam, 2013), or in his words, the "apparatus of kingship":

> You have not forgotten, Brutus, my remarks following the death of Caesar and your memorable Ides of March. I spoke of . . . the great storm which loomed over the republic. You had dispelled a great plague, and expunged a great stain from the Roman people . . . but the apparatus of kingship had been passed down. (Cicero, trans 2008, p. 268)

The letters of Cicero (trans. 2008) provide a detailed and moving testament to the attempts to preserve the Roman republic against Julius Caesar and other would-be dictators. Cicero's letters provide a picture of a complex, nuanced mind that is anxious to prevent the subservience of Roman society to the wishes of a dictator. The republic that Cicero supported only gave opportunity for voice to an elite group of free men; women and slaves did not have political rights in the Roman Republic. Nevertheless, the struggle was an important one. A read of Cicero's letters reminds us of two things: First, long struggles may need to be waged by those motivated to achieve more open societies. Second, although the republic of the Roman Empire was different from modern democracies, the two share the foundational challenge of preventing rule by dictators.

The Roman republic that Cicero supported was fragile and overpowered by one dictator after another until the empire collapsed in 5th century AD. Such historical examples, and more recent examples, such as Germany in the 1930s and Venezuela, Iran, Russia, and Egypt in the early 21st century, demonstrate that societies can move backward and become less open. But even in the context of such backward movement, we find principled individuals, such as Socrates and Cicero, who struggled to prevent the return of dictatorship.

These early experiments with democracy hold lessons for us—two in particular. First, the urge and need to achieve open societies is ancient; for thousands of years, some individuals and groups have struggled to become free thinkers and to develop societies that are open and supportive of free thinking. This deep-rooted psychological need for freedom is like a flame that has sparked to life and even blazed in some historical eras. For the flame of freedom to survive, though, institutions supportive of freedom also must evolve. Second, these early experiments remind us yet again that change can lead not only to more open societies but back to closed societies and despotism.

This book focuses on the democratic citizen: What is the psychological profile of this person? I argue that democratic citizens, a preponderance of whom in a society is essential to sustain an open society, have certain key psychological characteristics that can be, and should be, nurtured. Although I accept that inherited factors have some influence on political outlook (Alford, Funk, & Hibbing, 2005; Block & Block, 2006), my proposition is that socialization processes are foundationally important in the political thinking of individuals. In discussions of this issue, I attempt to move beyond a reductionist, individualistic approach and, instead, adopt a cultural approach that focuses on collectively constructed and shared narratives. This is because an individual-based approach is incomplete (Harré & Moghaddam, 2012) and fails to explain the cultural changes required to move toward actualized democracy.

THE PSYCHOLOGY OF BECOMING DEMOCRATIC

> Democratic politics should be ordered in ways that provide a basis for self-respect, that encourage the development of a sense of political competence, and that contribute to the formation of a sense of justice. (Cohen, 1989/1997, p. 144)

Terms such as *self-respect*, *sense of political competence*, and *sense of justice* are integral to models of democracy and are based on psychological assumptions about human cognition and action. When advocates of democracy make claims such as "people want the freedom to choose their own political leaders" and "people feel better and work better when they have a voice in decision making," they are making claims about the psychological characteristics of human beings.

The vitality of a democracy depends on the extent to which values and activities central to maintaining a functioning democracy are embraced by its citizens and their ingroup(s) and become integral to their identities. For example, does Joe see participation in elections as central to the sort of person he is and the sort of group to which he belongs? A central argument of this volume is that democracy functions best when the basic activities supportive of democracy, such as tolerance for differences, support of the rights and duties of all citizens, and respect for rule of law, become integral to the identities of individual citizens. For this to come about, democratic values and ideals must first become part of the collective narratives that regulate behavior in the wider society. It is through collective processes and collective identity that individuals develop their own personal, democratic identities (Harré & Moghaddam, 2012).

Interest in the cognitive styles of pro- and antidemocracy individuals spiked in the years following World War II. This interest was inspired in no small part by the authors of what became a classic work *The Authoritarian Personality* (Adorno, Frenkel-Brunswik, Levinson, & Sanford, 1950); they were concerned about the serious threat that dictatorial regimes posed for democracy during and after the war. *Tolerance for ambiguity*, a tendency to view ambiguous situations positively, was proposed as a relevant and important personality characteristic for the open society, first in Frenkel-Brunswik (1949) and then by Adorno et al. (1950). Research over subsequent decades has refined this basic idea that some individuals are better than others at coping with ambiguity (Furnham & Marks, 2013; Furnham & Ribchester, 1995) and they thereby have been seen as better capable of supporting democracy. The practical implications of this research has posed that those individuals high on tolerance for ambiguity enjoyed various advantages, such as being more creative in an educational setting (Zenasni, Besancon, & Lubart, 2008) and being better managers and leaders in an era of (ethnic, religious, linguistic, and cultural) diversity and globalization (Herman, Stevens, Bird, Mendenhall, & Oddou, 2010).

Related to the research on tolerance for ambiguity is research on open-mindedness (Baehr, 2011), which involves the ability and willingness to seriously reconsider the merits and shortcomings of a current cognitive standpoint. Hare (1979) described the ideal open-minded person as

> disposed to revise or reject the position he holds if sound objections are brought against it, or, in the situation in which the person has no opinion on some issue, he is disposed to make up his mind in the light of available evidence and argument as objectively and impartially as possible. (p. 9)

Ideally, open-minded individuals are aware of their own fallibility in decision making and cognitive assessment (Riggs, 2010). Open-mindedness also is considered an essential feature of critical thinking and a desirable goal in educational training (see discussions in Hare & Portelli, 2007).

However, several lines of psychological research have explored the possibility that open-mindedness in practice is different from open-mindedness in the ideal as described by Hare (1979) and others. One line of research, following Shweder (1991) and Peng and Nisbett (1999), is that open-mindedness is not a universal individual-level characteristic; rather, cultures vary in how accepting people are toward contradictions and changes (Spencer-Rodgers, Williams, & Peng, 2010). Compared with Westerners, East Asians have cognitive styles characterized by "naïve dialectivism," meaning that they tend more to see the world as "internally contradictory, inextricably interconnected, and inevitably in flux" (Spencer-Rodgers et al., 2010, p. 308). This greater tolerance for ambiguity and contradictions among East Asians might seem unexpected, given that East Asian states tend to be authoritarian, rather than democratic, and tolerance for ambiguity and change traditionally is associated with democracy. However, as I learned during my years of living in Iran, high tolerance for contradictions is a necessary requirement for survival in authoritarian societies. In closed societies, it is impossible to take political action against the many contradictions inherent in the workings of the regime and its effect on one's everyday life. In essence, tolerance for contradictions is developed in authoritarian systems because one has no choice but to tolerate those contradictions.

An alternative interpretation of open-mindedness in practice, as opposed to in the ideal, came from Kruglanski's (2004) research on motivated cognition. The starting observation is that thinking is for doing; it is goal oriented and has a temporal dimension. That is, goals can be turned on or off by situational and other factors. Depending on whether a goal is being pursued actively or not, the individual will be open-minded or closed-minded toward information that enhances or opposes that particular goal. Thus, being open or closed-minded is not a static, stable feature of individual behavior, but can vary across situations. For example, consider the case of individuals with a high *need for closure*, a desire for information that would allow them to reach a conclusion on a previously ambiguous issue. These individuals can become temporarily open minded to take in new information that ultimately helps attain closure. In contrast, the same person can become closed-minded and reject new information when it contradicts his or her goals. From this perspective, voters are not irrational when they become closed-minded and reject new information; they are maintaining goal consistency (Kruglanski & Boyatzi, 2012).

ACTIONS AND CONVICTIONS OF THE DEMOCRATIC CITIZEN

The democratic citizen is guided in action by a critical, open mind to the universe within the person and to the rest of the world. For democratic actualization to occur, the democratic citizen must develop the appropriate social skills to implement action based on the following convictions:

1. I could be wrong.
2. I must critically question everything, including the sacred beliefs of my society.
3. I must revise my opinions as the evidence requires.
4. I must seek to understand those who are different from me.
5. I can learn from those who are different from me.
6. I must seek information and opinions from different sources.
7. I should be actively open to new experiences.
8. I should be open to creating new experiences for others.
9. There are principles of right and wrong.
10. I should actively seek experiences of higher value.

I have represented these 10 convictions in a circle rather than a hierarchy (see Figure 2.1) because more than one can develop at the same time within

Figure 2.1. Ten convictions of the democratic citizen.

the same person. A circle is suitable because the order in which these convictions develop can vary across individuals and across societies. For example, for some individuals and people in some societies, *I should be actively open to new experiences* develops before *I should actively seek experiences of higher value*, but for some individuals and for some societies, the reverse is true. An elaboration on each conviction follows:

- *I could be wrong.* A foundational feature of the democratic citizen is self-doubt, not in the crippling sense of being unable to make up one's mind, make decisions, and take action, but in the positive, affirmative sense of being open to the possibility that *I could be wrong*, even with respect to one's most deeply held sacred beliefs.

- *I must critically question everything, including the sacred beliefs of my society.* Related to the acceptance that *I could be wrong* is a willingness to critically question one's own personal beliefs and values, and the beliefs and values of the larger society. Of course, the extent to which one can publicly adopt such a strategy depends largely on one's context: It is hazardous to one's health to serve as a critical questioner in a dictatorship, as Socrates discovered.

- *I must revise my opinions as the evidence requires.* As the saying goes, "Everyone is entitled to their own opinions, but not to their own facts." The democratic citizen is a seeker of information and, just as important, is willing and able to change his or her opinions as necessary on the basis of newly acquired knowledge. The model for such an open-minded approach is exemplified in scientific research, whereby the researcher will change his or her theory of the world as newly acquired evidence requires. This process involves continual change and adaptation.

- *I must seek to understand those who are different from me.* How should we treat those who are different from us? Imagine a continuum with "Immediately Rejected" at one extreme and "Given Full Consideration" at the other extreme. The vast research on intergroup relations, as reflected by the concept of ethnocentrism (Moghaddam, 2008a, 2008b), has suggested that, most of the time, humans react to people they perceive to be outsiders in a manner that is closer to immediate rejection than to giving full consideration. The democratic citizen seeks to interact with and gain a deep understanding of outgroup members and outgroup cultures.

- *I can learn from those who are different from me.* A characteristic of democratic citizens is that they approach even dissimilar outgroups with the belief that they can learn from them. What is required is an open mind and a willingness to interpret group-based differences in a constructive, positive manner, rather than viewing their ingroup's way of life as "naturally" superior.

- *I must seek information and opinions from different sources.* The democratic citizen actively seeks information from diverse sources and is equally critical toward ingroup and outgroup sources. Rather than preferring information that reflects group biases, such as information that shows similarity with the ingroup and dissimilarity with the outgroup (Wilder & Allen, 1978), the democratic citizen evaluates information independent from the source.

- *I should be actively open to new experiences.* The acquisition of information and ideas from new sources will only come about if and when a person is actively open to new experiences. What is required is that a person does not just passively tolerate differences but actively seeks to learn from lifestyles and belief systems that are different from his or her own.

- *I should be open to creating new experiences for others.* The process of learning from new experiences oneself has a corresponding process: being open to share with others so as to provide them with new experiences from which they can learn. Of course, helping others gain new experiences at the same time is a learning experience for the self.

- *There are principles of right and wrong.* The openness of the democratic citizen might (wrongly) lead to the conclusion that this individual has a relativistic outlook on life, an outlook that says that all values are as good as one another. This, however, would be a complete mistake. The democratic citizen is strongly wedded to certain principles of freedom, justice, and democracy. This individual has reached the stage of what developmental psychologist Lawrence Kohlberg (1927–1987; see Kohlberg, 1963) designated as principled or postconventional moral decision making, that is, universal moral principles are applied in the same way across different contexts (Kohlberg's research is discussed in more depth in later chapters).

- *I should actively seek experiences of higher value.* On the basis of their principles, democratic citizens judge experiences to be of unequal value and actively seek out experiences that are of higher value—in the sense that such experiences are more in line with progress toward actualized democracy. With respect to the criteria by which we evaluate experiences, a starting point is human rights and duties as recognized by the United Nations (1948) Universal Declaration of Human Rights. Further criteria should be adopted in line with the needs of developing the collective talents of society and the talents of individuals toward democratic citizenship. This active seeking of experiences necessarily involves active neglect and also rejection of other experiences.

CONCLUSION

This chapter outlined the psychological characteristics individuals need to develop in the process of becoming democratic citizens. The development of these characteristics is aided by additive features of globalization, but hindered by subtractive features of globalization (see Chapter 1).

Democratic citizens play an essential role in the struggle for the success of open societies; Socrates and Cicero are historic examples of such individuals; in modern times, they would be in the 40% or so of participants who, in Milgram's (1974) seminal studies on obedience to authority, refused to obey the authority figure. The context for nurturing democratic citizens is diminished by the persistence and even expansion of dictatorships. This context also is hampered by the trend toward more divergent democracies and the resource inequalities that characterize them. When resources are overwhelmingly concentrated in the hands of the few, the open society is diminished and less fertile ground is available to nurture democratic citizens because, in such a situation, the masses do not have the means or opportunities to develop their talents—either as individuals or as part of the larger society. Even the rich suffer in such a situation (Marmot, 2004). To paraphrase John Donne (1572–1631), no person is an island; every person is part of the whole. That which diminishes one person diminishes us all.

II

PSYCHOLOGY AND THE
NECESSARY CONDITIONS
FOR DEMOCRACY

In Part II, I explore the collective psychological journey societies need to undertake to achieve democratic actualization. This is far more difficult and important than the journey taken by individual citizens in becoming democratic. There are many instances in which a number of individuals have become developed democratic citizens, but failed to move society forward toward democratic actualization. On the path of democratic progress, collective change is far more important and difficult than individual change.

In Chapter 3, I outline the main ingredients necessary for actualized democracy, and in Chapters 4 through 12, I explore in greater detail the individual components. Supporters of democracy must act in the belief that although the achievement of actualized democracy is feasible, progress toward this goal is far from inevitable. There are very strong forces still intent on moving societies in the opposite direction, away from democracy. Such forces sometimes include leaders with popular support, and even elected leaders who are popular among the majority but use mass support to concentrate power in their own hands and eventually weaken democracy. It is a paradox inherent in democracy that charismatic leadership with majority support sometimes proves to be antidemocratic. This paradoxical trend has a long tradition, in modern times having Napoleon Bonaparte (1769–1821) as a prime example: far from eliminating monarchy, he crowned himself emperor and established some of his family members as kings and queens around Europe. Of course, Napoleon did introduce many reforms, but his own leadership style was far from democratic.

Tensions underlying leadership style remain at the heart of the struggle for greater democracy in many contemporary countries. This is why I have placed "leadership style" at the center of the circle of democracy discussed in Chapter 3. Prodemocracy leadership plays a pivotal role in achieving both the characteristics needed to achieve democratic citizenship discussed in Chapter 2, and those needed to achieve the democratic society discussed in Chapters 4 through 12. Progress toward actualized democracy depends on the inter-dependent three-way relationship between leadership style, citizenship characteristics, and societal characteristics. Because of the context provided for individual behavior by societal characteristics, I devote the chapters in Part II to collective processes.

3

THE DEMOCRACY CIRCLE

Into a world of hierarchy, the franchise decreed men equal for a day. Into the subtle interplay of local power and unwritten custom, it inserted a universal, written law and mandated its display in every polling station in the country. Into the face-to-face community, where boundaries were fluid and most secrets were open ones, it introduced one private act of will: voting.

—Margaret Lavinia Anderson (2000, p. 62)

In 1867, a radically new practice was introduced into politics in Germany: manhood suffrage. This new right to vote by secret ballot, given to every adult male regardless of property distinction, immediately ran up against the practices of priests, landowners, military officers, and other authority figures. By tradition, these authorities were accustomed to telling people of the "lower ranks" how to think and act in their lives, particularly in domains pertaining to power and resource distribution. Catholic priests continued to tell parishioners how they must vote as good Catholics, landowners told their tenants who to vote for as a matter of duty and loyalty, military officers expected the men under their commands to follow their examples in politics. Despite the forceful hand of traditional authority, democratic ideas about voting as independent, thoughtful citizens with individual rights slowly gained ground. As Anderson (2000) outlined in her innovative examination of the democratic practices introduced into imperial Germany, the introduction

http://dx.doi.org/10.1037/14806-004
The Psychology of Democracy, by F. M. Moghaddam

of suffrage made male voters slightly more independent and incrementally less subservient to authority by the end of the 19th century. The practice of voting by secret ballot, with the egalitarian protection for privacy that it afforded, provided concrete support for independent thinking and action.

Democratic practices in Germany and Western societies in general evolved gradually over relatively long periods against strong headwinds of traditional hierarchies and inequalities. The path to the 21st century, still-evolving Western democracy we know today has been a slow, conflict-ridden, step-by-step process. What we often assume to be revolutionary democratic breakthroughs were only initial, limited, tentative steps toward what is as yet still a weak form of democracy as practiced in the second decade of the 21st century. That progress toward fuller democracy will continue is not guaranteed; it could devolve in places toward dictatorship. The ratification of the U.S. Constitution in 1787 following the Declaration of Independence in America in 1776—events considered milestones on the march to contemporary democracy—only led to voting rights for White male citizens with property. The French Revolution in 1789 eventually did lead to universal male suffrage in France in 1792. However, it was not until well over a century and half later that all women and men gained the vote in these "liberated" countries.

In their analysis of women's suffrage around the world, Ramirez, Soysal, and Shanahan (1997) identified an important difference between the early wave of countries that had granted women the right to vote and a more contemporary wave. Their analysis shows that women's suffrage

> was preceded by national independence and male suffrage in the late nineteenth and early twentieth centuries, but since 1930 these three events increasingly have become a single political process. . . . The earlier temporal sequence, from national independence to male suffrage to female suffrage, is not repeated in a single case. (p. 743)

For example, India and Pakistan gave women and men the right to vote at the same time, when the two countries gained their independence in 1947. This all-at-once change puts Pakistan, the first Islamic Republic, ahead chronologically—at least on paper—of Western democracies like Switzerland in granting voting rights to women. Switzerland began the long march toward democracy centuries before Pakistan but did not give women the right to vote until 1971 (see discussions on the development of the modern Swiss nation-state and Swiss federalism in Kriesi & Trechsel, 2008).

An unintended consequence of the slow, step-by-step movement toward greater democracy is that people can have more opportunities to gradually learn the psychological and social skills required to serve as democratic citizens. The post-1930 trend that Ramirez et al. (1997) identified—of countries gaining most or even all major democratic rights in one step and on paper—often requires a difficult psychological leap. People who first developed cognitive and social skills in the context of dictatorship instantly have to develop and put into practice skills required to function in, and maintain, a democracy. Thus, in 1947, Pakistanis who developed social and cognitive skills under the British colonial system that was framed by authoritarian religious traditions suddenly were given the opportunity to live in a democracy (Talbot, 2009). This does not mean that such opportunities should be denied; rather, the challenges associated with such opportunities have to be better understood and overcome.

Whereas democracy requires toleration of differences and accommodation for diversity, Pakistani independence involved a rejection of pluralism in that it set up a state that explicitly included Muslims as the majority. The percentage of minorities was down to about 8% in 2002 (Malik, 2002) but has declined further as a result of increased activities by Islamic fundamentalists. Although accurate estimates of this decline in minorities are unavailable, mass media reports have indicated that most Hindus and Sikhs have ended up in Bangladesh (formerly East Pakistan) and other minorities also have come under pressure to leave Pakistan. Although the prodemocracy institutions were weak, religious institutions and authoritarian traditions stood strong; they supported ethnocentrism and rejected an open society. Given this cultural and historical context (Talbot, 2009), it is not surprising that the movement toward democracy has been painfully slow in Pakistan and punctuated by military coups and surges of Islamic fundamentalism. Since the 1947 independence, Pakistan has experienced its first peaceful transfer of power, in 2013, from one democratically elected government to another.

The distinction needs to be made between expressed verbal support for democracy and the behavioral and cognitive skills that support democracy. On the one hand, international surveys have shown robust attitudinal support for democracy across different societies (Inglehart, 2003, p. 52, Table 1) and research has suggested a link between mass attitudes and actual level of democracy (Inglehart, 2003, p. 54, Table 3). However, almost a century of psychological research has highlighted the rift that often exists between what people say and what they do (Ajzen & Fishbein, 2005). This rift has arisen from a variety of factors, but, for the purposes of this discussion, the most important one is a lack of the 10 characteristics of the prodemocracy individual described in Chapter 2, as well as the necessary institutional support for democratic practices.

In the context of 21st-century globalization and the spread of politically correct Western values, most people, at least in urban centers in major societies, are aware that democracy is supposed to be favorably evaluated. For the majority of educated, urban individuals, it simply is politically incorrect to express antidemocratic sentiments and beliefs. Nobody wants to be seen as antidemocratic. Even in harsh dictatorships, widespread attempts are made to present a democratic front and claim popular support by pressuring people to participate in elections in which candidates are prevetted to support the ruling despots and no critical voices are permitted (Moghaddam, 2013).

Expressed attitudes, though, can be, and often are, different from actual state practices. The role played by this rift is particularly important in the modern history of dictatorships. For example, in 1963, the last shah of Iran held a national referendum ostensibly to give the Iranian people an opportunity to express their approval or disapproval for the shah's White Revolution (which mostly involved land reform). In his seminal work on the last shah, Milani (2011) noted that

> the fact that voters were required to vote in open ballot boxes, under the watchful eyes of the police, made the results highly suspect. Not surprisingly, 99.5 percent of those who voted cast a ballot in favor of the White Revolution, with a little more than 4,000 people out of an electorate of nearly 6 million daring to ask for a "No" ballot. (p. 294)

Even major revolutions are not necessarily enough to transform such situations. In the case of Iran, where I was participant observer in the post-revolution period of 1979 to 1984, the elections held have continued the nondemocratic tradition: The state has screened candidates so they offer no real alternatives to the current ruling dictatorship. The challenge of moving from dictatorship to democracy in a one-step process proved too much. The general population was not given enough time after the 1979 revolution to make behavioral and cognitive adjustments to move toward democracy. Fundamentalists intent on reestablishing a dictatorship quickly ended freedoms after 1979, and Iran once again has become a closed and corrupt society—a fate common to a number of populations that have attempted rapid movement from dictatorship to democracy without constructive leadership (Moghaddam, 2013).

In this chapter, I provide a broad outline of the changes that a society needs to become a full-fledged democracy. In the chapters that follow (Chapters 4–13), I provide a more in-depth discussion of each component that is outlined briefly in this chapter. My focus here is on collective social and psychological processes, whereas in Chapter 2, I examined individual-level processes. I argue that, irrespective of whether a society moves step-by-step toward greater democracy—as has happened in the case of the United Kingdom and most other Western societies—or acquires democracy on paper in a single step—such as occurred in India and Pakistan in 1947, for example—the collective psychological changes required in the population are the same. Moreover, these psychological changes can be speeded up only through systematic education and training designed to enhance prodemocracy skills and thinking styles. Unfortunately, the elites have neglected, and sometimes even resisted, such education and training. Consequently, many of the countries that became democratic on paper in a one-step procedure have struggled to transform themselves without the support of strong prodemocracy education and training. It has been impossible to transform the actual behavior of the populations, either the political leaders or the masses, to implement the democracy described in their formal law.

Relatively fast transformation from dictatorship to democracy is more feasible when a prodemocracy leader is at the center. A variety of factors, including the role of chance, means that some societies enjoy the benefits of relatively more constructive, prodemocracy leadership. Sometimes, seemingly miraculously, leaders emerge who pave the way for further movement away from dictatorship and toward democracy. An important feature of such leaders is their reluctance to hold on to power and their willingness to step away from power after their "turn" has ended. They feel that they have done what they could to move society forward. A prime example is the first president of the United States, George Washington (1732–1799), who voluntarily handed over power to a successor. Quoting King George III, who was officially Washington's enemy, Seymour Lipset (1998) captured Washington's exceptional behavior:

> The king asked the painter Jonathan Trumbull, freshly arrived from America, what he thought Washington would do when the war ended. "Go back to his farm," Trumbull replied. "If he does that, he will be the greatest man in the world," rejoined the king. And that *is* what Washington did, twice—first when the war ended, and later after his second term as president of the United States. Following his second withdrawal, King George reiterated his opinion, saying that these actions "placed [Washington] in a light the most distinguished of any man living," and made him "the greatest character of the age." (p. 24)

King George's extraordinary praise was based on Washington's willingness to step away from power and "go back to his farm." More recently, Nelson Mandela of South Africa showed the same extraordinary capacity by stepping away from the highest political position even though adoring crowds supported his continued power. Unfortunately, in many other cases, leaders who come to power in countries with the potential to emerge from dictatorship simply take the country back to dictatorship. For example, consider the fate of the Arab Spring and Egypt, in particular, with the reestablishment of a military dictatorship.

THE PSYCHOLOGY OF BECOMING DEMOCRATIC AS A SOCIETY

Societies are dynamic entities that typically are in a state of continual change. We should not assume that any society is fixed and stable in the kind or level of democracy or dictatorship it has achieved, or that change is only in one direction: toward strengthened democracy. As Keane (2009) persuasively argued in *The Life and Death of Democracy*, "Democracy is not the timeless fulfillment of our political destiny. It is not a way of doing politics that has always been with us, or that will be our companion for the rest of history" (p. xiv).

Well-developed democracies can weaken and even slip into dictatorship, as the example of Germany in the 1930s clearly demonstrates. Adolf Hitler's rise to his appointment as chancellor in 1933 and the relative success of the Nazis in the Reichstag elections that same year were associated with a change in popular sentiment. Germans seemed willing to sacrifice freedoms to gain what they thought would be economic progress and political stability. Once in a position of considerable power, Hitler acted swiftly: "By the end of 1933 the democratic regime established by the Weimar Constitution had succumbed to a one-party state which was fast becoming totalitarian" (Raff, trans. 1988, p. 279). From the snuffing out of Athenian democracy around 2,500 years ago to the present are numerous reminders of the shifting nature of societies and what Keane (2009) has referred to as "the brittle contingency of democracy" (p. xiv).

Collective–Individual Integration

> He did not even realize that the new life was not given him for nothing, that he would have to pay a great price for it, that he would have to pay for it by a great act of heroism in the future. But that is the beginning of a new story, the story of the gradual rebirth of a man, the story of his gradual regeneration, of his gradual passing from one world to another, of his acquaintance with a new and hitherto unknown reality. (Dostoevsky, 1866/1951, p. 559)

> The Mind of the universe is social. (Aurelius, 180/1964, p. 88)

Raskolnikov, the central character in Dostoevsky's (1866/1951) *Crime and Punishment*, undergoes deep psychological changes after he kills and robs an old woman. He escapes discovery by the police but cannot escape his own conscience. Gradually and painfully, he becomes increasingly isolated. He eventually recognizes that, only by confessing his guilt, becoming enveloped by human law, and accepting punishment sanctioned by society can he rejoin society and experience a rebirth. Raskolnikov's conscience is symbolic of an invisible cord that binds individuals together to create human society. It is through their social relationships and active participation in collective life that individuals realize their own potentialities as humans.

Becoming democratic as individuals and becoming a democracy as a society involve long-term psychological processes; democracy is a becoming and a gradual journey for both individuals and societies. This process of becoming democratic can best be understood by exploring the dynamic relationship between the individual and society: how the individual enters into society, and how society enters into the individual. Traditional psychology has explored this theme by focusing primarily on individual minds. Swiss psychologist Jean Piaget (1896–1980), probably the most influential developmental psychologist in history, explored two cognitive processes within individuals that are particularly relevant here:

> *assimilation*, the process whereby an action is actively reproduced and comes to incorporate new objects into itself . . . and accommodation, the process whereby the schemes of assimilation themselves becomes modified in being applied to a diversity of objects. (Piaget, trans. 1970, p. 63)

In Piaget's system, the individual becomes integrated into the social world through cognitive processes in which existing cognitive schemas are applied to new problems or objects (assimilation), or existing cognitive schemas are modified to fit new problems or objects (accommodation). This way of looking at individual–society integration is limited because the focus remains so much on individual minds outside their social interactions.

An alternative approach, inspired by the ideas of Russian developmentalist Lev Vygotsky (1896–1934) and others (see Harré & Moghaddam, 2012), focuses on social processes as the origin or source of individual-level processes:

> Every function in the child's cultural development appears twice: first, on the social level, and later, on the individual level, first between people (interpsychological) and then inside the child (intrapsychological). . . . All the higher functions originate as actual relationships between individuals. (Vygotsky, 1978, p. 57)

This idea of psychological processes originating outside the person in social relationships runs contrary not only to traditional conceptions of Western psychology but to the assumptions and individualistic expectations of Western, particularly American, culture. In American culture, causes typically are assumed to reside within individuals: If Joe is out of work and Mary is poor, it must be because Joe and Mary are lazy, lack talent, or both.

The Actualization of Democracy

> Self-actualization . . . may be loosely described as the full use and exploitation of talents, capacities, potentialities, and the like. Such people seem

to be fulfilling themselves and to be doing the best that they are capable of doing. . . . They are people who have developed or are developing to the full stature of which they are capable. (Maslow, 1970, p. 126)

American psychologist Abraham Maslow (1908–1970) famously discussed actualization at the individual level by describing a hierarchy of needs from basic physiological needs, to safety needs, relationship needs, esteem and status needs, and self-actualization. According to Maslow's scheme, which typically is presented as a pyramid with "physiological needs" at the base and "self-actualization" needs at the pinnacle, human needs are satisfied in a stepwise manner and needs are triggered one at a time. Individuals take action to try to satisfy a higher need only after they have satisfied lower ones. Clayton Alderfer (1972) presented a more flexible conceptualization of human needs, whereby a person can pursue more than one need simultaneously (Oyedele, 2010). Alderfer grouped human needs into three categories: existence, relatedness, and growth. Existence corresponds to Maslow's basic physiological and safety needs; relatedness, to relationship and social needs; and growth, to self-actualization.

The vast majority of discussions about the models Maslow and Alderfer proposed have focused on individual needs and individual growth or actualization but have paid little attention to collective or what I term *societal actualization*. This innovative term refers to a society that is fulfilling its potential and operating at its highest capacity morally, cultural, politically, and economically. The neglect of collective processes is unsurprising, given the cultural context of the United States in which Maslow, Alderfer, and other major researchers have worked. American culture is characterized by what I have called the *embryonic fallacy*, the assumption that, as soon as life begins, the individual becomes the source of psychological experiences (Moghaddam, 2010). This fallacy is in line with the individualistic self-help ideology of American society, which is epitomized by the *American Dream*, the notion that American society is open so that anyone can make it, and a belief that the success of individuals depends solely on their own merits rather than their group characteristics, such as how rich or poor a family they are born into. An intimate link exists between individual and societal levels: Societal actualization serves as the springboard to individual actualization. Although individual characteristics play an important role, certain contexts better enable individuals to self-actualize, as is clear from the historical cycles of human creativity, particularly excellence achieved in science, architecture, fine arts, literature, theater, cinema, sports, and other domains of human activity. The brilliant output of geniuses, such as Leonardo da Vinci in Renaissance Italy, Jane Austen and Charles Darwin in 19th-century England, Sigmund Freud in late 19th-century/early 20th-century Vienna, Charlie

Chaplin in 20th-century America, and others, was not simply a result of their individual characteristics but was, in large part, because of the times and societal context in which they were socialized.

THE DEMOCRACY CIRCLE AND PSYCHOLOGY

The path to democratic actualization at the societal level can be represented as a circle with nine components (see Figure 2 in the Introduction to this book). "Leadership Style" at the center of the circle represents the influence the behavioral style of a leader exerts in enhancing or hindering movement away from dictatorship and toward democratic actualization. For example, consider how Nelson Mandela moved South Africa toward democracy after the collapse of Apartheid in 1990 and how Ruhollah Khomeini moved Iran back to dictatorship after the 1979 revolution. Even when a society is an absolute dictatorship, if the leader happens to become more responsive to the citizens' wishes, doing so can help bring about change toward democracy.

The actualization of democracy involves the completion of the nine components, which are discussed in detail in Chapters 4 through 12. No society has yet completed all the components, and it is not guaranteed that they will be completed in the future. The nine components involved in democratic actualization are depicted as a circle because the order in which they are achieved can differ across societies. For example, consider how the order in which progress on universal suffrage and minority rights may be fulfilled can differ across societies. A society might provide universal suffrage in practice before implementing minority rights. Pakistan and Iran are two examples: Although all citizens, including minorities, in these two societies are allowed to vote in political elections, the rights of many minorities, particularly religious ones, are not protected in practice. The reverse is true for gay people in Western societies: They had the right to vote before they gained equal rights (e.g., the right to marry) as a minority group.

Another feature of the democracy circle is that components can simultaneously be the focus of prodemocracy movements. For example, evolution toward rule of law can occur at the same time as winning greater freedom of speech. This is not necessarily a stepwise process. The fluidity of the order and simultaneous evolution of components makes this similar to Alderfer's (1972) model discussed previously.

My starting observation before proceeding to the chapters on the components of democracy is that no major society has completed all nine and achieved actualized democracy. The so-called advanced societies of North America and Western Europe have not even fully fulfilled the majority of these components. Some societies popularly known as dictatorships have made some progress on just a few components: Their leaders, have, at times, been responsive to their citizens and, in some instances, have implemented rule of law.

Progress on the nine components of democracy requires psychological changes. The objection could be made that humans currently do not have the psychological characteristics needed to reach actualized democracy. My response is twofold: First, the psychological characteristics can be taught and acquired through appropriate socialization. Second, a small number of individuals already possess all of the required characteristics. The challenge is to increase the size of this group until reaching a tipping point, when the collective movement toward democratic actualization accelerates and becomes more probable in outcome.

CONCLUSION

The ideal of democratic actualization is a long-term goal that human societies can achieve through appropriate socialization practices and institution-building. The role of appropriate institutions to provide contextual support is essential. By articulating this ideal and describing the components involved, we can facilitate progress along this journey. The journey to actualized democracy involves long-term collective processes—often over centuries of change. The outcome is not inevitable, but the probability of success is increased through more critical and detailed articulation of the key components and the psychological processes involved.

4

LEADERS RESPONSIVE TO THE WISHES OF CITIZENS

Well-ordered states and wise princes have studied diligently not to drive the nobles to desperation, and to satisfy the populace and keep it contented, for this is one of the most important matters a prince has to deal with.
— Niccolò Machiavelli (1532/1950, p. 69)

It is for us the living . . . to be . . . dedicated to the great task remaining before us . . . that government of the people, by the people, for the people, shall not perish from the earth.
— Abraham Lincoln (1863) in Gettysburg, Pennsylvania

A common theme in both realist and idealist discussions of government is the idea that rulers should be responsive to the wishes of the people. Views vary considerably as to the ways and extent responsiveness is believed necessary, and who among the subject population needs to be responded to. Who exactly are "the people"? All of the population in a society or simply those who command considerable wealth and power of their own? The resourceful individuals and groups who are effectively represented by lobbyists and various agents? The minorities with least power and resources? The much referred to middle class?

Machiavelli's (1532/1950) response to such questions is that the leader should do what is necessary to keep power and thus should consider the people's needs as a means of retaining power rather than as an end in itself. This realist approach contrasts with Lincoln's (1863) lofty ideal of "government of the people, by the people, for the people." Although, in

http://dx.doi.org/10.1037/14806-005
The Psychology of Democracy, by F. M. Moghaddam

practice, Lincoln and other idealist politicians have fallen short of this standard, and sometimes have defined *people* in a way that excludes certain groups, they have helped establish the legitimacy of leader as follower and democracy as entailing being led, directly or indirectly, by the people, meaning all or at least the majority of a nation's population. In this idealist approach, service to the people is the end and the leadership's power is the means. Thus, we can conceptualize a continuum with two extremes: "Leader Unresponsive to People's Needs" at one end and "Leader as People's Servant" at the other.

In this chapter, the main focus is on what can be a first step toward democracy: political leadership that becomes more responsive to the wishes of its people. In recent history at least, rulers typically have started by responding to the wishes of elite power groups, then gradually responding to the wishes of additional groups. For example, in the English context, King John's signing of the Magna Carta in 1215 was in response to the demands of the powerful barons in his realm, and over subsequent centuries, English monarchs began responding to a wider circle of people. The decline in absolute power of the English monarch corresponded to the rise in power of the English Parliament; the execution of Charles I in 1649 and the Glorious Revolution of 1688 were key turning points. By the 19th century, Britain had *constitutional monarchy*, that is, the monarch had limited decision-making authority. Those changes were accompanied by the extension of voting rights until, finally, in the 20th century, the leadership ceded voting rights to all adults, including women. A similar process of leaders' becoming more responsive to followers took place in many other countries, but this process involved many violent struggles. Leaders did not give up absolute power without a struggle.

As Machiavelli (1532/1950) suggested, a major reason for a leader's positive response to pressure from groups for more rights was to undercut opposition and retain power. Dictatorships survive largely by keeping the ruling elite cohesive: forming a united front that will use violence when necessary to control the masses (Moghaddam, 2013). However, even a leadership with a power monopoly that is utterly self-serving has a strong reason to appear responsive to the masses, at the least, to forestall rising popular demands. For example, consider how the Chinese leadership in its response to the 2014 protests in Hong Kong insisted that its goal was to protect the interests of the Chinese people by implementing rule of law and reestablishing law and order. The Chinese leadership claimed that the protests in Hong Kong disrupted the lives of ordinary citizens and worked against the interests of the wider Chinese society. Clearly, this is a case of leaders' refusing to be more responsive to the people's needs and demands.

LEADERSHIP IN EARLY COMMUNITIES

A focus on the development of governments and the responsiveness of rulers in Britain and other countries might give the impression that all societies and even small communities began with absolute rulers. This is not the case. Some early societies had more communal leadership, and *ubuntu* or traditional African models of communal leadership are attracting more attention today. Studies on leadership in human prehistory (before written records existed) have suggested that variation in leadership styles evolved over time in different societies: from shared and communal leadership styles to authoritarian, centralized styles (Earle, 1991; Mills, 2000; Sveiby, 2011). However, traditional leadership research has neglected this variety in decision-making styles, instead focusing more on individual than on collective leadership. This trend reflects what happened centuries earlier when Western colonists came across non-Western cultures, such as Aboriginal societies in Australia, that practiced collective leadership and communal decision making:

> British colonial governments . . . could not cope with a people who neither recognized chiefs with positional power nor political leaders, and they concluded that they had encountered a people who were so "primitive" that they did not even have leaders. (Sveiby, 2011, p. 386)

As a solution, colonial powers often introduced individual leadership where there traditionally had been collective leadership: "The forced introduction of hierarchical leadership by a foreign power on people practicing a [collective] leadership culture . . . had disastrous social effects" (Sveiby, 2011, p. 386). But, despite colonial intervention, collective leadership has survived in smaller communities. For example, communal traditions and decision making regarding land and water use has survived in parts of rural Africa and Asia despite the introduction of private ownership and individualistic leadership rules by Western governments and companies. Collective leadership was more feasible when early humans lived in small groups numbering no more than several hundred.

Another issue regarding the nature of leadership concerns the survival of leadership styles over long periods. From an evolutionary perspective, the question is, what functional characteristics have certain leadership styles had to enable them to survive? For supporters of the open society, evidence related to this question has led to both hope and despair. On the hopeful side, the emergence of democracy together with the development of and support for adherence to universal human rights (Finkel & Moghaddam, 2005) have resulted in a decline in violence and more humane attitudes (Pinker, 2011).

From this perspective, democratic leadership seems to be functional, at least in certain contexts. On the side of despair, dictatorships continue and, indeed, seem to be thriving. Major powers, such as China and Russia, still are under essentially dictatorial leadership, and the early promise of the Arab Spring democratization efforts was short-lived. From this perspective, one could argue that dictatorship remains functional and competitive as a political system in the 21st-century context.

LEADER MOTIVATION AND THE "WISHES OF THE PEOPLE"

To shake all cares and business from our age,
Conferring them on younger strengths, while we
Unburthened crawl toward death. (William Shakespeare, *King Lear*,
1.1.37–39; see Evans, 1997)

King Lear, in the play of the same name, and Prospero in *The Tempest* are the most notable examples of Shakespearian characters who attempt to step aside from power, although, in the case of Prospero, without formally abdicating. Lear transfers his power and wealth to two of his daughters (the third, unable to put on shows of affection and loyalty to Lear's satisfaction, receives nothing from her father). Prospero abandons power by losing himself in his studies; he neglects to attend to his duties as duke. The attempt to sidestep the responsibilities of power end in disaster: Lear, misused by the two daughters he empowered, ends up mad and abandoned in the wilderness; Prospero is stranded with his daughter on an isolated island after Prospero's brother conspires against him and takes over the dukedom.

If the fate of those who attempt to evade the responsibilities of power is disastrous in Shakespeare's plays, the fate of those who directly and intentionally seek greater power is equally as tragic. Notable examples are Macbeth and Richard III (in plays of the same names), Claudius in *Hamlet*, and Mark Antony and his co-conspirators in *Julius Caesar*. Antony says of Caesar, for example, "As Caesar loved me, I weep for him. As he was fortunate, I rejoice at it. As he was valiant, I honour him. But as he was ambitious, I slew him" (*Julius Caesar*, 3.2.23–25; see Evans, 1997). Macbeth is moved to kill King Duncan, a host in his castle at the time, and usurp the crown because of his self-confessed "vaulting ambition which o'erleaps itself" (*Macbeth*, 1.7.27; see Evans, 1997). Richard III is moved by greed for power to systematically kill every person between himself and the crown. On his way to grabbing the kingdom, he uses outrageous ploys and cunning to persuade the grieving queen to marry him, the murderer of her husband, and presents himself to the people in the company of holy men—a ploy not neglected by 21st-century political leaders in various societies. Shakespeare's skepticism of ambition for power leads to the question, Can a person rise to political leadership without greed for power? Surely, without the resolute focus on attaining power and the willingness to act in a determined and even ruthless way, the leader may fear Hamlet's predicament—rudderless in a sea of self-doubt, wavering between action and inaction, and moved to rash actions by circumstances and chance events.

The ability of leaders to retain power depends not only on responding to dissatisfactions they recognize in the realm but being in a psychological state to perceive reasonably accurately what is occurring around them. This idea is underlined by research on leadership in organizations that has shown that leaders can lose power as a result of misperceiving their relationships with others as overly positive: Leaders sometimes assume they are liked when they are disliked, and have support when they do not (Brion & Anderson, 2013). This particular bias is an example of a general self-serving bias well known to attributional researchers who study behavior from an early age (e.g., Boseovski, 2010).

A movement toward follower-centered leadership (Lord & Brown, 2004) is in line with a number of major psychological schools and theories. For example, from a behaviorist perspective, it is easier to lead along the lines of existing behavioral tendencies than to attempt to reshape the behavior of followers. If followers are prejudiced against particular minorities, it is easier for leadership to endorse such prejudices rather than to try to end or change them. From a social exchange theory perspective, followers are more likely to be satisfied with leadership, not surprisingly, if they perceive there to be a fair give-and-take between leaders and followers. Modern research has supported the view that when managers respond favorably to requests from employees, attitudes and actions of employees improve the employee–employer relationship (Shore, Sy, & Strauss, 2006).

SERVANT LEADERSHIP

The servant leader is servant first. It begins with the natural feeling that one wants to serve. . . . The best test is: do those served grow as persons . . . become healthier, wiser, freer, more autonomous, more likely themselves to become servants? And, what is the effect on the least privileged in society; will they benefit, or, at least, not be further deprived? (Greenleaf, 1977/2002, p. 27)

Robert Greenleaf (1904–1990) was the innovator of servant leadership described in the preceding quote. Critics have answered Greenleaf (1977/2002) with doubts, claiming that servant leadership is too idealistic. After all, servant leadership as described by Greenleaf establishes an ideal, but it is unclear that the kinds of individuals who are motivated to become leaders also are motivated, or even capable, of acting as servant leaders. Nevertheless, Greenleaf's work, particularly as interpreted by Spears (1998), has increasingly affected an understanding of leadership in part because leadership has become a major focus of higher education programs. Servant leadership also is becoming a particular focus in some universities (Polleys, 2002) perhaps because the ideals of servant leadership fit well with liberal academic ideals. It is associated with a reevaluation of the "greed is good" culture that has influenced the business sector in Western and, in particular, American society. Thus, servant leadership can be seen as an antidote to the extreme swing toward selfishness prevalent in capitalist societies.

Justice and Servant Leadership

The implications of servant leadership for justice could take one or more forms. The priority given to leader responsiveness could lead to a more just and democratic leadership style. However, it is unclear if this priority lines up more with a focus on *procedural justice*, the fairness of processes through which decisions are made and resources are distributed (Lind & Tyler, 1988), compared with *distributive justice*, the actual allocation of resources among individuals and groups in a society. Being responsive to the resource needs of group members is only one type of responsiveness. The leader can be responsive in a myriad of ways, including in the style of interpersonal interactions (De Cremer & Tyler, 2005). In an organizational setting, both formal and informal aspects of decision-making processes are influential in shaping how people feel about fairness (Blader & Tyler, 2003). It is not only what the formal rules say about how people should be treated and involved in decision-making processes, it is also the informal, tacit, implicit aspects of social relationships that influence perceptions of fairness.

Thus, servant leadership can become effective not just by influencing the distribution of rewards but, even more broadly, by shaping how people feel about the processes of decision making. This effectiveness is reinforced by a variety of intangibles, qualities such as charisma leaders may possess (Conger, 1989) that improve leader–follower relationships. Some leaders have the ability to make people feel good through a communication style that uses a peripheral route to persuasion (Petty & Cacioppo, 1986). The peripheral route relies less on cognitive engagement or rational analysis and more on implicit process or subtle cues that often remain outside conscious experience. An implication of the potential efficacy of the peripheral route is that many factors other than the amount of resources received may influence popular perceptions of fairness.

Social Identity and Justice

Perhaps the most important nonmaterial factor that shapes perceptions of procedural justice is identity (Blader & Tyler, 2009), and identity, in turn, is centrally important to shaping behavior in organizations (Haslam, 2004). How followers perceive procedural fairness is a key to their sense of belongingness (Cornelis, Van Hiel, & De Cremer, 2012). When an individual feels that a group's procedures are fair, that individual is more likely to become part of a group, identify as a group member, conform to group norms, and cooperate in group activities (Lind, 2001).

In some contexts, economic incentives shape behavior through their influence on social identity (Blader & Tyler, 2009); that is, economic incentives signal to individuals that they are valued and belong (see Kamenica, 2012, on incentives and psychological factors). This becomes clear in situations in which economic incentives are not by themselves significant but gain significance through how they are interpreted. In most North American universities, and increasingly in most competitive universities around the world, for example, university faculty annually evaluate their peers and allocate points in the areas of teaching, research, and service (i.e., the faculty grade one another). The salary increase of each faculty member for the following year depends partly on these peer evaluations. Given the amount of annual salary increase for faculty at my university, the actual dollar difference between receiving, for example, a 7.5 rather than 8.0 out of 10.0 for teaching, or research, or service is often not more than $100 over the course of a year. This is not a large financial incentive—but it still influences behavior.

However, at some universities, conflicts and rivalries among academics over points or grades in the annual merit review typically become fierce, far more fierce than the dollar amounts would warrant. New assistant professors starting their university careers quickly learn that, despite the financial stakes being low, academic politics often is quite intense. The sense of identity among academics is seriously influenced by the points or grades they receive in their merit evaluations. Moreover, by using rankings of journals and other publications outlets as a basis for evaluation, so that mainstream publications receive higher ratings, this evaluation system enforces conformity in academic research; in effect, those who publish research in nonmainstream publication outlets are punished. The result is greater conformity and less democracy in the sense that being different is punished. In addition to such real-life examples, experimental demonstrations have indicated that identity can be evaluated by objectively trivial criteria, just as $100 is relatively trivial as an annual salary increase in the economic context of Western societies.

That people often use objectively trivial criteria as a basis for social categorization and intergroup bias has been shown repeatedly by minimal group paradigm research (Moghaddam, 2008b). In the late 1970s, Henri Tajfel and his associates developed the minimal group paradigm with the initial goal of creating minimal groups, groups that do not have the usual characteristics associated with group cohesion and intergroup bias, such as common goals, shared leadership, and personal relationships (Tajfel, Billig, Bundy, & Flament, 1971).

Minimal group paradigm research has two basic stages. In the first stage, individuals carry out a trivial task, such as estimating the number of dots flashed on a screen. In the second stage, the participants are divided between Group X and Group Y, ostensibly on the basis of their answers on the trivial task (actually, all participants are placed in the same group, and performance on the trivial task is unrelated to group membership). The participants are then asked to allocate points to the members of Groups X and Y. When a participant asks, "On what basis should I allocate points?" he or she is told, "On any basis you want." In allocating points, the participants do not know the identity of others either in their own group or the outgroup, and they do not receive any of the points they allocate. They do not know anything about the groups, other than that one group is labeled X and the other, Y, and that they are in Group X.

Despite the minimal nature of the groups in which they are placed, participants systematically show a bias in favor of the ingroup. In showing bias, participants are giving importance to what, in other conditions, would be a trivial or minimal basis for intergroup differences (Moghaddam & Stringer, 1986). For example, consider a situation in which people give importance to the colors red and green associated with two rival sports teams. Team supporters might even get involved in physical violence against the supporters of rival teams wearing the "wrong" colors. In a different context, the same individuals might not even notice if the colors red and green are present. Although the criteria for group differentiation and intergroup bias can change across contexts, there is consistency across contexts in that people want to be evaluated favorably and to be seen as, to some extent, being different on the basis of that evaluation. The basic effect of social categorization on a trivial basis has been shown in many different populations and with different age groups (e.g., preschoolers; MacDonald, Schug, Chase, & Barth, 2013).

Since the 1970s, an impressive body of research evidence based on the minimal group paradigm has supported the social identity theory proposal that individuals are motivated to achieve positive and distinct identities (Tajfel & Turner, 1979). People try to belong to groups that enable them to achieve such an identity. Rather than simply being an end in itself, having more material resources may serve as a means to bolster a positive and distinct identity (Blader & Tyler, 2009; Dukerich, Golden, & Shortell, 2002).

The role of trivial factors in identity construction is important because it opens the door to leaders' influencing and, in some cases, manipulating group behavior. Such manipulation can move groups and nations away from democracy. Prominent examples include U.S. Senator Joseph McCarthy's (1908–1957) supposed anticommunist campaign in the 1950s and the endorsement of torture and mass spying by U.S. presidents and congressional leaders as part of the 21st-century so-called war on terror.

LEADERSHIP AND IDENTITY CONSTRUCTION

A soldier will sacrifice himself for a many-colored scrap of stuff on a pole, because it has become the symbol of his fatherland, and no one thinks that neurotic. (Freud, 1895/1950, p. 349)

Freud's (1921/1955) analysis of the relationship between leaders and followers revealed how behaviors that have come to be seen as normative are often based on irrational processes. He explored how leaders direct the energies of group members in particular directions and strengthen identification with certain group constructions, even without the leaders and followers being aware of how and why they are behaving in particular ways. For example, in the modern era, national leaders have encouraged nationalism and have developed feelings of national pride, sacrifice, and glorification often through symbols, such as the national flag, which serves as a cultural carrier of values, norms, and beliefs, and a propagator of culture more broadly (Moghaddam, 2002). Children learn to salute and value a national flag, as evidenced by the allegiance to the flag ceremonies for U.S. schoolchildren. To sacrifice for the flag has become the heroic fate of many young men and women in wars waged in far-off lands that have been inspired and led by leaders living in luxury back home. Whereas the kings of old often fought, lived, and died with their troops in battle, 21st-century leaders stay in safe and pampered shelters from which they encourage their armies to set about annihilating the enemy while members of those armies are themselves killed.

Carriers and Groups

There are surface differences among *carriers*, means by which cultures are propagated and continuity is achieved across generations. For example, consider the Islamic *hijab*, the clothing that certain Muslim authorities, who in Muslim societies are invariably male, insist that women must wear to preserve their modesty. Like the national flag, the Islamic *hijab* is just a piece of cloth and does not have intrinsic value as such. However, the symbolic value of the *hijab* could not be greater for certain Muslim men who are ready to sacrifice their lives to defend it. The important role of cultural carriers in mobilizing people to make sacrifices for the sake of the group underlines the potency of group identity and the considerable influence of leaders who are adept at shaping group identity and identification to their own ends.

Carriers play a pivotal role in strengthening nationalism and mobilizing people to participate in national movements, including going to war against other nations. From the national flag to the awarding of medals to military personnel for sacrifice and bravery, from physical spaces (e.g., Arlington National Cemetery) to pieces of music and poetry (e.g., national anthem) and special days (e.g., Independence Day, Memorial Day), the variety of carriers that support nationalism and strengthen nationalist feelings is almost endless. The role of these carriers is reinforced continually by leadership, such as when the U.S. president is shown on television saluting the flag.

As suggested by findings from the minimal group paradigm (Tajfel et al., 1971), the leader can influence the creation and mobilization of a group on the basis of a criterion that is objectively trivial. Consider, for example, how leaders magnify the role of sport in 21st-century nationalism, such as by attending sports events and celebrating star athletes. At one level, soccer only involves 22 individuals kicking a ball within the boundaries of an oblong surrounded by crowds of spectators. The 22 individuals typically wear shirts of two different colors, such as red and blue. Such surface differences as shirt colors could mislead us to believe that soccer is just a game and only plays a minor role in identity construction and group mobilization. However, sport plays an enormously important role in reinforcing and influencing the direction of nationalism (see readings in Smith & Porter, 2004). The question of who wins in international soccer matches is highly influential in the everyday lives of hundreds of millions of people and helps to shape and give meaning to national sentiments. I learned this lesson the hard way years ago, when, together with some other pedestrians, I was beaten up by drunken English soccer fans who were unhappy that their team had lost.

A central issue concerning what shapes group behavior in domains such as sports and nationalism concerns the relationship between, on the one hand, material interests and, on the other hand, identity and meanings (Gutmann, 2003; Huddy, 2013). This issue reflects a broader debate among scholars who have argued for a materialist explanation of group and intergroup dynamics and those who have advocated for the primacy of psychological factors (Moghaddam, 2008b). From the perspective of materialist theories, which include a variety of Marxist theories, resource mobilization theory, system justification theory, and realistic conflict theory (Moghaddam, 2008b), the most important underlying factors are shared instrumental interests that could serve as a basis for group formation and mobilization. That shared instrumental interests do not always serve as a basis for group formation and mobilization reflects, according to the Marxist tradition (Marx, 1852/1979; Marx & Engels, 1848/1967), *false consciousness*, the inability of individuals to accurately perceive their own group membership and what are assumed to be their social class interests.

Identity groups are characterized by identification with particular social markers rather than shared instrumental interests as the main basis for group formation (Gutmann, 2003). Consider, for example, the case of individuals who, in terms of phenotypic characteristics, could pass as White but choose to identify themselves as African American to show solidarity with a disadvantaged group. For such individuals, identity and identification is driven by ideology rather than material self-centered interests—which would have led them to identify with the dominant White group.

The extensive literature on identity politics has recognized the powerful role of identity in politics and in social movements (Calhoun, 1994). Some research has suggested that, at the root of democratic movements, such as the collective mobilization of immigrant groups struggling for their rights (Brodkin, 2007), is the challenge of developing coherent group identities. In addition to coherence, *distinctiveness* of identity becomes particularly important when the political policies and interests of competitors are similar. For example, only small policy differences existed between the policies of Barack Obama and Hillary Clinton, the two main Democratic candidates for the 2008 Democratic Party presidential nomination. However, to attract followers, the candidates had to demonstrate some level of distinctiveness, such as in moral positions (Iyer, Graham, Koleva, Ditto, & Haidt, 2010).

CONCLUSION

Group identities of various kinds that are based on religious, ethnic, linguistic, nationality, sport club, and other such criteria for categorization are alive and well in the 21st century, as is evident from the fact that leaders continue to mobilize support for themselves by appealing to such group identities. Observing fans during the football World Cup with their team colors, dances, and chants, and their extreme fervor reminds us how deep group sentiments are among 21st-century humans. Leaders still find it convenient and effective to use these primitive sentiments to mobilize collective support for themselves, particularly by manufacturing and highlighting intergroup differences and identifying certain groups as "the other." To paraphrase Freud (1930/1961, p. 114), manipulative leaders can get the ingroup to love one another, as long as some people are left over to hate as the outgroup.

In both Western and non-Western societies, leaders continue to use hatred of outgroups to boost their own following. It can be claimed that, even in servant leadership, the leader is helping an ingroup and by default opposing outgroups because that is what ingroup members want. However, what people want is not static; rather, what people want is constructed to some degree by the leadership and can move in more constructive, less tribal directions. This movement is part of the journey to actualized democracy.

Progress on the path to democratic actualization, short of a revolutionary rupture, requires that leaders guide and inspire collectives to realize their democratic potential. The leader himself or herself must have a pro-democracy style and not be motivated to monopolize power and resources. Unfortunately, in many countries, the main motivation of individuals to attain leadership positions is to accumulate power and resources. The failure of revolutions to move from dictatorship toward democracy, as recently occurred in Iran, Egypt, Russia, and some other nations, is partly because the leaders who emerge are primarily motivated to monopolize their own power rather than step aside in a timely manner (e.g., as Nelson Mandela did) and establish a democratic tradition of turn-taking in their societies.

5

RULE OF LAW

All are equal before the law and are entitled without any discrimination
to equal protection of the law.
—Article 7, United Nations (UN, 1948) Universal Declaration of
Human Rights

The idea that the law should apply equally to all people has a long
history (Tamanaha, 2004). In Aristotle's (trans. 1943) *Politics* and Plato's
(trans. 1987) *The Republic*, law was set above men as something that should
govern everyone. No citizen would be subjected to arbitrary arrest, and those
correctly arrested would be subject to the same legal procedures and enjoy
the same legal rights. This did not mean society was conceived as egalitarian,
and, as in Plato's case, certainly was not democratic. In Plato's *The Republic*,
rulers had gold in their makeup, auxiliaries had silver, and farmers and other
workers had iron and bronze. However, even rulers had to be governed
by laws, and, indeed, Plato explicitly proposed that the laws should serve
as the foundation of meritocracy so that bronze children born to gold or
silver parents would be allowed to slide down the status hierarchy, whereas
gold children born to bronze or silver parents would be permitted to rise up
and become rulers (Plato, trans. 1987, *Book III* 415b, c, d). Thus, power and

http://dx.doi.org/10.1037/14806-006
The Psychology of Democracy, by F. M. Moghaddam

status would be distributed on the basis of individual merit, rather than group membership (e.g., the family one is born into). Failure to allow such social mobility would result in the collapse of society. Thus, although Plato was critical of democracy, he supported meritocracy.

Tensions inherent in rule of law, such as those involving meritocracy and democracy, are reflected in the debates of the ancients. In his timeless play *Antigone* (written around 442 BC), Sophocles (497 or 496 BC–406 or 405 BC) highlighted the tension between the formal law of society and the law as dictated by private individual conscience, as well as between the ruler and the people as enforcers of law. Antigone defies formal law: She buries her brother, the rebel Polyneices, instead of allowing his body to be exposed to the elements and eaten by wild animals, as formal law dictates. But when the ruler, Creon, wants to punish her, he is reminded that the people, if asked, will side with Antigone. She follows her private conscience, saying, "I will bury the brother I love" (Sophocles, trans. 1977, p. 188). The same tensions have continued in modern times: Henry David Thoreau's (1817–1862) essay on civil disobedience (Thoreau, 2008) gives voice to a modern strand of civil protest, which includes the heroic nonviolent political campaigns of Mohandas Gandhi (1869–1948) and Martin Luther King, Jr. (1929–1968). For example, Gandhi protested British taxes by leading a nearly 240-mile march in 1930, and King led a boycott of segregated buses in Montgomery, Alabama, in 1955–1956. Those individuals followed their moral conscience, even when it conflicted with formal law. Their disobedience inspired entire movements to go against, and ultimately change, the formal law of the land.

Thus, sometimes a tension and even a contradiction exist between formal law and ethical precepts citizens may feel compelled to follow. Reform of formal law ultimately may occur through this clash. When a sufficient number of people with material and intellectual resources recognize that formal law is supporting an immoral system and that basic human rights are being violated, a collective movement takes place to arrive at rights from wrongs (Dershowitz, 2004). For example, until the 1865 ratification of the U.S. Constitution's Thirteenth Amendment, which outlawed slavery throughout the United States, slavery was backed by formal law in much of what had been, before the secession of the South, the United States. But increasing numbers of individuals and groups followed their private conscience and acted to end slavery. They developed the Underground Railroad to help slaves escape to freedom, although such action was illegal. This turning away from the wrongs of slavery gained momentum until the rights to freedom became widely accepted. The wide acceptance eventually forced reform in formal law.

Despite the tension between formal law and private morality, the application of formal law in an equal manner across all individuals and groups is seen to be an essential part of national development. According to the UN (2011), *rule of law*

> refers to a principle of governance in which all persons, institutions and entities, public and private, including the State itself, are accountable to laws that are publicly promulgated, equally enforced and independently adjudicated, and which are consistent with international human rights norms and standards. It requires, as well, measures to ensure adherence to the principles of supremacy of law, equality before the law, account-ability to the law, fairness in the application of the law, separation of powers, participation in decision-making, avoidance of arbitrariness and procedural and legal transparency. (pp. v–vi)

RULE OF LAW, NATIONAL DEVELOPMENT, AND THE ESTABLISHMENT OF THE MODERN STATE

> Nothing distinguishes more clearly conditions in a free country from those in a country under arbitrary government than the observance in the former of the great principles known as the Rule of Law. Stripped of all its technicalities, this means that the government in all its actions is bound by rules fixed and announced beforehand. (Hayek, 1944/1969, p. 72)

The importance of rule of law has elevated it as a central topic in a broader conversation about its necessity for robust national development. A variety of factors shape national development and economic growth, including social infrastructure, geography, and international trade (which, in turn, depends on adherence to international agreements—in other words, rule of law). Some researchers have argued that national development and economic growth are driven by *social infrastructure*, that is, social assets that include schools, hospitals, and community housing, that is based on the qual-ity of institutions and government policies—integral to which is rule of law (Hall & Jones, 1999). When rule of law is in place, and more broadly when institutions and government policies are of high quality, the conditions are conducive to entrepreneurship, investment, and trade. People can plan for the future and accurately assess the level of risk involved in business and other ventures, so they are more comfortable developing innovative prac-tices. Rodrik, Subramanian, and Trebbi (2004) found support for this social infrastructure explanation of national development and economic growth that was tested against two other explanations: the geography and the market integration models.

The best-known advocate of the *geography thesis* is Jared M. Diamond (2005), who, in his bestselling book *Guns, Germs, and Steel*, argued that environmental factors, and not biological differences, have determined the different rates of development on different continents. The centralized political organizations and sophisticated technologies that developed in some parts of the world were made possible by food surpluses, which could only come about where concentrated and stable farming populations with domesticated animals emerged. J. M. Diamond (2005) identified nine such farming population centers, which gradually became the dominant powers of the world. The technologies, cultures and other key features of these powers—their guns, germs, and steel—spread to help them dominate the modern world.

Another explanation of national development and economic growth is the *market integration view*, which proposes that international trade is the underlying motor for change (Dollar & Kraay, 2004). When countries lower tariffs, facilitate free trade, and take steps to increase international trade, their peoples benefit from being integrated into and profiting from the global economy, or so the argument goes. Increased commerce then is supposed to lead to increased growth and poverty reduction. But this view assumes that market integration takes place on a level playing field. In practice, the playing field is uneven: More powerful countries are the center of international companies that set the rules for trade. For example, the major pharmaceutical companies are based in Western countries and regulate prices for medications throughout the world.

All three of the aforementioned perspectives are, to some degree, valid, and rule of law, the focus of this chapter, does have an important role in national development. However, there are serious criticisms of rule of law and the role envisaged for it in national development. The following is a review of the limitations of rule of law; I attempt to show how, nevertheless, rule of law can have a constructive influence on the journey to democratic actualization. An important condition for such positive influence is a nation's acceptance of and respect for universal rights and duties. Embrace of the UN (1948) Universal Declaration of Human Rights, the International Criminal Court (ICC), and other key international declarations and organizations provides a constructive start for meeting this challenge.

PSYCHOLOGICAL ASSUMPTIONS AND LIMITATIONS OF THE RULE OF LAW

The psychological assumption that underlies rule of law is the assumed rationality of humans. I discuss how rule of law relies heavily on a central authority, typically a federal government, for implementation—and the problem this poses, namely, the central authority might itself violate the rule of law. On the international stage, the superpower role of the United States means that America can, and has, stood outside the law on important issues, for example. I also discuss two potential and more subtle shortcomings: (a) rule of law is a necessary but insufficient condition for justice; in addition to the rule of law, the law itself must be just. And (b) multiple laws sometimes contradict one another, which poses a problem for the rule-of-law concept, at least on paper. I examine a common misunderstanding that has resulted in political solutions being vilified and rule of law being seen as superior. I argue that, in some conditions, political solutions can be more inclusive and fair than rule of law.

Rule of Law and the Assumption of Rationality

> Anyone who takes up psycho-analytic work will quickly discover that a symptom has more than one meaning and serves to represent several unconscious mental processes simultaneously. (Freud, 1901–1905/1953, p. 11)

> I often cringe when my work with Amos [Tversky, Kahneman's frequent collaborator] is credited with demonstrating that human choices are irrational, when in fact our research only showed that Humans are not well described by the rational-agent model. Although Humans are not irrational, they often need help to make more accurate judgments and better decisions. (Kahneman, 2011, p. 411)

The idea that the law should apply to all people equally rests on a number of important psychological assumptions among which is the assumption that people are rational and conscious of the factors that influence their behavior, including the factors that influence their attempts to apply the law in an inclusive manner. Of course, it could be argued that rule of law requires fairness but not necessarily rationality. However, rationality is a prerequisite for fairness: A system based on irrationality is arbitrary and, as such, is more likely to have unfair outcomes.

At least two research traditions in psychology challenge the assumption of rationality. First, the psychoanalytic research tradition, shaped largely by Freud (1856–1939) initially, directly challenges the assumption of human rationality: It proposes that behavior is strongly influenced by unconscious factors. According to this tradition, a myriad of unconscious factors could influence people in how they interpret and apply the law. Consequently, even though the conscious intention might be to establish rule of law as a rational process, the actual outcome may be different in practice. For example, racial profiling continues in the United States, even though it is deemed illegal and often is officially frowned upon (Harris, 2003). It persists in part because some of the cognitive processes involved in profiling are not conscious to the individuals who are committing the profiling. Such unconscious factors, along with racial prejudice and other factors, result in some great injustices: "Imprisonment rates for black Americans have long been five to seven times higher than those for whites" (Tonry, 2010, p. 273).

Second, the more recent tradition of cognitive research, represented by Kahneman (2011) and others, highlights serious shortcomings in how people make decisions and judgments. The focus here is on cool automatic processes rather than hot motivated biases highlighted in the Freudian tradition. People are unaware of shortcomings in their decision making (although Kahneman, 2011, argued that this represents faulty decision making, not irrationality). In another strand of this second tradition is a growing literature on the controversial (Arkes & Tetlock, 2004) Implicit Association Test (IAT), which supposedly measures biases of which we ourselves are unaware (A. G. Greenwald, Poehlman, Uhlmann, & Banaji, 2009). Results from the IAT have been used to argue that racial prejudice and discrimination persist, particularly against African Americans in the United States.

One interpretation of this new cognitive tradition is that some biases are associated with rapid, split-second thinking and arise from the functional demands of survival. For example, security needs often lead us to make split-second decisions about the trustworthiness of strangers on the basis of mere physical appearance. This decision making involves fast, automatic cognitive processing. In contrast, the Freudian tradition depicts irrationality as arising from a dynamic process of psychological experiences that are pushed into the unconscious. The push comes from the clash among individual desires, motives, and inclinations, and the taboos of society. Despite these differences, the two approaches are similar in that they highlight how rule of law can become faulty in both design and implementation.

The Danger of Government's Monopoly Power

The sole end for which mankind are warranted, individually or collectively, in interfering with the liberty of action of any of their number, is self-protection. That the only purpose for which power can be rightfully exercised over any member of a civilized community, against his will, is to prevent harm to others. His own good, either physical or moral, is not a sufficient warrant. . . . In the part which merely concerns himself, his independence is, of right, absolute. Over himself, over his own body and mind, the individual is sovereign. (Mill, 1859/1975, pp. 10–11)

The notion of mental illness implies (1) the positive value of "mental health," and (2) certain criteria according to which states of mental health and illness can be "diagnosed." In the name of this value . . . the same sorts of actions may be undertaken as were carried out by medieval man marching under the banner of God and Christ. . . . First, those who are considered especially strong and healthy . . . are rewarded. The ath-

letes, the beauty queens, the movie stars are the modern day "saints. . . ."
Who are the people who are persecuted and victimized in the name of
"health" and "happiness"? . . . In their front ranks are the mentally ill, and
especially those who are so defined by others rather than by themselves.
(Szasz, 1961, pp. 218–219)

If rule of law is to be implemented, presumably it must be largely,
although not exclusively, through government action. As such, it creates a
danger that the government will stand above and beyond rule of law. Such a
danger has been recognized by numerous thinkers, including John Stuart Mill
(1859/1975) in his seminal work *On Liberty*. Mill adopted the position that
the government has no right to restrict the freedoms of citizens, even when
such government intervention is for "his own good, either physical or moral"
(p. 6), except to protect other citizens from harm (of course, this government
duty to protect other citizens from harm opens the door to government intervention in areas such as environmental pollution). This position was taken
up more recently by the antipsychiatry thinkers led by Thomas Szasz (1961)
and R. D. Laing (Laing & Esterson, 1964). They argued that mental health
experts and other authorities are wrong to label as schizophrenic, manic-
depressive, and the like, those whom they deem to be insane. These labels are
particularly damaging when government-sanctioned authorities use them.
This broad critique is against the overwhelming power of the state and goes
beyond the accusation that, in some communist states, some political prisoners were said to suffer from serious mental disorders (even if no signs of it were
evident) and incarcerated in mental institutions (Munro, 2000).

Hayek (1944/1969), well liked by conservative politicians such as
Ronald Reagan and Margaret Thatcher, was one of a number of right-wing
thinkers who had been critical of selected government interventions, particularly in the economic sphere. He assumed that rule of law helps contain
the power of the government in cultural and other domains. However, the
sheer expanse and complexity of technology wielded by government agencies
means that it has become difficult for citizens groups to track government
activities—even while the government is itself monitoring citizens groups
in illegal ways (Granick & Sprigman, 2013). Ironically, the central government has increased surveillance under both conservative (e.g., George W.
Bush, 2000–2008 administration) and liberal (Barack Obama, 2009–2016
administration) U.S. presidents.

Rule of law has not prevented expansion of government power, nor
has it been able to remedy the relative powerlessness of the masses in the
21st century. Labor unions have become weaker in the era of globalization. Ordinary citizens are left relatively powerless in comparison with the
power of both private-sector international corporations and central governments. Globalization has particularly empowered international business

corporations. However, the danger that governments pose to civil liberties is in some respects even greater, as is evident in the case of the National Security Agency (NSA), the U.S. agency that has been monitoring private communications of hundreds of millions of people around the world—in some cases, illegally. The NSA case raises serious questions about how U.S. government practices can be monitored in their adherence to rule of law (Granick & Sprigman, 2013).

The historic practice of many states' directly using the legal system for their ideological goals becomes clear after reviewing major revolutions. Historically, revolutionaries have acted to change the legal system in line with their ideologies. After the 1917 Russian Revolution, for example, Vladimir Lenin embarked on changing the legal system in line with the goals of communism (Varga, 1982/1992b). I witnessed a similar trend in Iran, where, after the 1979 revolution, Ruhollah Khomeini and his followers "Islamicized" the Iranian legal system according to Khomeini's interpretation of Islam. Earlier in the 20th century, the Nazis took over the German legal system and made the "will of the Fuehrer" law (N. S. Marsh, 1946/1992, p. 566). These examples suggest that international organizations will need to try to serve as a last line of defense against local tyranny. Fanatical movements inspired by fascist ideology and religions tend to spill across national borders, and require international cooperation to defeat.

RULE OF LAW AND "FAIRNESS" IN AN INTERNATIONAL CONTEXT

Rule of law has come to have a central and important role in the international system, and is given high priority by the UN, the World Bank, and other international organizations. In the UN (2011) discussion of rule of law, a central place is given to international human rights norms. The clear implication is that it is not enough to abide by any law: The law itself must be just.

"Might Is Right": International Organizations and U.S. Support

International organizations can only become effective in supporting rule of law if they have support from major countries. Unfortunately, the United States presently refuses to ratify some important international treaties, including those that support the ICC (see Hafner's, 2005, interesting defense of the U.S. position). In the U.S. view, it seems that might is right and, in practice, rule of law only applies to the weaker nations. Whereas African leaders, such as Charles Taylor, former leader of the National Patriotic Front of Liberia, have been arrested and put on trial for crimes against humanity,

American leaders remain immune from such persecution despite accusations of serious crimes. Renowned Stanford researcher Philip Zimbardo (2007) argued, for example, that the George W. Bush administration, with "The Vice President of Torture" Dick Cheney (p. 432), became an exemplar of "administrative evil" (p. 437).

The African scholar Charles Villa-Vicencio (2009) rightly criticized the might-is-right foundation of the way national leaders are held accountable. Discussing the case of the former Iraqi dictator Saddam Hussein (a case the United States did not put before the ICC), Villa-Vicencio (2009) wrote,

> He was convicted of crimes against humanity, for the killing and torture of 148 Shiite villagers in Dujail following a failed assassination attempt in 1982. He was sentenced to death and subsequently hanged. The courts did not address the more extensive record of his reign of terror. Questions about America and the West encouraging Hussein to invade Iran in 1980—an invasion that led to the deaths of 1.5 million people—were not posed. The supply of chemical weapons components, with which Saddam drenched Iran and the Kurds; the anarchy unleashed by American and British troops in the aftermath of what was described as a "mission accomplished"; and the use of Saddam's Abu Ghraib torture chambers by American torturers are not part of the court record. (p. 109)

Such serious criticisms from major international scholars reflect the complexity of applying rule of law. Institutions such as the ICC can bring benefits (Glasius, 2006), but only when every nation and its leaders are equal before the law. This is not the case at present. Critics have helped highlight the role of cultural context in applying law, a topic I discuss next.

Legal Pluralism Versus Legal Uniformity

The idea of rule of law raises the question, Whose law? As discussed earlier, historical and contemporary evidence can be cited to support the view that rule of law sometimes translates to might is right. Those who enjoy greater power can shape the law to be biased in favor of their own interests. This trend is evident in the colonial context of the 16th to 19th centuries, when Western powers, such as France, Spain, and Great Britain, colonized African, Asian, Australian, and the American lands. In each colony, the colonial powers swept aside local legal systems and established their own. Typically, the colonies, such as India, went from legal pluralism to legal uniformity.

Rule of law in the colonies implemented colonial law through the influence of a Western-trained indigenous elite. The multiplicity of local customs, informal norms, rules, and alternative dispute resolution procedures were seen as backward. This change from legal pluralism to legal uniformity helped bind the economies of the colonies to the colonial powers, which brought long-term problems associated with economic exploitation to the colonies (Ma & van Zanden, 2011).

The irony in this situation is that, even within the Western societies, different legal traditions have developed, such as those giving priority to common law (law developed by judges), or civil law (codified law originating from Roman law), or socialist law (civil law influenced by communist ideology; Chloros, 1978/1992). Ellickson's (1991) studies examined how disputes are settled between neighbors in the U.S. West, such as when animals stray into a neighboring ranch and cause damage. Locals often use their own informal methods for resolving conflicts. That research showed that, even in contemporary Western societies, in practice, a high level of legal pluralism exists.

Formalist Versus Substantivist Interpretations of Law

> For my friends, everything; for my enemies, the law. (Vargas, see O'Donnell, 2004, p. 40)

Rule of law is not enough to achieve justice because the law can be, and has been, used instead as a means for supporting injustice. For dictators such as President Getúlio Vargas (1882–1954) of Brazil, the law can be a weapon against political opponents. In Iran before the 1979 revolution, it was the corrupt shah and his extended family and friends who framed and misused the law to expand their own personal power and profits. After the revolution, the new constitution of the Islamic Republic of Iran gave absolute power to one man, the so-called Supreme Leader. According to the law, this one man (of course, it can never be a woman) has the right to decide on every single aspect of life for the rest of the 80 million Iranian population. A formalist interpretation of rule of law is in line with such practices because a formalist interpretation is unconcerned with the justice of the law.

According to an alternative *substantivist* interpretation of law, which assumes certain rights are integral to rule of law, it is not enough to apply the law to everyone consistently, but the law also has to be correct. I support this perspective. But, according to what criteria do we decide about the "correctness" of law? This is where international standards become relevant, starting with the UN (1948) Universal Declaration of Human Rights.

The application of international standards raises questions about the relative value of local standards and moral orders. Is there not a danger that the most powerful nations will determine international standards and thus force smaller societies to bend to their will through the force of international law? In the next section, I discuss the merits of political solutions as answers to these questions.

Rule of Law Versus "Political Solutions"

Rule of law has been put forward as a *neutral* solution, meaning unbiased, and has been contrasted with *political*, meaning partisan, solutions that are supposedly biased. It is useful to reassess this perspective and not oversimplify rule of law as neutral and politics as completely partisan. Rule of law often is advocated as a neutral or objective solution by those who argue that nonpolitical solutions to problems are needed. The opposite is argued by Aristotle (trans. 1943) in his *Aristotle's Politics*, by Machiavelli (1531/2003) in his *The Discourses*, and, most recently, by Crick (1962).

The Aristotelian tradition is to see politics, in its best form, as different groups and individuals in society who are actively participating in the political system and working out solutions that reflect their various, and sometimes contradictory, interests. This is inevitably a messy process involving forced compromises or ending in gridlock. However, the process of arriving at an agreement between parties with opposing ideologies and interests itself strengthens the state because it requires the participation of citizens from diverse groups who are achieving a political goal. The state that has a politically involved citizenry is ultimately stronger because it has citizens as defenders.

Of course, to function effectively, politics interpreted this way must involve groups and individuals wedded to the same basic ideals of freedom and who are willing to compromise when negotiating. Fundamentalism of every kind, particularly religious fundamentalism, will bring an end to this kind of balanced politics. This is a point highlighted by Ian Buruma (2007) in this vivid description of a fanatical Muslim's brutal murder in Amsterdam of Theo van Gogh, a Dutch filmmaker who criticized Islam:

> An essential part of enlightenment thinking is that everything, especially claims to "nonnegotiable" and "fundamental" values, should be open to criticism. The whole point of liberal democracy, its greatest strength, especially in the Netherlands, is that conflicting faiths, interests, and views can be resolved only through negotiation. The only thing that cannot be negotiated is the use of violence. (pp. 34–35)

We have to pause at this point and question the claim that everything is negotiable except the use of violence. This perspective, too, is problematic for at least two reasons. First, it endorses an extreme form of relativism, which works particularly against the interests of minority groups (Moghaddam, 1992). In situations in which everything is negotiable, those with most power usually prevail and enforce their own standards through force. Universal rights and duties are the best protection for those with less power. The second reason why this perspective is problematic is that it assumes that only extremists have nonnegotiable positions. This is not true: it is not only Islamic fundamentalists, right-wing-nationalists, neo-Nazi groups, and other extremists who have nonnegotiable positions.

Back to the Challenge of Relativism

Are we on firm ground when we claim that there are universals in justice? This position seems to be undermined by variations in formal law and different legal systems around the world, as documented through comparative legal studies (Varga, 1992a) and translations of non-Western legal systems (see, e.g., Doniger, 1991). The UN (1948) Universal Declaration of Human Rights was created after the end of World War II, particularly through the efforts of Eleanor Roosevelt (1884–1962), the first chair of the U.N. Commission on Human Rights. Research showed that these rights are being adopted around the world, particularly by younger people (Doise, 2002). Does this adoption demonstrate that certain rights are universal?

A number of arguments can be made for universals in human rights. For example, the idea that law is necessary for national development implies that all societies need to achieve a certain type of legal system and conception of law to develop according to the traditional criteria (e.g., improved gross domestic product). On the other hand, this assumption about the relationship between law and national development has been criticized severely (Carty, 1992b). Critics have argued that it is a continuation of colonial thinking (Carty, 1992a, referred to it as the "Legal imperialism debate," p. xi): To make progress, non-Western societies need to adopt Western ways of doing things, including adopting Western courts of justice. My position is that basic human rights are a necessary foundation for healthy national development.

Just as I put forward the nine components of actualized democracy as a universal ideal, I argue that certain duties and rights need to be universally adopted. The duties and rights I have in mind are those necessary to achieve actualized democracy. These duties and rights are reflected in, but are not confined to, the UN (1948) Universal Declaration of Human Rights. The U.N. declaration fails to give adequate importance to *collective* duties and rights, which form the basis for progress in distributive justice and other important steps toward actualized democracy.

CONCLUSION

My focus has been on the conditions to be met so that rule of law will achieve its constructive role in the journey to actualized democracy. First and foremost, the law itself must be just. In many parts of the world, including my own country of origin, Iran, the law is unjust and undemocratic, and leads to the treatment of power minorities (e.g., women) as second-class citizens. In other major countries, such as Russia and China, rulers change the law to perpetuate their own power monopolies. Obviously, rule of law fails to benefit the vast majority of people in these countries.

At the international level, the United States, in some instances, has adopted a might-is-right attitude toward the UN and some other aspects of the international system, including international law. The United States, as we have seen, has, in some instances, also refused to apply international law to its own leadership and its own actions, including in the use of electronic surveillance. These behaviors need to be reformed for progress to be made toward democratic actualization.

6

LEADERS REMOVABLE THROUGH POPULAR WILL

Chaeronea changed Greece forever. Even ancient writers recognized the magnitude of Philip's victory: "with the bodies of those who fell here was buried the freedom of the Greeks," the Athenian orator Lycurgus lamented.

—Ian Worthington (2013, p. 254)

The defeat of the Greeks at the battle of Chaeronea (338 BC) gave Philip of Macedon (382–336 BC), the father of Alexander the Great, considerable power over Athens. Philip could have destroyed Athens, but he proved to be a shrewd leader. Although he was an absolute monarch, he recognized that his rule over the Greeks would be far more effective and efficient if he treated Athens judiciously and maneuvered the Athenians to cooperate with him. Consequently, the defeat of Greece and the eventual demise of Athenian democracy did not mean that King Philip, and Alexander the Great who followed, completely disregarded the wishes of the people of Greece.

Well before the emergence of modern democracies, insightful leaders, even the absolute monarchs, recognized that governance would be easier when the people cooperated with the ruler and at least despised the ruler less. Machiavelli (1532/1950) provided advice along these lines in *The Prince*: "The prince must . . . avoid those things which will make him hated or despised" (p. 66) and

http://dx.doi.org/10.1037/14806-007
The Psychology of Democracy, by F. M. Moghaddam

one of the most potent remedies that a prince has against conspiracies, is that of not being hated by the mass of the people; for whoever conspires always believes that he will satisfy the people by the death of their prince; but if he thought to offend them by doing this, he would fear to engage in such an undertaking. (pp. 67–68)

This idea (as discussed in Chapter 4) that the likes and dislikes of the people matter, even in strong monarchies, is supported by evidence from China, England, and other countries where emperors or monarchs were toppled after ruling for long periods on the basis of a divine right (Perry, 2001). As Charles I (1600–1649), the king of England, Scotland, and Ireland who was executed in 1649, discovered, even though he was not brought to power by popular acclaim, he could be toppled by a popular revolt.

The idea that leaders should be removable by popular will is an important and essential step in the journey toward actualized democracy. This idea did not arise in a vacuum. Rather, it arose from a historical context integral to which is the idea of a social contract between citizens and rulers. In the first section of this chapter, I examine the social contract from a psychological perspective and explores the concept of the psychological social contract that was introduced in Chapter 1. The emergence of the idea that leaders should be removable by popular will, it turns out, is closely associated with changes in the psychological justification for rule by a leader. In the chapter's second section, I examine how the justification for leader authority has changed over time and how this change is associated with psychological research.

THE PSYCHOLOGICAL SOCIAL CONTRACT

The concept of social contract is reflected in the works of Plato and others who wrote in the era of classical Greece 2,500 years ago. In Plato's (trans. 1987) *The Republic*, the state must arrive at the cardinal qualities of wisdom, courage, discipline, and justice by achieving harmony among the different social classes. The Guardians who rule come to an agreement with the lower classes they govern because everyone understands it benefits society to function in this stratified and orderly manner. Being the numerically smallest group, the Guardians exercise authority through wisdom rather than by force:

So the state founded on natural principles is wise as a whole in virtue of the knowledge inherent in its smallest constituent part or class, which exercises authority over the rest. And it appears further that the naturally smallest class is the one which is endowed with that form of knowledge which alone of all others deserves the title of wisdom. (Plato, trans. 1987, *Book Four* 198–199e)

The concept of social contract is taken up more explicitly more than 2,000 years later during the classical era of social contract theory, most notably in the work of Thomas Hobbes (1588–1679; see Hobbes, 1651/1991), John Locke (1632–1704), David Hume (1711–1776; see Hume, 1748/1948), and Jean-Jacques Rousseau (1712–1778). John Rawls (1921–2002) made a major contribution to this tradition in more recent times.

An underlying theme in the classic 17th- and 18th-century writings on the subject was the assumption that, sometime in the historical past, the rulers and the ruled had agreed on some kind of contract. As Hume (1748/1948) put it, when we trace government to its original roots before the development of modern settlements, it must have been through "their own consent, and their sense of the advantages resulting from peace and order" (p. 149) that people came to agree to be governed by a central authority. Because people are fairly equal in their strengths and abilities, it would have been impossible to force the majority to accept governance by a minority without majority agreement. No traces of this original contract exist because it was before the development of writing, but "we trace it plainly in the nature of man" (Hume, 1748/1948, p. 149). Thus, the recognition that life in society is safer and more comfortable led people to submit to government authority, or as Hobbes (1651/1991) put it, "Fear of oppression, disposeth a man . . . to seek ayd by society: for there is no other way by which a man can secure his life and liberty" (pp. 71–72).

Lack of Empirical Basis for the Logical Social Contract

This logical social contract supposed by Hume, Hobbes, and others does not have a basis in anthropological or historical data. Furthermore, it assumed people to be rational, understand their own interests, and select paths to best satisfy those personal interests. The same assumptions of rationality underlie Rawls's (1971, p. 12) proposal that people should make decisions "in a veil of ignorance" about their own group memberships. Rawls assumed that, under conditions in which I do not know which group I will fall into—whether I am rich or poor, Black or White, male or female, and so on—I will be fair in my decision making. After all, if I make decisions that are biased against a particular group, I may well end up being a member of the group against which I have shown biases. For example, if I support racist policies, I might find that I myself am an ethnic minority member and a target of racism. Moreover, the veil of ignorance assumes that individuals will follow paths that maximize their interests. However, in practice, some individuals and groups are ready to destroy themselves to destroy others. Consider, for example, suicide terrorists. An even more devastating example is leaders, such as Saddam Hussein and Ruhollah Khomeini, who have dragged their nations through years of destructive warfare to try to destroy the other. Their hatred of others, and sometimes themselves, is overwhelming (Moghaddam, 2006).

The power of the logical social contract lay not in its rationalist assumptions but in its revolutionary implications: If the original social contract had arisen in the distant past, when the people consented to be governed by leaders, then the people *could take back* their consent. If the people in the past decided it would be beneficial to live in a society and be ruled by an elite, then they *could decide* that the benefits were insufficient to continue that arrangement. The people could dismiss the leaders they had *chosen* to be ruled by. This is one interpretation of revolutions against leadership and the executions of Charles I in England in 1649, Louis XVI in France in 1792, and Nicholas II in Russia in 1918.

However, a number of ideological justifications were developed in an attempt to nullify the revolutionary implications of the logical social contract. These ideological justifications varied across time and across cultures, but their basic function was to legitimize and extend the rule of unelected leaders. The justifications served to negate the idea that the people could demand a different system of organization or a different leadership—for themselves and for society. For example, kings justified their rule by the ideology of the divine right of kings, which proposed that the monarch was God's representative on earth. As James I (1566–1625), king of Scotland and England, put it, "Kings are . . . Gods Lieutenants upon earth . . . and sit upon Gods throne" (quoted in Burgess, 1992, p. 837). Although this ideology faded in Western societies, the divine right of kings continued into the modern era to serve as a basis for monarchical rule in some countries, such as Iran in the age of the shah (Milani, 2011).

If God can assign kings to be rulers, then religious leaders also can be favored in this way. Indeed, according to traditional thinking, religious leaders are even more likely to receive such favors from God. The new constitution established in Iran after the 1979 revolution gave absolute and final decision-making power to a supreme religious leader assumed to be the representative of the absent imam on earth. The implication is that rebellion against the government in postrevolution Iran is a rebellion against God's representative on earth. The pope used similar justifications for his rule when he also was emperor. When unelected and unchecked rulers become the head of both the systems of government and religion, corruption and despotism soar.

The Shift From Duties to Rights

Industrialization in Western societies was associated with major changes in the characteristics of psychological citizens and leader–follower relations. The psychological citizen in preindustrialized societies was socialized to function within, and to sustain, social relationships and leader–follower relations based on *duties*, or what an individual owes to others. The progress made in preindustrial societies toward establishing rule of law initially was focused on codifying and getting agreement about duties first and foremost. The important progressive step forward represented by the Magna Carta, agreed to by King John at Runnymede, England, in 1215, formalized the duties of the king, particularly toward freemen. Medieval psychological citizens functioned through networks of duties that bound them to their lords and to the monarch, and to one another. Considerable power disparities existed, and society was highly stratified, but both the rulers and the ruled were bound by their obligations to one another.

Industrialization and the development of capitalism transformed social relationships so that duties began to take a backseat to *rights*, or what a person is owed. Moreover, in the context of capitalist democracies, rights have been interpreted as belonging to individuals rather than collectives (the collective receives almost no attention in the United Nations Universal Declaration of Human Rights, adopted by the UN General Assembly in 1948; the collective is mentioned only once, in Article 29, in a discussion of the duty of everyone to the community). This shift of focus from duties to individual rights was associated with a decline in the importance of land and a rise in the importance of capital, particularly from the 18th century onward. As long as land was the main source of wealth, those who worked the land in various ways owed duties to landowners. These duty-based relationships served as the backbone of social order. After the rise in importance of capital, industrial production, and urbanization, the population became far more mobile, geographically and, to some degree, socially (although social mobility has been shown to be less than generally suggested by ideas such as the American Dream over the past few centuries; see Clark, 2014).

The decline in the traditional landed gentry in power and the rise of the new capitalist class are reflected in the great novels of the 19th century. When Jane Austen (1775–1817) was publishing her most important works at the start of the 19th century, the major characters who enjoyed power in her novels, such as Mr. Darcy in *Pride and Prejudice* (1813) and Mr. John Dashwood in *Sense and Sensibility* (1811), derived their status and wealth from land rather than from business and fluid capital. In a slightly later work, *Mansfield Park* (1814), however, Sir Thomas Bertram relies heavily on trade associated with his estate in Antigua. This trade reflects a shrinking world in which slavery and other forms of exploitation are part of international business. However, his business is still based on land and people tied to land in the form of plantations worked by slaves.

By the time George Eliot (1819–1880) was publishing her masterpieces later in the 19th century, the major characters in her novels reflected the shift of power from the traditional landed gentry to the new capitalist class. In Eliot's (1872/1964) *Middlemarch*, the influence of Sir James Chettam and other traditional landed gentry is overshadowed by the banker Mr. Bulstrode and other men of commerce. Mr. Bulstrode has capital, is mobile, and is not rooted to any particular location or community. He leaves the town of Middlemarch at the end of the novel just as easily as he entered it earlier to set up his banking business.

In *Middlemarch*, Eliot (1872/1964) also charts the changes occurring in psychological citizens. These changes are clearly reflected in Will Ladislaw, a young man who points the way to the new, more democratic and rights-based political movements sweeping across many Western societies at that time. In England, the rising power of the middle class brought to center stage new types of political leaders: ones more directly beholden to middle-class voters than to the landed gentry for their power. Revolutions broke out across Europe in 1848 (the *Communist Manifesto* was published in the same year; see Marx & Engels, 1848/1967), and eventually Ladislaw was elected as a politician beholden to the people and progressive ideas. The psychological citizens who emerged in 19th-century England gradually brought individual rights to the forefront and diminished the importance of duties to traditional authority figures and land-owning gentry.

If belief in individual rights is a central characteristic of the psychological citizen that emerged with capitalism, capitalism also brought group-based inequalities based on new social relationships. Capital accumulated in the hands of a tiny minority that was able to buy the labor of the majority. Both working class and professional middle-class people sold their skills on the marketplace. The buyers were the owners of capital. New legitimization ideologies were needed to make individual rights and group-based inequalities compatible. In Western societies, and gradually more globally, certain strains of the science of psychology have come to play just such a legitimization role.

PSYCHOLOGICAL RESEARCH AND EMERGING JUSTIFICATIONS FOR LEADERSHIP

Many women who do not dress modestly lead young men astray and spread adultery in society which increases earthquakes. (Sediqi, "Iranian Cleric Blames Quakes on Promiscuous Women," 2010)

When discussing changes in how leadership is legitimized, a first point to highlight is the persistence of important 21st-century cross-cultural variations. In Iran, Saudi Arabia, and certain other dictatorships, leadership, obedience, and authority generally are justified using religion. Even earthquakes have been interpreted as resulting from disobedience. However, in Europe, North America, and many other parts of the world where there is greater openness and movement toward actualized democracy, religion, the divine right of kings, and other traditional means of legitimizing leadership have given way to explanations often tied to psychological research. Thus, so-called science has taken over the legitimizing role of religion.

The most important of such scientific explanations is associated with justifications of *meritocracy*, the idea that the position individuals attain in society should be determined by their personal merits, rather than birth, inheritance, apparent selection by divine powers, or any other such factors. The term *meritocracy* was introduced and popularized by British sociologist Michael Young's (1958/1994) satirical work *The Rise of the Meritocracy*. Young used the term critically and pointed out that this "new" social system based on "scientific" intelligence tests would perpetuate inequalities and create a new system of stratification. Rather ironically (see discussions in Dench, 2006), *meritocracy* has taken on a different connotation in the 21st century: It is now viewed as favorable. A meritocratic society is often referred to as an ideal goal (in Chapter 11, I discuss the kind of meritocracy that can be constructive).

In the society Young envisaged, social position is a result of ability plus effort, and intelligence tests become efficient at predicting the success of individuals. In Young's (1958/1994) novel, the age at which intelligence tests reliably predict success becomes lower and lower, so that soon tests administered to 3-year-old children provide highly accurate predictions about their adult success. As a consequence of the highly unequal rewards given, inequalities arise based on merit. This new system is justly unequal as opposed to the old system of inherited position, which was unjustly unequal. Of course, inequality continues.

Intelligence and Meritocracy

Two critical points need to be highlighted with respect to Young's (1958/1994) novel. First, although the term *meritocracy* was coined by Young, the main idea it depicts is ancient. The teachings of Confucius serve as a source for meritocratic policies in the East (Chan, 2007). The civil service examinations were used to select government officials for more than 1,000 years in China. In the Western tradition, Plato (trans. 1987) explicitly advocated a meritocratic system in *The Republic* (*Book III* 415b, c, d), a point not adequately appreciated by critics, such as Popper (1966).

A second point is that the revival of themes in Young's work in more recent psychological research on intelligence. For example, in their controversial work *The Bell Curve*, Herrnstein and Murray (1994) assumed that American society is functioning as a meritocracy, and that, just as Young predicted in 1958 (Young, 1958/1994), IQ is the most important factor that determines the position of an individual in the social hierarchy. Herrnstein and Murray pointed out enormous problems that an IQ-based meritocracy will face in the future. For example, according to Herrnstein and Murray, American government policies are encouraging lower IQ females to have more children than higher IQ females. Because IQ is, according to these authors, highly inherited and because people select marriage partners who are similar in IQ to themselves, this trend inevitably will result in the general U.S. population's experiencing a decline in IQ:

> Putting the pieces together—higher fertility and a faster generational cycle among the less intelligent and an immigrant population that is probably somewhat below the native-born average—the case is strong that something worth worrying about is happening to the cognitive capital of the country. (Herrnstein & Murray, 1994, p. 364)

According to Herrnstein and Murray, the meritocracy based on IQ will result in U.S. society's becoming

> something resembling a caste society, with the underclass mired ever more firmly at the bottom and the cognitive elite ever more firmly anchored at the top, restructuring the rules of society so that it becomes harder and harder for them to lose. (p. 509)

Thus, according to this picture, meritocratic processes will ensure that those with higher IQ will not only rise to the top but will influence the rules so their supremacy becomes more difficult to challenge. It will become increasingly difficult for the masses to select their leaders, particularly if the IQ of the masses is in decline.

Many criticisms have been raised about the shortcomings of *The Bell Curve* (e.g., see Devlin, Fienberg, Resnick, & Roeder, 1997), but, for now, I limit my comments to two points. First, Herrnstein and Murray (1994) were flatly wrong about a factual claim central to their work: IQ scores are not declining; they are rising (Flynn, 2007). This so-called Flynn effect is well documented in the United States and in many other countries. Explanations for the rise in IQ scores include better nutrition and better test preparation. A great deal of evidence has demonstrated that, far from being a test of intelligence independent of experience and education, IQ test scores are significantly influenced by preparation.

Test scores have increased across the board partly because young people are now routinely trained in taking IQ-type tests from kindergarten on. Furthermore, although increased exposure to IQ-type tests have resulted in improvements of scores for the general population, the rich have enormous advantages both in test preparation and entrance to prestigious schools and universities. The rich also benefit from access to the best private tutoring and test-preparation. In addition, monetary contributions to elite universities and legacy advantages of various kinds move the rich well ahead in the race for entrance to elite educational institutions.

Second, Herrnstein and Murray's (1994) concern that an entrenched elite will restructure "the rules of society so that it becomes harder and harder for them to lose" (p. 509) has been echoed by other researchers, but on a completely different basis. Instead of assuming that a meritocracy has enabled those with the highest IQ to reach the top, an alternative explanation has been that those with the greatest economic and political resources have prevented a meritocracy and, instead, have given their families and other ingroup members huge advantages to succeed. Other researchers have agreed with the claim that an entrenched elite has come to power, but have disagreed with Herrnstein and Murray's explanation of higher IQ's being the basis of this power.

Rather than use higher IQ as the explanation for the emergence of an entrenched elite, Thomas Piketty's (2014) analysis pointed to characteristics of the capitalist system. If unchecked, capitalist development inevitably results in an increased accumulation of capital in the hands of a small elite—with dire consequences for democracy:

> The overall conclusion of this study is that a market economy based on private property, if left to itself, contains powerful forces of convergence, associated in particular with the diffusion of knowledge and skills; but it also contains powerful forces of divergence, which are potentially threatening to democratic societies and to the values of social justice on which they are based. (Piketty, 2014, p. 571)

Piketty's solution to the problems arising from having an entrenched elite is not focused on policies related to IQ or other assumed characteristics of individuals. Rather, Piketty put forward a macrolevel solution:

> If democracy is to regain control over the globalized financial capitalism of this century, it must also invent new tools, adapted to today's challenges. The ideal tool would be a progressive global tax on capital, coupled with a very high level of international financial transparency. (Piketty, 2014, p. 515)

Thus, both Herrnstein and Murray (1994) and Piketty (2014) saw problems associated with the emergence of an entrenched elite, but foundational differences existed in what they argued were the sources and solutions. Herrnstein and Murray assumed that a meritocratic system has been enabling those with higher IQ to rise to greater positions of power and influence, and that the danger exists that the highest IQ individuals will rearrange the rules so that their position will become unassailable, and the meritocracy presumably will be damaged or even ended. According to this viewpoint, the characteristics of individuals, specifically in terms of IQ, will shape social structure. This is a bottom-up process. Piketty, on the other hand, adopted a top-down process; he viewed the emergence of an entrenched elite as a result of the accumulation of capital in the hands of the few and suggested an economic–political solution.

Social Mobility and Its Determinants

An argument consistently used against the ability and right of the people to recall a leader is that society is open, social mobility is high, and leaders become leaders by their individual talents. These talents can include the leader's being selected by God or being in some other way special and beyond the power of ordinary people. In modern Western societies, particularly the United States, the assumed high talents of the leader is associated with meritocracy. The American Dream suggests that anyone can make it in the Land of Opportunity, and so those who have reached the most powerful positions of leadership are the most talented individuals, as indicated by higher IQ, for example.

Two issues need to be examined further. The first concerns whether and to what degree there is social mobility. The second is the question of what factors determine social mobility. With respect to the first, the traditional rhetoric of the American Dream, particularly as perpetuated by right-wing thinkers, including Herrnstein and Murray (1994), is that there is a high level of social mobility in capitalist democracies, and particularly in the United States. The empirical evidence has strongly suggested that social mobility in the United States is actually lower than in some European countries, such as the Scandinavian societies. It is about the same as in England, with its governments led by elites who attend schools such as Eton, entrance to which is a birthright for some families. But even the low levels of social mobility identified by traditional research may be an exaggeration.

Clark (2014) argued that conventional mobility studies have suffered from a fatal flaw: They are mostly one-generational studies. They generally

> overestimate overall mobility. Further, they overestimate mobility in later generations even for single aspects of mobility, such as income. They also overestimate even single aspects of mobility for social, ethnic, and religious groups such as Jews, Muslims, Black Americans, and Latinos. The rate of regression to mean [moving to the population average] social status for these groups is much slower than conventional estimates would imply. So, for almost all the issues of social mobility we care about, these estimates are not useful. (p. 11)

Clark adopted a new method for tracking social mobility by using surnames to examine the rise and fall of families across centuries in Sweden, the United States, England, India, China, Taiwan, Japan, Korea, and Chile. His conclusion was that long-term social mobility is far lower than predicted by the traditional studies.

As to what factors determine social mobility, Clark (2014) identified an important role for inherited abilities and randomness. *Randomness* means that the elite includes individuals who do not have particular personal talents that might imply "elite" to the casual observer, just as the lower classes include individuals who have the personal talents that one might expect among the elite.

> The curse of the elite is that they are surrounded by imposters, possibly including themselves, and thus the marriage market for the upper classes is full of prospects likely to underperform as carriers of a lineage. In contrast, the bottom of the marriage market is full of potential overperformers. (Clark, 2014, p. 282)

This quote reminds us of Plato's (trans. 1987, *Book III* 415b, c, d) warning that some children of gold parents will be of bronze and silver quality, whereas some children of bronze parents will be of gold and silver quality. Even from Plato's time, the controversy over inheritance and intelligence has persisted.

At the heart of the contemporary IQ wars (Devlin et al., 1997) is disagreement about the extent to which society is open for individuals to freely move up and down the social hierarchy based on their individual talents. On the one side are those (e.g., Herrnstein & Murray, 1994; Murray, 2012) who see American society as meritocratic, with IQ as the key determinant of social position. On the other hand, some believe that the elite, in part through their enormous influence in elite schools and universities, use their power and resources to buy privileges for themselves and their children.

This disagreement about social mobility has important practical implications for leadership. If we assume that the system is open and meritocratic, then we expect leaders to rise (and fall) according to their IQ levels. An alternative view is that what really determine the rise of leaders are the economic interests they represent and the resources driving their campaigns. Thus, the IQ of the leader is only one factor among many. Accountability to the people, a hallmark of actualized democracy, becomes far more difficult to achieve in this second scenario. The U.S. Supreme Court 2010 decision (*Citizens United v. Federal Election Commission*, in Liptak, 2010) to open the floodgates to unlimited money from special interest groups made accountability to the people particularly difficult to achieve. The danger is that now U.S. political campaigns are less about buying some votes and more about buying entire elections. Political leaders have become even more beholden to the largest financial donors and less accountable to ordinary voters.

WHY LEADER ACCOUNTABILITY MATTERS: PSYCHOLOGICAL RESEARCH

Why should leaders be removable through popular will? I address this question with reference to psychological research on power, decision making, and the conditions under which corruption emerges and grows. In my personal experience of living in and researching dictatorships, the key determinant of the low quality of life in dictatorships is the lack of opportunity for people to criticize authorities and demand improvements. This absence of opportunity to provide critical feedback and hold officials accountable for their actions means that authorities and leadership become increasingly corrupt and inefficient. In an actualized democracy, institutional support would ensure that leaders are open to receiving critical feedback on their performance and that people can and do routinely replace the leader.

Leadership, Power, and Corruption

> How can one fit monarchy into any sound system of ethics, when it allows a man to do whatever he likes without any responsibility or control? Even the best of men raised to such a position would be bound to change for the worse. (Otanes, quoted in Herodotus (5th century BC/1954, p. 209)

Writing in the era of classical Greek scholarship, Herodotus (c. 484–425 BC) reported a debate between a group of Persians about the kind of government they should adopt. Otanes argued that monarchy brings corruption because the monarch has absolute power. Unfortunately, Darius used trickery to become king and fulfilled the prediction that the monarch becomes corrupt. The dictum "Power corrupts, absolute power corrupts absolutely," an idea, usually attributed to Lord Acton (1832–1902), was very much on my mind when I experienced life in Iran during the early 1980s. The flickers of freedom that sprang up after the 1979 anti-Shah revolution were fading by 1980, and the U.S. embassy hostage crisis, together with the start of the Iran–Iraq war (1980–1988), was used by Islamic fundamentalists to squash freedoms. With Ruhollah Khomeini's followers wiping out all opposition and gaining absolute power, we learned about corruption under the guise of religion. Unfortunately, billions around the world living in closed societies and closed organizations live and breathe the idea that absolute power corrupts absolutely. They know from personal experience that when a leader has absolute power, when the whims and words of the leader are tantamount to law, corruption seeps into all corners and crevices of life.

But we should not assume that power corrupts only in relatively closed societies. Political power has been associated with hypocrisy in Western societies (Runciman, 2008). Psychological research in Western societies has shown that power leads people to condemn others for cheating and for moral transgressions while they themselves cheat more and overlook their own moral transgressions (Lammers, Stapel, & Galinsky, 2010). Experimental results also have suggested that power leads people to overlook constraints on their actions. They are then more apt to seek their own (often self-serving) goals (Keltner, Gruenfeld, & Anderson, 2003; Whitson et al., 2013) and not understand the perspective of others (Galinsky, Magee, Ena Inesi, & Gruenfeld, 2006; Lammers, Gordijn, & Otten, 2008; Overbeck & Droutman, 2013).

One ray of hope provided by such experimental evidence is that when the powerful feel they are illegitimately in their positions, they will be more constrained (Lammers, Galinsky, Gordijn, & Otten, 2008). However, this is a dim ray of hope. Those who monopolize power also monopolize the manufacturing of ideology, particularly through the media and the education system, and the use of violence to establish and reify the legitimacy of their leadership positions. Even when the masses view the leader as illegitimate, as is often the case in more closed societies, the leader can use violence to reinforce legitimacy (Moghaddam, 2013). Citizens with guns pointed at their heads are not inclined to dispute the legitimacy of the ruling clique or "Supreme Leader."

Can the Group Be a Force for Democracy?

The idea that power corrupts and therefore leadership power must be constrained might be challenged with the assertion that psychological research casts doubt on group wisdom. If the leader cannot be trusted, then neither can the group. For example, a long line of research on conformity, from Muzafer Sherif's classic studies in the 1930s to more recent research using brain imaging technology to track brain activity associated with conformity (Berns et al., 2005) has demonstrated that individuals can be influenced to conform to incorrect norms. Research on groupthink (Janis, 1972; see also review by Esser, 1998) has demonstrated that even highly intelligent individuals can be influenced to dumb down their thoughts and become part of a collective decision-making process that leads to disasters. Recent examples of groupthink abound, from the Bay of Pigs in 1961 to the invasion of Iraq in 2003. The Bay of Pigs, which moved ahead with the consent of President John F. Kennedy (1917–1963) and his advisers, was a failed Central Intelligence Agency–backed attempt to invade Cuba and replace Fidel Castro as the leader. The invasion of Iraq proved to be equally disastrous; it went ahead with the blessing of President George W. Bush and the majority of the U.S. Congress, including prominent Democrats and Republicans and their advisors.

Despite this tradition, an alternative picture of collective wisdom is emerging from empirical research. This alternative view began in Francis

Galton's (1907) study that endorsed *vox populi* (the wisdom of the crowd). Crowds were asked to estimate the weight of an ox and were accurate within 1% of the actual value. The wisdom of the crowd also is reflected in current studies on *swarm intelligence*, the idea that group life develops solutions to cognitive problems that individuals are incapable of developing (Krause, Ruxton, & Krause, 2010). For example, swarm intelligence has been shown to help find better solutions to dealing with terrorist attacks (L. J. Marcus, McNulty, Dorn, & Goralnick, 2014). New and better tactics sometimes emerge from collective decision-making processes. In a series of studies, Nemeth and her associates found that when critical debate rather than getting along is encouraged in groups and when group members challenge received wisdom, more constructive outcomes are achieved (Nemeth & Ormiston, 2007; Nemeth, Personnaz, Personnaz, & Goncalo, 2004). The empirical research on participatory or democratic decision making in humans has been supplemented by research on a surprising topic: democracy in animals (Conradt & Roper, 2007). Evolutionary research is now pushing aside the simplistic stereotype of animal groups being ruled by strong male leaders. The research has presented a nuanced picture of group decision making in which conflicts of interest exist between members and, through more collective processes, dominant members sometimes make decisions (Dyer, Johansson, Helbing, Couzin, & Krause, 2009). Through an extensive study of honeybee democracy, Seeley (2010) arrived at a number of lessons for decision making in human societies, including "minimize the leader's influence on the group's thinking" (p. 221), "seek diverse solutions to the problem" (p. 224), and "aggregate the group's knowledge through debate" (p. 226).

Corruption, Plain and Simple

There is general agreement that corruption is associated with regime type. More democracy and openness means less corruption (Norris, 2012). Countries with more dictatorial political systems have relatively more corruption. This relationship becomes clear when examining country profiles provided by organizations, such as Transparency International (see http://www.transparency.org/country). Unfortunately, many of the societies that have more closed political systems are also the ones with the least-developed economies and the lowest living standards for the general population.

In defense of corruption in more closed societies, a relativistic argument is occasionally put forward: "This is not corruption, this is part of our culture" or "This is our local way of doing business." I once listened to a prominent mullah in Iran argue that there is nothing wrong with a citizen's providing a government official with a gift in exchange for a service—that it is simply a sort of kindness. Of course, because the Supreme Leader and the rest of the political mullahs have a power monopoly in Iran, they are the recipients of most such kindnesses. This relativist argument has crept into discussions by economists and other experts who have added an intriguing grease-the-wheels twist: "In the context of pervasive and cumbersome regulations in developing countries, corruption may actually improve efficiency and help growth" (Bardhan, 1997, p. 1322).

Such a relativist defense of corruption assumes that we have to accept the entire corrupt political system. In practice, not even petty corruption helps the economies of developing societies, because it actually results in greater inefficiency (see Jain, 2001, p. 92). This is not to say that accountability is fully achieved and corruption ended in the more democratic countries; the complexity of advanced political and economic systems makes accountability more difficult (Mulgan, 2003). In addition, the personalization of politics (Garzia, 2011) means that the personality of leaders and their projected images, rather than consequential issues, become the focus of political campaigns. Voting in economically advanced societies is increasingly influenced by leader personality rather than important public policy issues (Pakulski & Körösényi, 2012). Voting based on the personality of the leader, almost by definition, distracts from candidates' key ideological and policy positions. However, a more critical characteristic of more open societies may be support and protection for whistle-blowers. On the path toward actualized democracy, it is essential that such protection is expanded and strengthened.

CONCLUSION

How people react to holding power is not just a function of some abstract relation of dominance, but of the identity, beliefs, values and theories of the people involved and the political and social content of their relationship. (Turner, 2005, p. 18)

Claims that success in a democracy depends on paying court to the audience, flattering it, seducing it with pleasure, create an analogy between the democratic and the tyrannical audience. Both pursue irresponsible pleasures and force those who address them to conform and say only what they want to hear. (Morgan, 2003, p. 203)

It is essential that people are able to replace political leaders and enable turn-taking. As President Vladimir Putin of Russia, former President Hugo Chávez of Venezuela, and others have demonstrated in societies that are more closed, leaders can manipulate the façade of democracy to continue their power monopolies under different guises. Justification for the rule of leaders without real accountability to the people traditionally has relied on religion, as presently happens in Iran, Saudi Arabia, and other such religious states.

However, psychology and the so-called science of IQ have provided a more nuanced, sophisticated, and seemingly objective ideological justification for the rule of unaccountable leadership.

According to the IQ-meritocracy argument, in the United States and some other societies, we now have a meritocracy, and leadership and superior social position are based on IQ differences. Similarly, in this view, some groups enjoy resource advantages because they are superior on the basis of inherited IQ. These claims have no scientific merit. Despite the rhetoric of the American Dream, the United States is not a meritocracy, does not have high social mobility, and IQ tests being used in America do not test ability independent of wealth, context, and experience (the same is true for the United Kingdom and other Western nations). In short, leaders do not become leaders because they are the best and the brightest; inherited wealth, status, and the interests represented by leaders play a crucial role in determining leadership in contemporary Western societies. Thus, it is even more critical that leaders be accountable to citizens.

7

FREEDOM OF SPEECH

What is being abolished is autonomous man—the inner man, the homunculus, the possessing demon, the man defended by the literature of freedom and dignity. His abolition is long overdue. Autonomous man is a device used to explain what we cannot explain in any other way.
—B. F. Skinner (1971, p. 200)

Inflated perceptions of the link between thought and action . . . may explain why people experience an illusion of conscious will at all. The person experiencing will . . . is in the same position as someone perceiving causation as one billiard ball strikes another.
—Daniel M. Wegner (2005, p. 654)

Most often . . . when social scientists rely on their empirical work to address the concerns of democratic theorists, the core question of citizen competence arises. Ideal characteristics of ideal citizens are posited with regard to qualities such as political knowledge and expertise, understanding and internalization of democratic norms and values, political interest and involvement, rational deliberations and emotional passions, and so on. Accordingly, social scientists have concluded, based on several decades of empirical research, that American citizens, despite participating in a long-standing and reasonably robust democracy, fall far short on almost every normative criterion.
—Eugene Borgida, Christopher M. Federico, and John L. Sullivan
(2009, pp. 2–3)

In Shakespeare's play *As You Like It*, Celia says to her cousin Rosalind as they flee from Duke Frederick (her father) and his court to a life of banishment in the country and the Forest of Arden:

Now go we in content
To liberty, and not to banishment. (I.iii.131–132; see Evans, 1997)

http://dx.doi.org/10.1037/14806-008
The Psychology of Democracy, by F. M. Moghaddam

At court, Celia and Rosalind were forced to censor themselves and hide their true thoughts. The newfound freedom of the forest allowed them to develop new relationships and an alternative society: one based on liberty, openness, and free expression. The transition from the dictatorship at court to a participatory, open society in the countryside is achieved by a simple change of scene in Shakespeare's play, but, of course, is a far, far slower and less certain transition outside the theater.

Many citizens who live in democracies such as the United States remain unengaged and uninformed in politics (Delli Caprini & Keeter, 1996); this is the image depicted by research, as Borgida et al. (2009) noted in the preceding quote. Psychological research has been particularly effective at undermining the idea that the country is populated by an active, informed, open-minded citizenry (Taber & Lodge, 2006). Over recent decades, psychologists have launched a range of the attacks against the *autonomous individual*, a person with some measure of free will and rational decision-making ability. Behaviorist B. F. Skinner (1971) argued that we must abandon archaic conceptions of freedom and dignity, and our assumption that we are autonomous individuals. Instead, we must accept that we are essentially playthings of environmental stimuli. As Frazier, a stand-in for Skinner in his novel *Walden Two*, declares, "I deny that freedom exists at all. I must deny it—or my program would be absurd. You can't have a science about a subject matter which hops capriciously about" (Skinner, 1948/1962, p. 257). Cognitive psychologist Wegner discussed the illusory nature of a conscious will: He questioned intentional decision making through informed assessment of alternative choices (for a full account, see Wegner, 2002). One interpretation of this broad array of attacks is that freedom of speech and other essential features of actualized democracy are impossible to realize. After all, how can a being that lacks a will and/or is controlled by environmental stimuli be able to exercise free speech? However, an alternative interpretation is that there are shortcomings in the model traditional psychology has developed of humans. In particular, traditional psychology has failed to put forward a picture of the psychological characteristics and social context required for individuals and societies to become fully democratic.

THE "HUMAN ORGANISM" ACCORDING TO TRADITIONAL PSYCHOLOGY

The Party taught that the proles were natural inferiors . . . Heavy physical work, the care of home and children, petty quarrels with neighbors, films, football, beer, and, above all, gambling filled up the horizons of their minds. To keep them in control was not difficult. . . . All that was required of them was a primitive patriotism. (Orwell, 1949, pp. 61–62)

There are at least three different ways in which traditional psychological research has undermined the idea that ordinary people can be engaged, active citizens supportive of democracy and capable of constructively using freedom of speech. A first way is to claim that people are more or less unsuitable to participate fully in democracy because of their own evolutionarily developed characteristics. New brain-imaging technologies have enabled researchers to track brain activity as people engage in different types of thinking and action. This research has pointed to the apparent inability of individuals to have conscious awareness of the assumed causes of their own behavior. The claim is that the human brain evolved to function in this way and uses heuristics to make split-second decisions that improve individual survival chances but remain a mystery to the actor (Harré & Moghaddam, 2012). Thus, traditional psychological research seems to have provided an explanation and even a justification for why it is that so many people in democracies seem disengaged, ill informed, and apparently unsuitable to serve as active participants in democratic life. But this fails to explain why considerable differences exist among groups as to the extent of their being informed and engaged. Why are affluent White males more involved in politics than economically deprived minorities?

A second way in which traditional psychology has undermined the image of ordinary citizens capable of participating in democratic governance is by highlighting the tendency for people to learn and use the dominant ideologies that are false but serve to justify the prevailing group-based inequalities. A central concept here is that of false consciousness (discussed in Chapter 4), the idea that the members of the working class are immobilized by the false ideology dominant in society that prevents them from recognizing and protecting their own collective interests.

George Orwell's (1949) novel *1984* is traditionally interpreted as an attack on totalitarian regimes, but, in some respects, it also is a critique of resource and power inequalities and their consequences in capitalist democracies. The naturally inferior "proles" Orwell described are the working class whose minds and horizons are filled with films, football, beer, and, above all, gambling. The lives of the working class are filled with meaningless entertainment, their education is shallow, and their knowledge of society and politics is gained from news outlets dominated by celebrity gossip. In the real 21st-century world, such news sources are controlled by the likes of the billionaire media mogul Rupert Murdoch, who applies the same formula whenever he moves into a business: Fill news sources with sex, gossip, and violence, and dismantle labor unions and worker security. The theme of false consciousness is reflected clearly in current psychological research on how people are socialized to think in ways that justify the group-based inequalities in society (see Moghaddam, 2008b). The trash culture fed to the masses may prompt people to think and act in ways that seems to justify the very political system that keeps them immobilized, lacking resources, and powerless.

Third, traditional psychological research has failed to present a picture of what psychological characteristics are needed for a society to function as a democracy, and for individuals to serve as active participants in a democratic society. Psychologist Gordon Allport (1955) aptly pointed this out more than half a century ago:

> Up to now the "behavioral sciences," including psychology, have not provided us with a picture of man capable of creating or living in a democracy. These sciences in large part have imitated the billiard ball model of physics, now of course outmoded. . . . The theory of democracy requires . . . that man possess a measure of rationality, a portion of freedom, a generic conscience, propriate ideals, and unique value. (p. 100)

What, then, is the ideal psychological citizen for achieving actualized democracy? Aside from characteristics discussed in other chapters, an essential part of the answer to this question concerns freedom of speech: having not only the opportunity to speak freely but also the ability to fully use speech in a constructive way. To explore this issue, I begin by discussing the opportunity to speak freely and the consequences of not having such an opportunity. I then define the requirements of constructive free expression.

THE OPPORTUNITY FOR FREE EXPRESSION, AND ITS PSYCHOLOGICAL CONSEQUENCES

> Joseph Priestly was now well known—not so much as an eminent scientist and theologian but as a sympathizer with the French. He set up a Constitutional Society in Birmingham [England] where he now lived, its first act being to hold a "Gallic Commemoration Dinner" on 14 July 1791 to honor the second anniversary of the storming of the Bastille. Pro-Government newspapers condemned it. Such was the intensity of their attacks that Priestly withdrew from the event, but that did not discourage an angry Church-and-King mob organized by local magistrates from setting fire to his house, laboratory, and library. They then went on a spree: four meeting houses and twenty-seven domestic residences were destroyed; eight rioters and one special constable were killed and many others injured. (Wu, 2008, p. 48)

Nationalist Sentiment and Citizen Silence

When I returned to Iran to participate in the "spring of revolution" in 1979, ordinary Iranians had suddenly found themselves in the extraordinary position of having considerable freedom of speech. In the streets, in bath-houses, in classrooms and school playgrounds, in restaurants, in mosques, in coffee houses (which only serve tea), in shops, at bus stops, in sports stadiums, on the radio, everywhere in Iran, I found people speaking out and expressing themselves. Imagine a society held down by political repression that has suddenly found freedom. The dam had been burst, the river was rushing down, and it seemed that nobody could push the water back up the mountain again. Inspired by an exhilarating atmosphere in which every political persuasion—from Marxist–Leninist to Muslim fundamentalist and even liberal democrat—was represented in a tidal wave of freedom, I began teaching in universities in Tehran. This was truly a revolutionary experience—for Iranians to be able to speak freely in public and to participate in open political debates where competing points of view were represented. Before the revolution, freedom of speech had been almost nonexistent in the shah's police state. Now, we were suddenly giddy with freedom.

Unfortunately, the postrevolution freedom did not even last a year. Women and religious minorities began to be pushed back step by step into dark silence. It started with seemingly random acts of violence: acid thrown into the face of a woman who refused to wear the hijab, violent raids into the homes of outspoken religious minorities, the disappearance of political activists who did not accept Ruhollah Khomeini's brand of Islam. Iranians were muzzled again. Individuals could still criticize the government in brief nervous comments exchanged in a taxi or a street corner, but there was no more organized collective action against repression. Two events helped bring about this dark public silence: the hostage crisis (1979–1980) and the Iran–Iraq war (1980–1988).

The hostage crisis began on November 4, 1979, and lasted for 455 days. The world saw that American diplomats were taken hostage, but few recognized that prodemocracy Iranians were, in a different way, also now hostages. The hostage crisis accentuated the sense of threat and instability in the country; in this stifling political atmosphere, anyone in Iran who spoke in favor of democracy and against the dictatorship of Khomeini was immediately branded an American stooge and violently attacked. As if this were not enough, the 1980–1988 Iran–Iraq war gave the fundamentalists even greater license to muzzle dissenting voices. Saddam Hussein was encouraged by some Western nations and certain Iranian dissidents to invade Iran on the assumption that a country that had just experienced a revolution would not be able to defend itself, and Iran would quickly fall. Instead, nationalist sentiments soared, and the Iranian population mobilized to fight the invaders. I was in Tehran at the time and witnessed buses, trucks, and private cars being loaded up with people and supplies to rush to the war front to defend Iran. The mullahs used this opportunity to crush their opponents. Anyone who dared disagree with the ruling mullahs was branded a traitor, a collaborator with the enemy at a time of war. Saddam Hussein was ready to sign a peace treaty as early as 1983, but Khomeini insisted on continuing the war for 8 years because it served his political purposes. The longer the war dragged on, the more political dissidents were rounded up as collaborators with Iran's enemies. By the end of the war, all organized opposition had been squashed, as had freedom of speech. Iran had returned to the dark ages of political repression.

Using war to pummel internal opposition to the ruling power is a continuous theme in human history. It's a near universal in group dynamics that external threat leads to political repression, internal cohesion, and stronger support for aggressive leadership. The universality of this principle suggests deep evolutionary roots (Gneezy & Fessler, 2012). In his erudite biography of William Hazlitt (1778–1830), D. Wu (2008) described the political atmosphere in England during the Napoleonic wars, for example, and the intense pressures put on and violence experienced by dissenters, such as Joseph Priestly (1733–1804). The perceived threat posed by Napoleon Bonaparte and the French Revolution resulted in what D. Wu (2008) called the "Church-and-King mob" (p. 48) that hammered dissenting voices and bred fear and mistrust of others.

Declining Trust and the Mass Media

> Freedom of the press belongs to those who own one. (Liebling, quoted in Baker, 2007, p. 2)

> If one were to take stock of global media and democracy, there will be little to celebrate. . . . Social clauses that once limited media monopolies have now been revoked at national levels, intellectual property rights especially copyright and patents have been used by industry to reinforce property rights in the media, new media such as the Internet, that in its inception promised to be a people's communication tool, is now firmly advancing down the commercial track, the audio-visual spectrum is in danger of migrating from the hands of government to that of a handful of media combines and people's right to information is being compromised by post-11 September policies that have enhanced public and private surveillance, resulted in restrictions to the public scrutiny of certain government institutions, ostensibly for reasons of national security, the manufacture of wall to wall, 24 hours media propaganda and to palpable efforts aimed at curbing the media's right to independently report in the context of war situations such as Afghanistan and Iraq. (Thomas, 2004, pp. 293–294)

In his critical analysis of why media ownership matters for democracy, Baker (2007) identified three particularly important factors. First, giving more people greater power to communicate is supportive of democracy. But, second, this dispersal of communicative power needs to be backed by structural safeguards against what Baker (2007) called the *Berlusconi effect* (p. 18). This term refers to Silvio Berlusconi, the Italian media mogul who used mass media to manipulate and corrupt political processes in Italy for decades until he was convicted of tax fraud in 2013. Third, dispersed ownership is more likely to result in a mass media that pursues objectives more in line with the interests of the larger society rather than the interests of only the super-rich.

Some studies of mass media ownership concentration in America have concluded that although the concentration has increased, it is not above the level found in other major industries (Noam, 2009). Why, then, is there such a concern about the mass media and democracy (e.g., see N. Bowles, Hamilton, & Levy, 2014; Rice, 2008)? Two major reasons have to do with a change in the focus of the media from news to entertainment. Increasingly, the line between news programs and entertainment programs has become blurred, so that informative news programs are disappearing and opinions are replacing factual information. Even programs with a religious mission are masquerading as news programs. This shift from news to entertainment means that the public is receiving less factual information and more biased opinions sponsored by rich donors. Second, recent U.S. Supreme Court rulings have opened the way for almost unlimited media campaigns by the rich.

In theory, all citizens in the United States and other Western societies enjoy some space for free expression. On the other hand, in America, the rich have gained great influence through decisions of the U.S. Supreme Court led by Chief Justice John G. Roberts. A 2013 Supreme Court decision opened the door much wider to rich donors' influencing political elections. Writing for the dissenting minority in *McCutcheon et al. v. Federal Election Commission* (2014), Justice Stephen Breyer argued that the Supreme Court ruling

> creates a loophole that will allow a single individual to contribute millions of dollars to a political party or to a candidate's campaign. Taken together with, Citizens United v. Federal Election Comm'n, 558 U.S. 310 (2010) [*Citizens United v. Federal Election Commission* (2010)], today's decision eviscerates our Nation's campaign finance laws, severely truncating our ability to deal with the grave problems of democratic legitimacy that these laws were intended to resolve.

The Roberts court decisions opened the floodgate of money into political campaigns, detrimentally influencing the climate of politics in America. At the same time, the Edward Snowden–National Security Agency (NSA) scandal has dealt another blow to trust in government, as well as in America's established media outlets (see G. Greenwald, 2014). These media outlets are willing to expose wrongdoing when the target is an individual, such as President Richard Nixon during the Watergate affair in the early 1970s, but they are unwilling to challenge the political system. Snowden, a 29-year-old computer contractor, exposed an enormous systemic problem: that government agents often illegally gathered and shared (including with certain foreign countries) about 20 billion e-mail and telephone records on a daily basis. The assumption now is that any and all communications in America, and indeed around the world, could be and often are monitored by the NSA. In such a situation, it is not surprising that distrust is high among ordinary citizens.

Thus, the current political climate in the United States involves a combination of unlimited spending by the rich using the mass media they also own, transformation of "news programs" to entertainment programs with less informational content, and a sense among ordinary people that their views do not really make a difference. Similar trends are apparent in other Western societies.

PSYCHOLOGICAL REQUIREMENTS FOR CONSTRUCTIVE FREE EXPRESSION

An essential feature of actualized democracy is *constructive free expression*, which involves at least the following three skill sets: empathic listening, critical thinking and identity integration, and constructive and open response. The broad public only can develop each of these skill sets when there is a supportive and enriching societal context for expression and debate. At present, such contexts are rarely available. A few individuals are able to develop constructive free expression without a supportive environment, but the vast majority needs the supportive societal context that institutions and appropriate government policies can supply.

Empathic Listening

> To sense the client's private world as if it were your own, but without ever losing the "as if" quality—this is empathy. (Rogers, 1957, p. 99)

In contemporary industrialized societies, a great deal of time and effort is invested in developing listening skills in individuals who work in therapy, counseling, communications, and related fields. Such education is based on the idea that listening skills can and should be developed, and that the experience of being listened to is an essential experience in healthy social relationships (S. Myers, 2000). The skill of empathic listening has been central to therapy, in particular, humanistic therapy, from the earliest years of the modern verbal therapy movement (Rogers, 1951). More broadly, effective listening has long been seen as important in human communications

(Bodie, 2011). Surprisingly, very little of this sentiment and knowledge has been transferred to the political arena and particularly to discussions about citizenship education.

The same emphasis that is placed on listening in therapy, communications, and related fields needs to be placed on listening in the political context. Democracy requires that citizens have the ability to constructively use freedom of expression and the ability to empathically listen to others exercising this right. If people do not listen effectively, freedom of expression is of little use. Developing these skills should be a priority in socializing new immigrants to Western societies and should be part of the general education in schools and universities. Just as it is essential to develop good listening skills in the context of therapy, it is essential to develop good listening skills in the context of politics. Listening is, in some respects, even more essential to the democratic development of societies than is speaking, and greater efforts should be made to develop empathic listening skills to bolster democratic potential. Politicians themselves need to develop skills to listen to scientists and knowledge producers (Haas, 2004), and to use blogs and new technologies to listen to the public (Coleman, 2005).

Critical Thinking and Identity Change

> Becoming a more central participant in society is not just a matter of acquiring knowledge and skills. It also implies becoming a member of a community of practice. This requires people to see themselves *as* members, taking responsibility for their actions (including the use of knowledge and skills) in that position. The learning process thus implies a change in personal identity, in the way one presents oneself to others and to oneself. (ten Dam & Volman, 2004, p. 371)

Critical thinking has been discussed as central to education in democratic societies (Lipman, 2003) and has received attention from psychologists interested in socialization and developmental processes (Kuhn, 1999). By *critical thinking*, I mean ideally developing the 10 characteristics discussed in Chapter 2. Essential components of these characteristics are being open to new information and interpretations, being aware of one's own fallibility, and being willing to recognize more valid positions and to adopt them, even though doing so requires abandoning former positions. My point of departure here is ten Dam and Volman's (2004) focus on learning processes as part of identity changes. This is in line with my general theoretical outlook that democratization involves, first, a change in collective identity, with people coming to see and present themselves as a democratic society, and, second, a change in how individuals see and present themselves as individually democratic.

In the development of actualized democracy, critical thinking becomes integral to identity changes. Individuals come to associate thinking critically as part of, and normative to, who we are and who I am. Constructive free expression will be most beneficial when it occurs in a context in which people collectively and individually see themselves to be, and act as, critical thinkers.

Constructive and Open Response

The practice of freedom of speech in actualized democracy is different from saying anything I feel like saying. Expressions in such truly democratic conditions are constructive and interactive: Each person in the community attempts to positively integrate and build on the contributions made by others. Empathic listening enables individuals to understand and identify the most valuable contributions, despite major disagreements in viewpoints. Next, the individual integrates these contributions and constructs a response to move the dialogue forward.

For dialogue to be creative and to instigate change, individuals must feel they can make a difference. The responses must be open, in the sense that individuals should not feel compelled to reach particular conclusions. Psychologists have recognized that such empowerment must be a feature of communities and relationships, not just individuals. The concern is actual empowerment and not just perceptions (Christens, 2012). To take an extreme example, by the end of 1979, when I was teaching in universities in Iran, the Islamic fundamentalists had already established a suffocating level of pressure against free expression. Class discussions became difficult because the students and professors were aware that they had to remain within the confines of Khomeini's pro-dictatorship interpretation of an Islamic society.

The Role of a Supportive Context to Nurture Constructive Free Expression

> And what is it we have seen? Not aggression, for there is no anger, vindictiveness, or hatred in those who shocked the victim. Men do become angry; they do act hatefully and explode in rage against others. But not here. Something far more dangerous is revealed: the capacity for man to abandon his humanity, indeed, the inevitability that he does so, as he merges his unique personality into larger institutional structures. (Milgram, 1974, p. 188)

> Both public and private organizations, because they operate within a legal framework, not an ethical framework, can inflict suffering, even death, on people by following cold rationality for achieving the goals of their ideology, a master plan, a cost–benefit equation, or the bottom line

of profit. Under these circumstances, their ends always justify efficient means. (Zimbardo, 2007, pp. 381–382)

Stanley Milgram and Philip Zimbardo are the most influential exponents of a situational perspective in psychology. The situational perspective highlights the power of context to shape behavior, as demonstrated famously by Milgram's (1974) experimental studies of obedience to authority and Zimbardo's (1972) Stanford prison study. In those studies, participants were healthy males with normal personality characteristics who were influenced by the power of the situation to inflict sever harm on others (Milgram's study was replicated with female participants, with the same results). In Milgram's study, about 60% of participants followed orders to inflict what they believed to be lethal electric shocks to a stranger. In Zimbardo's prison study, participants randomly assigned to the task of acting as guards in a makeshift prison severely mistreated other participants randomly assigned to the task of acting as prisoners. The participants in these studies were behaving wrongly by severely harming others, but, simultaneously, they were themselves victims of the situation. They could reasonably have claimed, "We are ordinary people. You are not different from us. You would have done the same if you were in our situation."

The clear implication is that when we witness wrongdoing, we must take care not to commit the fundamental attribution error, which is to judge the individual as the source of the event. Keeping in mind the power of the situation, Zimbardo (2007) interpreted the terrible mistreatment of Iraqi prisoners in Abu Ghraib prison as arising from the government policies of the George W. Bush administration and the ends justify the means culture of the era created by Vice President Dick Cheney, rather than from evil lurking within individual prison guards.

The situational perspective leads us to view the practice of free speech as shaped largely by the context, rather than as inherent in the personalities of individuals. The validity of this viewpoint becomes clear when we consider differences between societies in which people are censored and those in which they do enjoy more free expression. In countries such as China, Russia, Cuba, Saudi Arabia, North Korea, and Iran, even the Internet is strongly censored, and citizens have limited opportunity for free expression. Relatively greater opportunities for free expression are enjoyed by citizens of Western Europe and North America. Clearly, these differences in how much free expression is enjoyed in different countries are explained by differences in government policies and the general climate of communications created by the authorities.

In the context of the United States and other Western societies, the limitations on speech arise less from legal restrictions on free expression and more from the enormous influence of the super-rich, the owners of the mass media, and rich sponsors of commercial advertising and political campaigns. Free speech becomes practically meaningless when ordinary citizens have relatively little control over the mass media and feel they will make little difference in political outcomes. Part of the solution is the development of critical thinking skills, as set out in Chapter 2, through reforms in the education system. But another part of the solution is change in the laws regulating spending in political campaigns and mass media ownership concentration.

CONCLUSION

For freedom of speech to contribute to progress toward actualized democracy, such expression must be constructive and coupled with empathic listening. Countries such as China, Iran, Saudi Arabia, North Korea, Cuba, and Russia fail to meet even the minimum requirement of allowing citizens to openly criticize authorities. Western societies, and the United States in particular, fail to provide opportunities and skills for ordinary people to critically engage in politics in a way that makes a difference. Increasingly in America, effective freedom of speech is available only to individuals and groups with enormous financial assets. Helped by the Roberts Supreme Court decisions, the free market mentality has overwhelmed the political system and made it less democratic.

To strengthen free expression, there also needs to be a change in the larger context, including the laws regulating spending in political campaigns. Furthermore, a systematic and genuine effort needs to be undertaken to teach empathic listening and constructive free expression. This can best begin with programs in schools and the training of the young, as well as the socialization of new immigrants. Both educational institutions and the mass media should be participants in this effort. Such a strategy would help to eventually remedy the disengagement, apathy, and cynicism common to the masses in Western societies toward politicians and the political system.

8

MINORITY RIGHTS

My actual release time was set for 3 p.m. . . . Warrant Officer Swart prepared a final meal for all of us, and I thanked him not only for the food he had provided for the last two years but the companionship. . . . Men like Swart . . . reinforced my belief in the essential humanity even of those who had kept me behind bars for the previous twenty-seven and a half years.

—Nelson Mandela (1994, p. 562)

He began with the argument that we whites, from the point of development we have arrived at, "must necessarily appear to them [savages] in the nature of supernatural beings—we approach them with the might as of a deity. . . . By the simple exercise of our will we can exert a power for good practically unbounded," etc., etc. From that point he soared and took me with him. . . . There were no practical hints to interrupt the magic current of phrases, unless a kind of note at the foot of the last page, scrawled evidently much later. . . . It was very simple, and at the end of that moving appeal to every altruistic sentiment it blazed at you, luminous and terrifying, like a flash of lightening in a serene sky: "Exterminate all the brutes!"

—Joseph Conrad (1899/1958, p. 274)

A first striking fact about the treatment of *minorities*, groups that might be the numerical majority but nevertheless enjoy less power and resources than a nation's dominant group, is its enormous range, from generally benevolent to deeply malevolent, from empathy to hatred and aggressive destruction. On the benevolent side, when Nelson Mandela (1918–2013) finally was released from prison and became the first democratically elected leader of a postapartheid South Africa, he used his power and influence to support intergroup harmony, peace, and acceptance of minority groups and the former

http://dx.doi.org/10.1037/14806-009
The Psychology of Democracy, by F. M. Moghaddam

ruling Whites (Mandela, 1994). He insisted on seeing and giving priority to humanity in others, even when those others had treated him inhumanely. Unfortunately, few revolutions end so constructively.

The violence, subjugation, and exploitation typically used against minorities is brilliantly depicted by Joseph Conrad (1857–1924) in *Heart of Darkness* (Conrad, 1899/1958), a short novel about a Belgian trading company in the Congo. In that story, Kurtz represents only the company interests, although he used to be a well-intentioned, well-rounded, and talented man. Over the years, as Kurtz exploits the native peoples and the natural resources of the Congo River region, he becomes increasingly corrupted morally. Symbolic of his shift from an idealistic young man to a tyrannical older man is his scrawl of "exterminate all the brutes!" on a report he had prepared as a younger man (Conrad, 1899/1958, p. 273). The level of savagery Conrad depicted toward indigenous people in the Congo is not exaggerated or fictional, as has been made clear by documentary evidence about Belgium's rule in the Congo, particularly during the reign of Belgium's King Leopold II (1835–1909; see Hochschild, 1999). Like Kurtz in Conrad's novel, King Leopold brutalized the indigenous people around the Congo River and made enormous fortunes through ivory and, later, rubber sales.

The vast range of behavior, from the most positive to the most negative, demonstrated by people toward minorities raises hopes and questions. It raises hopes because it suggests that a constructive, positive path is available that some people like Mandela take to huge social effect. Perhaps the rest of us could be socialized to follow Mandela's example. But the destructive behavior described by Conrad (1899/1958) raises questions about the best way to move society toward the more constructive path. How can we most effectively ensure that minorities have equal rights and opportunities? What policies toward minorities would be most compatible with movement toward actualized democracy?

That there can be considerable individual differences in how people think and act toward minorities has been shown, for example, by research on personality and prejudice (Duckitt, 2005) and extent of tolerance of majorities toward minorities (Phelps, Eilertsen, Türken, & Ommundsen, 2011). Whereas some individuals are tolerant and accepting toward minorities, others are antagonistic to the point of justifying the most savage collective violence against minorities. Where do differences between individuals, as measured by authoritarianism (Adorno, Frenkel-Brunswik, Levinson, & Sanford, 1950; Altemeyer, 1988) and the need to see the world in simplistic either–or, black–white terms (Kruglanski & Boyatzi, 2012), arise from? A long tradition of research on this topic has indicated that they arise to a large degree from "culture" (Adorno et al., 1950, p. 229), and are integrated in personality through socialization processes. The cumulative weight of research evidence has demonstrated that societal context largely shapes tolerance toward minorities (Gibson & Gouws, 2003; G. Marcus, Sullivan, Theiss-Morse, & Wood, 1995; Peffley & Rohrschneider, 2003; Weldon, 2006). Thus, although individual differences in tolerance toward minorities exist in any given cultural context, it is the cultural context that shapes the general trends among a population in their collective tolerance toward minorities (see the discussions on temperament and context in Wachs & Kohnstamm, 2001).

Individual differences function within the general biases afforded by cultural context and collective processes. To take a historical example, during the Nazi era, there were individual differences in tolerance toward Jews among Germans, but this was within the general cultural context and collective direction established by Nazi ideology. To take a contemporary example from my own experiences, I found that individual Iranians in Ruhollah Khomeini's regime varied in their tolerance toward religious minorities. However, the authorities fully supported intolerance toward minorities. The cultural context created by the ruling regime in Iran had established the general trend of persecution and intolerance toward particularly religious and ethnic minorities.

A central feature of cultural context with respect to minorities is policies adopted for managing diversity. What should be the primary goal of such policies? Should the goal be to achieve assimilation by absorbing ethnic and linguistic minorities into mainstream culture and melting away intergroup differences? Such an assimilationist policy would result in greater similarity and less focus on group-based differences. Should the goal of policies instead be to highlight, celebrate, and enhance the distinct characteristics of minority groups? These different policies would provide substantially different settings for the development of how individuals view and treat minorities.

THE PSYCHOLOGY OF ASSIMILATION POLICY: DIFFERENCE AS A THREAT

At the start of the second decade of the 21st century, the heads of state in France, Germany, and the United Kingdom—President Nicolas Sarkozy, Chancellor Angela Merkel, and Prime Minister David Cameron, respectively—criticized *multiculturalism*, the celebration, sharing, and strengthening of cultural differences. They declared multiculturalism to have failed and called for renewed efforts to develop their national identities with immigrant assimilation (Novoa & Moghaddam, 2014). This turn away from multiculturalism toward assimilation, the historically dominant policy in Western Europe and traditional immigrant-receiving societies, such as the United States, Canada, and Australia, is to some degree an attempt to find a solution to the Islamic radicalization and terrorism that has grabbed headlines since the tragedy of

9/11. The idea that multiculturalism would prove to be a solution for Islamic radicalization and terrorism by enabling Muslims to feel confident in their own identities and not experience collective identity threat in the face of the spread of Western secular values (Moghaddam, 2008a) has lost support because it has not ended or decreased these problems.

In the European Union (EU) in particular, the focus of debates about minorities has been the Muslim population. Although size estimates of the Muslim population in Europe differ, according to the Open Society Institute (2010), approximately 15 million to 20 million Muslims now live in the EU, and this population is expected to double by 2025. Another estimate is that 44 million Muslims already live in Europe, and this number will increase to 55 million by 2030 (Islam, 2012). Despite such differences in estimates, general agreement is that the fertility rate of the Muslim population in Europe is increasing more rapidly than that of the indigenous population. The fertility rate among indigenous populations in Western European countries is well below the 2.1% annual increase needed to maintain their population level. Immigrants are replenishing the aging European labor force, and this replenishment is part of the larger international movement of populations in the 21st century (Lee, 2011).

The integration of Asian and African newcomers has been problematic in Europe, and evidence has suggested that Muslims, in particular, face discrimination. For example, Adida, Laitin, and Valfort (2010) found that a Muslim job applicant is 2.5 times less likely to receive a job interview callback than a Christian applicant with the same profile. The focus of mainstream discussions about Muslims, however, has tended to center around cultural and value differences, rather than bread-and-butter issues, such as job discrimination and economic disparities (Phillips, 2010). Discrimination against Muslims continues, despite evidence that the majority of Muslims in Europe are adopting mainstream values (Norris & Inglehart, 2012). From a minority perspective, it is the low economic and power status of Muslims in Europe, rather than their cultural characteristics, that should be the main focus.

How Should Group Differences Be Treated?

The presence of tens of millions of Muslims in the EU has highlighted the question: How should group-based differences, such as in culture, language, religion, ethnicity, and race, be interpreted and treated? Should they be highlighted, celebrated, and shared, as proposed by multiculturalism policy, or melted away, as required by assimilation? The multicultural approach is addressed in the next section of the chapter; here, I discuss the *assimilationist approach*, according to which group-based differences should remain within the private sphere of private family life rather than gain central prominence in public life.

The question of how group-based differences should be treated has gained practical significance in military (McDonald & Parks, 2012) and business settings (Holvino & Kamp, 2009). Some of the same questions that are raised in the context of business organizations and other applied settings also are important in the larger context of democracy (Harell & Stolle, 2010). For example, in their discussion of managing diversity in a business organization context, Holvino and Kamp (2009) asked whether individual or group differences should be given priority and examined the consequences of stressing group-based similarities rather than differences in organizations. Similar issues have arisen in the larger context of democracy and citizenship (Moghaddam, 2008c, 2013): How much should group-based similarities rather than differences be given priority in the larger society? The answer from the perspective of assimilation policy is clear: Group-based differences can become problematic and should be minimized. The focus should be on similarity—and not differences across groups.

Over the years, various researchers have assumed that greater ethnic, religious, racial, linguistic, and other such group-based differences will result in more intergroup conflicts in societies (Dahl, 1971; Horowitz, 1993; Worchel, 1999). One reason for such conflicts, particularly in politically more open societies, is that it is so tempting and convenient for political leaders to appeal for support based on ethnic, religious, racial, linguistic, and other such visible affiliations compared with appeals based on just as telling, but more abstract, characteristics, such as ideology and social class. As a consequence, critics have argued, there is too much danger of democratic politics breaking down into divisions based on ethnicity and religion, say, rather than political ideology. Supporters of these policies have argued that minimizing group differences is an important reason why an assimilationist policy should be adopted.

From a traditional Marxist perspective (Marx, 1852/1979; Marx & Engels, 1848/1967), divisions based on ethnicity, religion, gender, and language become highlighted in capitalist societies as a way to deflect attention from social class. Such divisions are part of the false consciousness that prevents the working class from giving allegiance to their own class membership and recognizing that the interests of their class are diametrically opposed to the interests of the capitalist class. Thus, in response to Frank's (2004) question, What's the Matter with Kansas?—a state that now votes predominantly for right-wing politicians who support policies that favor the rich instead of the majority of people in Kansas who are relatively poor—one answer is that Kansans suffer false consciousness. Heads of state President Sarkozy, Chancellor Merkel, and Prime Minister Cameron followed Marx when they declared that allegiance to ethnicity and other such groups is harmful. However, whereas Marx wanted a move from ethnic, race, religion, and other such allegiances to recognition and allegiance of social class, the heads of state in France, Germany, and the United Kingdom wanted priority to be given to nationhood (and increasingly also to a European identity).

Psychological Research and Group Differences

The lay public has had a tendency to focus on group divisions based on easily recognizable criteria, such as ethnicity and language, but are social science researchers also focused on such differences? According to a number of scholars (e.g., Lalonde, in press; Lamiell, 2004), psychological research also has been making foundational mistakes in how it treats differences. Research evidence has suggested that humans are prewired to categorize phenomena, both social and nonsocial, and to notice similarities and differences (Lalonde, in press; Moghaddam, 2008b, Chapter 2). However, Lalonde (in press) argued that biases in the mass media and social psychological research have resulted in differences being highlighted, rather than similarities. The media has used stereotypes such as "too smart Asians" and "fanatical Muslims" to represent particular groups as being different. Psychologists (and social scientists, in general) are trained to use experimental methods and statistical procedures that highlight differences, not similarities. Indeed, a failure to find significant differences between groups usually condemns a research study to being unpublishable in traditional journals.

The focus on differences has resulted in major shortcomings in social sciences research, according to Lamiell (2004). For example, researchers adopt statistical procedures to identify differences between groups and then assume that these differences are the causes of certain types of behavior. For example, a huge research literature has been built up on the assumption that differences between cultures on measures of individualism and collectivism are the cause of cultural variations in thought and action. Such presumption of differences between groups as a cause may lead to incorrect conclusions about the meanings of research data (Moghaddam & Harré, 2015). Just as important, from an applied perspective, the focus on differences leads to a turning away from assimilation as a policy for managing diversity.

Assimilation seems to be in line with democracy and democratic slogans, such as the French national motto "Liberté, Egalité, Fraternité." After all, if people are going to have liberty, equality, and fraternity, then whatever additional groups they are part of, they should feel themselves to be part of the larger group that coincides with the political nation—with a shared identity. For example, Italian Americans, Arab Americans, Jewish Americans, and Hispanic Americans should feel themselves to be first and foremost "Americans." Both *melting-pot assimilation*, whereby all groups melt into one another (e.g., to arrive at a new American culture, one that is new and different from the culture of any of the groups that compose America), and *minority assimilation*, in which minority groups adopt the culture of the majority group (e.g., minority groups melting into Western European culture), are compatible with democracy. However, political leaders, such as President Sarkozy, Chancellor Merkel, and Prime Minister Cameron, undoubtedly had minority assimilation in mind as the preferred policy when they criticized multiculturalism because, in minority assimilation, the majority Western European culture is preserved.

A PSYCHOLOGICAL PERSPECTIVE ON THE BENEFITS OF ASSIMILATION POLICY FOR DEMOCRACY

I explore here the benefits of assimilation policy for democracy by first clarifying the role of intergroup contact in improving intergroup relations.

Contact, Assimilation, and Democracy

One of the most important arguments for assimilation policy arises from psychological research that has shown that intergroup contact will lead to improved intergroup relations (Hodson & Hewstone, 2012). Allport (1954) postulated that contact will result in improved intergroup relations when groups enjoy equal status within the context in which the contact occurs, share common goals in this context, have cooperative rather than competitive relations, and enjoy the support of the community. These are difficult conditions to achieve in practice. However, in evaluating more than half a century of research on intergroup contact, Pettigrew and his associates (Pettigrew & Tropp, 2006, 2008, 2013; Pettigrew, Tropp, Wagner, & Christ, 2011; Tropp & Pettigrew, 2005) concluded that the effect of contact is greater when Allport's (1954) conditions are met; however, even when they are not met, contact can benefit intergroup relations. Studies with a focus on longer-term contact processes have been showing a similar trend too (Dhont, Van Hiel, & Hewstone, 2014).

The vast majority of research has focused on the effect of direct contact (Pettigrew & Tropp, 2013), but more attention also is being paid to alternative forms of contact. *Extended contact* shows that merely being aware that one of our group has a friend in the outgroup can lead us to be more positively disposed toward the outgroup (S. C. Wright, Aron, McLaughkin-Volpe, & Ropp, 1997). Even more dramatic from a psychological perspective is the demonstration of *imagined contact*, whereby imagining a positive contact with an outgroup member can result in more positive intergroup relations (Miles & Crisp, 2014).

We also must consider that intergroup contact can fail to result in more positive intergroup relations (see Chapter 12 in Pettigrew & Tropp, 2013) and that Western academic researchers are probably painting too rosy a picture. I am reminded of this harsh reality as news reached me about new waves of murderous violence in Iraq, Syria, and other parts of the Muslim world where I was born. Sunni and Shia Muslims have a great deal of contact with one another in these societies, yet this contact has not prevented events of extreme violence between them. I have no doubt that contact could help improve intergroup relations, but this beneficial outcome is not realized in some societies that are characterized by a history of violent intergroup rivalry. Even in Western societies, contact may reduce prejudice, but, in practice, prejudice also may reduce contact (Binder et al., 2009).

The assumption that contact leads to more positive intergroup relations is in line with the optimism of democracy: The more we get to know others, the more positively disposed we will become toward them, and the more positive our attitudes toward one another, the more harmonious society will be. This assumption is supposed to hold true even when others prove to be different from us. Psychological research has presented a serious challenge to this assumption. Next, I discuss research that has shown that similarity and not dissimilarity leads to attraction between individuals and groups.

Similarity-Attraction, Assimilation, and Democracy

A long line of research has supported the view that people are more positively disposed toward others whom they see as more similar to themselves (Berscheid & Reis, 1998; Byrne, 1971). This relationship is consistent across cultures (Schug, Yuki, Horikawa, & Takemura, 2009) and across actual and perceived similarity (Montoya, Horton, & Kirchner, 2008). From the perspective of the present discussion, a shortcoming of this research is that the vast majority of studies have been carried out on similarity and attraction between individuals, rather than between groups. In a direct test of the similarity-attraction hypothesis at the intergroup level, Osbeck, Moghaddam, and Perreault (1997) found strong support for the hypothesis in relationships among six different ethnic groups. The empirical research, then, has strongly supported the view that people are attracted to others who are similar to themselves. Therefore, an assimilation policy that leads the members of a society to change to become more similar will result in a society that is more cohesive.

Meritocracy, Assimilation, and Democracy

The most direct argument suggesting that assimilation is in line with democracy has focused on *meritocracy* (Moghaddam, 2008b), a system in which each individual's status depends on his or her personal merit (discussed in Chapter 11, this volume). When positions in society are filled on the basis of merit, then group-based prejudices are circumvented. Although meritocracy is not seen by all as being necessary for democracy, the argument has been made that social mobility based on individual merit is a necessary prerequisite for a successful society. In the modern era, meritocracy is supported by the ideal of the *American Dream*, the idea that anyone can make it in America as long as they have the talent and work hard enough. This ideology is reinforced by political rhetoric from leaders who emphasize self-help and individual responsibility.

The argument that priority should be given to individual responsibility seems to be supported by psychological research that has demonstrated that individuals show lower effort when the group, rather than individual group members, is given responsibility for group productivity (Latané, Williams, & Harkins, 1979; Kerr & Bruun, 1983). This social loafing or free riding is well known to students and others who have been given group assignments. When doing group assignments, group members sometimes find that individuals in the group fail to do their share of the work and essentially take a free ride on the efforts of other group members (discussed in Chapter 11, this volume). Perhaps most people assume that free riding will occur when they are attempting to move up the hierarchy from a lower status to a higher status group. This may explain their preference for trying to move up individually and on their own personal effort by gaining promotions for themselves personally, for example, rather than as part of the entire lower-status group and through collective effort (S. C. Wright, Taylor, & Moghaddam, 1990).

This tendency to try to achieve social mobility individually first lines up with arguments that, to make a fair and open competition possible, a policy of assimilation must be followed so that all individuals are as similar as possible in terms of cultural, linguistic, and other relevant group characteristics. Assimilation, it has been argued, will enable immigrant children to compete on a level playing field and give them a fair shot at moving up in the meritocratic system—including immigrant children's having the linguistic and cultural skills to compete on standardized tests in the education system.

THE PSYCHOLOGY OF MULTICULTURALISM POLICY: DIFFERENCES AS STRENGTH

The rise of ethnicity as a key theme of social science and politics has several roots, including post-1945 anti-colonial struggles, the U.S. ethnic revival and the 1960s and the post-communist re-ordering of Eastern Europe and Central Asia. (Castles, 2011, p. 23)

Globalization is taking place in a fractured manner (Moghaddam, 2008b) because it involves two opposite movements: a first toward increasing integration and the melting of different cultures into one world (e.g., young people around the world are increasingly sharing the same popular culture through the Internet) and a second toward independent local identities, particularly based on ethnicity and more recently on religion (e.g., as reflected in national–ethnic independence movements such as the Kurdish independence movement and in the rise of Islamic State and other extremist Islamic groups that are attempting to establish independent Islamic states). The first globalization movement endorses assimilation but is perceived by non-Western traditionalists and fundamentalists as an invasion of Western, particularly White Christian American, values. At the global level, the rise of radicalization and terrorism is one extreme reaction to this perceived crusader invasion of non-Western societies (Moghaddam, 2010). The second movement, involving fragmentation, differentiation, separatism, and the celebration of distinct, independent identities, has given rise to multiculturalism as a strategy, and sometimes official national policy, for managing diversity.

Successive waves of events since World War II have nurtured the ethnic revivals (see Castles, 2011), which eventually fed into the multiculturalism movement. For example, the Civil Rights movement in the United States eventually resulted in consciousness raising among African Americans, Hispanic Americans, and many other ethnic minority movements within and outside America. The opening up of higher education to larger numbers of ethnic minorities in North America and throughout the world also nurtured ethnic movements through the infusion of new intellectual resources into ethnic communities. In a sense, we are all multiculturalists now because support for multiculturalism—the celebration, sharing, and strengthening of cultural diversity—has become the pervasive ethos within education, at work, and within other major contexts. Thus, despite the lack of an official U.S. policy for managing diversity, the politically correct policy is now recognized to be multiculturalism, particularly in education (although different interpretations of multiculturalism in education still exist; see Sarat, 2008). Canada was the first country to officially adopt multiculturalism as government policy through the Canadian Multiculturalism Act of 1988. Australia and New Zealand followed Canada's example. The four key elements of Canadian multiculturalism (Berry, 1998) serve as a useful framework to discuss this policy: (a) preserving and developing distinct group identities, (b) promoting harmony and respect among groups as they develop distinct collective selves, (c) encouraging intergroup contact to promote mutual acceptance, and (d) encouraging learning official languages to guarantee equal participation.

Preserving and Developing Distinct Group Identities

The most important shift from assimilation to multiculturalism policy is the move to preserve and develop distinct group identities rather than abandon heritage identities and to melt into the mainstream identity. This shift to preserve distinct identities can be interpreted as supported by social identity theory (Tajfel & Turner, 1979), which postulates a universal motivation among humans to achieve a positive and distinct social identity. It is not enough for my group to be evaluated positively. According to social identity theory, I need to feel that my group enjoys distinctiveness and an identity that is, in some salient respects, special and not shared by other groups.

Are there—should there be—limits to support for multiculturalism policy? What about groups that have identities and cultures that subjugate women and minorities? For example, some Muslim women and men are delighted to escape the violation of human rights in countries such as Iran and Saudi Arabia. These individuals do not want to retain the distinctive group identity, which they see as subjugating women and minorities. There is a contradiction between *universal* human rights, as reflected by the United Nations (1948) Universal Declaration of Human Rights, and the relativist value that each society has a right to apply its own moral code (see Nussbaum, 2000, and Schlesinger, 1998, for criticisms of relativism). Female circumcision, forced hijab, polygamy, the exclusion of women from political leadership and power—there is a long list of cultural practices that groups such as fundamentalist Muslims claim are part of their distinct heritage culture. The relativism associated with multiculturalism does not seem to allow for clear lines to be drawn as to what group practices should be—or should not be—part of preserving and developing group identities.

Promoting Harmony and Respect Among Groups as They Develop Distinct Collective Selves

At the heart of multiculturalism policy is the *multiculturalism hypothesis*, which former Canadian Prime Minister Pierre Elliott Trudeau (1919–2000) postulated as involving "confidence in one's own individual identity" out of which can grow "respect for others and a willingness to share ideas, attitudes, and assumptions" (Trudeau, 1971/1992, p. 281). The multiculturalism hypothesis has been interpreted and tested in various ways by different researchers (Novoa & Moghaddam, 2014), but the contentious research question remains: What is the relationship between identification with the ingroup and bias against outgroups? Is it the case that the stronger one's identification is with the ingroup, the stronger one's bias against the outgroup will be? This question has been examined, especially in relation to the puzzling continuity of nationalism (Smith, 1995) and the rise of religious, particularly Muslim, radicalization (Moghaddam, 2008b).

Religiosity has been shown to increase bias against outgroups. This bias increases when *priming* (i.e., putting people through an experience that makes it easier for them to think of or recognize something else) is used to trigger religious thoughts and images (Johnson, Rowatt, & La Bouff, 2012). The more that religious people are reminded of religion, the more they become biased against outgroups. This picture is probably too simplistic because studies of the relationship between nationalism and outgroup bias have illuminated a more complex picture in which the characteristics of the context in which identification occurs influences outcomes (Pehrson, Brown, & Zagefka, 2009). For example, immigrants are seen as more of a threat by those who strongly identify with the nation, even when the population is seen as more heterogeneous (Falomir-Pichastor & Frederic, 2013). In another study that highlighted the role of context, stronger nationalism led to stronger bias against outgroups, but not when nationhood was associated with democratic values (Wagner, Becker, Christ, Pettigrew, & Schmidt, 2012).

Research on the identity context, then, has suggested a complex, situation-dependent relationship between identification with the ingroup and derogation of the outgroup. Historic examples also have highlighted this complexity. The Nazis had confidence in their own identity but were not at all accepting of outgroups. Similarly, Islamic fundamentalists express great confidence but are not accepting of others. Both research and real-world examples have raised serious questions about the validity of the multiculturalism hypothesis.

Encouraging Intergroup Contact to Promote Mutual Acceptance

Research on the contact hypothesis has suggested that, under certain conditions, greater contact among groups results in more positive relations between them. This is true for direct, extended, and even imagined contact, as discussed in the previous section. In one key respect, though, that research is misleading in the context of 21st-century developments when resource inequality between the richest and the rest is increasing (Dorling, 2014; Piketty, 2014; Stiglitz, 2012). Although contact research has tended to focus almost exclusively on ethnic groups, the role of social class largely has been neglected.

Research in the context of Europe (Dorling, 2014; Musterd, 2005) and North America (Iceland & Wilkes, 2006) has demonstrated that social class plays an important role in group-based geographical segregation. The role is highly complex because the influence of social class comes about through interactions with ethnicity. For example, in many major urban centers, ethnic minorities also are more likely to be economically poor. As a result, a policy recommendation is that "schools should look seriously at classroom segregation by class and race and design plans to lower it" (Orfield & Lee, 2005, p. 43). As resource inequalities have increased over the past few decades, researchers have given attention to the often highly subtle effect of social class in social life (see papers in Fiske & Markus, 2012). For example, the independent self model can be put into effect by the young growing up in more affluent families because their financial power enables a self-development based on agency, independence, and initiative. Children who grow up in poor families too often stumble when they try to put into effect such an independent self model because they do not have the scaffolding—the support system needed to enable success in a competitive educational and professional work environment. Even the working class language they use puts them at a disadvantage when competing with more affluent children taught from an early age to use "correct English" and abstract ideas.

Encouraging Learning Official Languages to Guarantee Equal Participation

The learning of "official language(s)" has been consistently highlighted as a prerequisite for the success of minority group members. In the Canadian context, the two official languages are English and French, but other major societies, such as the United States, Germany, France, and the United Kingdom, have one dominant language (the United States does not have an official national language, although English is clearly the dominant language). Proficiency in official, or dominant language(s), is associated with the success of minority groups in education (Barrett, Barile, Malm, & Weaver, 2012). However, language proficiency by itself does not guarantee the success of a minority group; the role of material resources and socioeconomic status is more important (Davis-Kean, 2005).

Books such as *Schooling in Capitalist America* (S. Bowles & Gintis, 1977/ 2011) and *Unequal Childhoods* (Lareau, 2011) have illuminated the large and, in some cases, growing resource inequalities of students in the 21st-century U.S. education system. These resource inequalities include the knowledge base and skills of children's parents, extended family, and neighborhood. A child born into a poor family and impoverished neighborhood most likely will attend a school that is relatively poorly resourced and staffed by less well-trained administrators and teachers. Not surprisingly, in a meta-analysis of studies involving 101,157 students in 6,871 schools, Sirin (2005) found an important association between socioeconomic status and academic achievement. This is in line with a broader trend that has shown that lower socioeconomic status is associated with poorer life outcomes generally, including poorer health of individuals (Luo & Waite, 2005). A common language, then, may be a necessary but not a sufficient condition for equal participation.

A PSYCHOLOGICAL REEVALUATION OF POLICIES FOR MANAGING DIVERSITY IN THE CONTEXT OF DEMOCRACY

> The recognition of cultural and linguistic diversity by and in EU institutions is normatively inconsistent, as it shows a pronounced bias towards the identities embodied by nation-states to the detriment of non-dominant and "minoritized" identities. (Kraus, 2011, pp. 30–31)

Economic and technological forces, including the globalization of commerce and the expanded reach of multinational corporations and Internet, are pushing toward assimilation within larger global and regional units. This increased global interconnectedness through commercial and technological forces is spreading mainstream Western lifestyles, languages, and values, and is placing increased pressure on cultural, linguistic, and religious minorities. The result is a sense of collective threat among traditionalists and fundamentalists strongly motivated to retain their heritage (i.e., traditional) ways of life (Moghaddam, 2008b, 2010). In the face of large-scale global and regional changes, such as the expanded reach of American culture and the English language, central governments are coming to the defense of national identity and national languages often to the detriment of local minority identities and languages. For example, although the French government defends the French language, regional language variations in France have almost disappeared (Moghaddam, 2008b). It is within this context of fractured globalization that the strains and stresses of diversity and democracy must be evaluated (Fish & Brooks, 2004).

Assimilation and Democracy

The discussion in the first part of this chapter shows that a strong case can be made that assimilation is the policy most compatible with democracy. An assimilated world in which people are more similar would seem to have important advantages: Similarity is associated with attraction. Also, similarity would seem to improve conditions allowing social positions to being open to merit because similarity can help create a level playing field. However, these advantages may be illusory.

Greater similarity can be a basis for greater attraction, but evidence has suggested that the motivation to differentiate and discriminate can result in the use of even the most trivial dissimilarity as a basis for intergroup bias (Moghaddam, 2008b). The minimal group paradigm, discussed in Chapter 4, clearly suggests that differences can be manufactured to justify intergroup discrimination, even when, objectively, such differences are trivial. After all, on what objective criteria is skin color important?

The assumption that assimilation will result in better conditions for merit-based social mobility is also problematic because assimilation, as it has been conceived, does not influence some of the most important factors relevant to meritocracy, including material resources. When President Sarkozy, Chancellor Merkel, Prime Minister Cameron, and others showed support for assimilation, they meant that minority groups should take on the dominant language and culture. They assumed this policy would enable minority group members to compete more effectively in the marketplace. Some minority group members will rise economically, but others may fall further behind. The likely overall outcome is that minorities remain at the bottom of the status hierarchy. President Sarkozy, Chancellor Merkel, and Prime Minister Cameron mean to continue the economic system as it is, not to change it so that group-based inequalities decrease. Consequently, they do not mean to eradicate the material sources of group-based inequalities.

Multiculturalism and Democracy

Multiculturalism has become the politically correct policy, and on the surface it seems to be in line with democracy. After all, surely it is a human right to celebrate and maintain one's own heritage culture without being forced to adopt the majority culture. Everyone should have the right to go his or her own way. Moreover, when people are made to feel confident in their own identities, won't they become open and accepting toward others? Unfortunately, this celebration of differences approach has fundamental flaws.

There is no straightforward relationship between confidence in one's own identity and acceptance of others. As discussed earlier, historic examples and empirical research has suggested that, in some cases, those individuals who most strongly identify with, and are most confident about, the ingroup also are most strongly biased against outgroups. Second, the celebration of differences quickly leads to the challenge of relativism and the plight of numerous underdogs within minority cultures. For example, Muslim women who have fled Saudi Arabia, Iran, and other such Islamic dictatorships do not want to perpetuate their own persecution as part of a multicultural policy in the EU or in North America. They do not want to recreate the culture that persecuted them. The solution to the plight of such women and other underdogs is the firm implementation of universal human rights and not the relativistic set of values associated with multiculturalism.

Omniculturalism and Democracy

Clearly, the established policies of assimilation and multiculturalism have fundamental shortcomings that have led to attempts to develop alternative policies. For example, historians (e.g., Kelley, 1999) have introduced the concept of *polyculturalism*, the belief that different ethnic and racial groups always have influenced each other's cultures. Agreement with polyculturalism is associated with more positive intergroup attitudes (Rosenthal, Levy, Katser, & Bazile, in press). However, polyculturalism is less of a policy than a set of beliefs about cultural origins. A more direct attempt to develop an alternative policy came with *omniculturalism*, which I put forward in light of the shortcomings of assimilation and multiculturalism (Moghaddam, 2012). Omniculturalism involves two stages of socialization. In the first stage, human commonalities are highlighted; in the second stage, group differences are recognized.

Omniculturalism attempts to be more compatible with democracy by first giving primacy to characteristics, including rights and duties, that all humans should have by virtue of being human. Second, omniculturalism makes room for group differences and distinctiveness in collective identities. The claim made by omniculturalism is that there is a scientific basis for establishing certain human commonalities and answering the question, What is a human being? Similarly, it is argued that all humans, irrespective of their group memberships, have certain rights and duties, and that a universal criteria must be applied to evaluating the actions of everyone, from private individuals to government authorities. In educating the young until the early teens, emphasis must be placed on human commonalities and on universal rights and duties. At a second stage, the education of the young includes explorations of group differences. However, in an omnicultural system, group differences do not become the main focus of the education system. In practice, this might mean that events such as African American Week or Hispanic American Week only take place in high school (not elementary school) and after children have been thoroughly trained to see the world through a lens of human commonalities.

CONCLUSION

The most important psychological characteristic of a democratic society with respect to minorities is that people develop the ability to treat all other individuals as humans with important shared characteristics and rights and duties common to all. This ability is associated with the worldview that perceives and gives priority to human commonalities. This ability also includes, at a secondary level, recognition of and value given to group-based differences. However, under no conditions should such group-based differences negate or override human commonalities. The policy for managing diversity that is most compatible with these requirements, I believe, is omniculturalism, not multiculturalism or assimilation. Progress toward actualized democracy necessitates a shift toward an omniculturalism policy.

9

INDEPENDENT JUDICIARY

Whoever attentively considers the different departments of power must perceive, that, in a government in which they are separated from each other, the judiciary, from the nature of its functions, will always be the least dangerous to the political rights of the Constitution; because it will be least in a capacity to annoy or injure them.

—Alexander Hamilton in *The Federalist* Papers
(Number 78; Hamilton, Madison, & Jay, 1787/1996, p. 490)

As courts, especially the highest courts, become more activist and autonomous in their decision-making by upholding challenges to the activities of the other branches of government and by dealing with hotly contested issues of public law, they attract much more political attention and criticism. Thus an increase in judicial autonomy and power means that the judiciary becomes more directly connected to a democratic society's politics.

—Peter H. Russell (2001, p. 301)

The Supreme Court is a Political Court.

—Richard A. Posner (2008, p. 269)

When the founding fathers of the United States discussed the separation of powers and the role of the judiciary at the end of the 18th century, the world provided numerous examples of what goes wrong when the judicial system is not independent from political authorities and ideologies. Judges influenced in their judicial decisions by bribes, by political pressure, by threats, by their own ideological biases—these are some of the detrimental outcomes when the judiciary fails to remain independent of politics. In this context, *independence* means not only remaining separate from political forces outside the court but also not basing decisions inside the court on one's own political ideology.

http://dx.doi.org/10.1037/14806-010
The Psychology of Democracy, by F. M. Moghaddam

A paradox is facing the judiciary in the United States and a number of other Western societies. On the one hand, Western thinkers are advancing an "independent judiciary" as a key goal that non-Western societies should adopt if they are to advance toward democracy. On the other hand, in the United States and some other Western societies, against the expectation of Hamilton (Hamilton et al., 1787/1996) and other founding fathers, the judiciary increasingly is being viewed as part of the larger political system—in the sense that Supreme Court judges are seen as making decisions based on their own political ideologies. In the United States, the judiciary is, by definition, political because it is part of the Constitution and the system of government. However, judges are supposed to leave their ideologies outside the courtroom. But, as Richard Posner (2008), a highly influential federal judge nominated by President Ronald Reagan, argued, the U.S. Supreme Court is political and, more broadly, judging is political (p. 369).

In this chapter, I argue that judicial independence must remain a goal integral to democratic societies. Indeed, democratic actualization is impossible without an independent judiciary. However, judging will remain political in some ways, such as the intrusion of unconscious biases; I discuss this topic later in this chapter. This apparent contradiction is solved by distinguishing between the institutional framework in which the judiciary works and the psychological processes involved in making judicial decisions. The institutional framework can and should be organized to enable the judiciary to act independently. However, psychological limits to political neutrality exist. Although the institutional safeguards necessary to establish an independent judiciary have been discussed considerably, far less attention has been given to the psychological factors that can and do often result in biases in the decisions that even an independent judiciary takes.

CONTEXT OF THE JUDICIARY AND MORAL THINKING

> After discriminating . . . in theory, the several classes of power, as they may in their nature be legislative, executive, or judiciary, the next and most difficult task is to provide some practical security for each, against the invasion of the others. What this security ought to be, is the great problem to be solved. (Madison, Number 48; Hamilton et al., 1787/1996, p. 343)

The founding fathers of the United States gave considerable attention to the separation of powers when they deliberated the U.S. Constitution in 1787–1788. Many deliberations on this matter are found, particularly in numbers 78 to 83 of *The Federalist* Papers, a series of articles by Alexander Hamilton (1757–1804), James Madison (1751–1836), and John Jay (1745–1829). As

Madison pointed out, the greatest challenge lies in the details of the practical security each power should have against the invasion of the other(s). Through the separation of powers, the founding fathers believed they were establishing a context in which moral decisions could be made more correctly. Later in this chapter, I discuss the psychological research on the development of such moral thinking.

The founding fathers developed ideas on the separation of powers by looking to different mixed government forms in ancient Greece, the Roman Republic, the English political system, and the French political philosopher Montesquieu's (1750/2011) work *The Spirit of Laws*, which is repeatedly referred to in *The Federalist* Papers (Hamilton et al., 1787/1996). Although many thinkers have agreed that the separation of powers is a desirable and even necessary requirement for democracy, there is less agreement on what judicial independence means (McNollgast, 2006, p. 105). Most commentators have viewed judicial independence from the executive to be particularly important. Tiede (2006) considered three approaches to defining judicial independence: (a) institutional, which focuses on institutional configurations and processes as neutral shapers of judicial outcomes; (b) the judicial rulings against government, which focuses on the ability of judges to "act without political manipulation" (p. 148); and (c) the strategic interaction, which assumes that "law is politics" (p. 150) and legal decisions arise out of interactions between the judiciary and other branches of government. Tiede's preference is to define *judicial independence* "as the judiciary's independence from the executive, as measured by the amount of discretion that individual judges exercise in particular policy areas" (p. 131).

In line with this realist approach, Clark (2011) discussed the results of his interviews with politicians, judges, and others, on the political pressures that shape and limit judicial independence. In essence, he argued that the judiciary is as independent as political support, including support in the form of public opinion, allows it to be. This view of judicial independence gives importance to power distribution and the sources of power, a topic that is particularly important in the context of international relations and national development.

JUDICIAL INDEPENDENCE AND NATIONAL DEVELOPMENT

If one is even to begin to understand the enormity of the task of development, one must unreservedly accept the extent to which the West, in particular England and France, have torn apart the political and economic structures of Third World societies and *used their legal systems* to do so. In other words, not only has law not had an automatically positive function in ensuring political and economic development, it has also had an ambiguous and even negative significance as the instrument used to subject these countries to exploitative trading relations, to land seizures, to discriminatory and even enslaving personal laws and to concepts of public order and administration which are intended to be incapacitating. (Carty, 1992a, p. xiii)

As discussed in Chapter 5, rule of law is no magic pill that will necessarily bring about justice and promote national development in non-Western (or even Western) societies. The law being implemented must itself be just; otherwise, rule of law extends injustice. And the kind of law that is implemented is determined largely by the power enjoyed by specific majority and minority groups, and power relations between groups (D. M. Taylor & Moghaddam, 1994). The mullahs who rule Iran do so through the force of the Republican Guards (an extremist Islamic military force with an army, navy, and air force); the Basij (a plainclothes security force comprising local informants and vigilantes); and an extensive secret security system, MISIRI (Ministry of Intelligence and National Security of the Islamic Republic of Iran). These forces have given the mullahs absolute power out of which has evolved absolute corruption. The injustice of the laws on the books in Iran, such as those giving absolute dictatorial power to an unelected supreme leader, means that rule of law would not bring justice, even if it were applied.

The tendency for rule of law to do harm when the law is unjust, and for the harm to be amplified when the judiciary is under the thumb of political authorities, is clear from the experiences of many Asian and African countries with colonialism and imperialism. As Carty (1992a) made clear in the preceding quote, Britain, France, and other powers used force to change the legal system of nations they colonized and brought the judiciary under the control of colonial authorities. In that way, exploitation of local resources by the colonists was interpreted as legal. Greenberg (1992) discussed numerous examples of exploitation made lawful through the control of the legal system by colonial (and later, neocolonial) power. For example,

> to prevent African farmers from competing with English settlers, the former were forbidden by law from growing export crops (e.g., coffee in Rhodesia), and railroads were located far from native reserves, where land was often malarial, swampy, or of generally poor quality. This, together with the imposition of a cash head tax, forced Africans to work on European plantations. (p. 102)

Such experiences of colonized nations highlight the need for institutional arrangements that safeguard judicial independence (Greenberg, 1992). Lifetime tenure for judges, a progressive judicial career structure, financial independence of the judiciary, and other measures can help make the judiciary less vulnerable. Another important factor is the selection of judges on ideological grounds by politicians who are intent on shaping the direction of judicial decision making, a process that has warped the U.S. Supreme Court in different eras, including the early 21st century. However, no matter how robust the institutional safeguards are against such ideologically driven practices, some biases are likely to creep into the decision-making process. Such biases have to do with the psychology of how judges think and how decisions are made in the process.

DECISION MAKING, INSTITUTIONS, AND MORAL THINKING

How are decisions made in the judicial system? Are decisions made strictly according to law, or do other factors influence decisions? Given the importance and political nature of this issue, it is not surprising that people have put forward and fervently supported differing opinions. Although some thinkers have argued that judges view law as a firm guide for their decisions, others have argued that judges "express their own political vision in deciding hard cases. . . . Respect for law does not determine their decisions" (Cooter, 2000, pp. 1598–1599). A variety of factors, including personality, personal taste, and political preferences, have been cited as influencing courtroom decisions. In an attack on this idea, Kozinski (1993) mockingly stated, "It is popular in some circles to suppose that judicial decision making can be explained largely by frivolous factors, perhaps for example the relationship between what judges eat and what they decide" (p. 993). He dismissed the position taken by critical realism and argued that far too many constraints—the presence of eager young law clerks ready to criticize; colleagues ready to provide corrective feedback; possible critical feedback from the Supreme Court and the political system and politicians; and legal precedent—are placed on judges for them to be able to make decisions based on their personal tastes. The idea that judicial decision making is based on principles, rather than personal intuitions and biases, has been bolstered by a highly influential line of research on the psychology of moral development that was pioneered by Lawrence Kohlberg (1927–1987).

The Kohlbergian Tradition

Using a research methodology that involves asking participants to make decisions on cases that raise moral questions with no easy answers, Kohlberg (1963) developed a broad and far-reaching model of moral development. The most famous is the *Heinz dilemma*, which is as follows:

> In Europe, a woman was near death from a very bad disease, a special kind of cancer. There was one drug that the doctors thought might save her. It was a form of radium for which a druggist was charging ten times what

the drug cost him to make. The sick woman's husband, Heinz, went to everyone he knew to borrow the money, but he could only get together about half of what it cost. He told the druggist that his wife was dying, and asked him to sell it cheaper or let him pay later. But the druggist said, "No, I discovered the drug and I'm going to make money from it." So Heinz got desperate and broke into the man's store to steal the drug for his wife. (Kohlberg, 1973, p. 638)

The responses of participants to such dilemmas are evaluated according to Kohlberg's (1963, 1973) stages of moral development: Level 1 is the preconventional level that involves behavior guided by reward and punishment. Level 2 is the conventional level that involves behavior guided by social conventions. Level 3 is the postconventional or principled level that involves behavior guided by general moral principles (within each of these levels are sublevels that need not concern us here). For example, a person on Level 1 would respond to the Heinz dilemma by saying, "He should only steal the drug if he is sure he will not get caught and punished. If he can escape punishment, he should do it." A person on Level 2 might respond, "If Heinz can find a good lawyer who will help him take the drug but remain within the law, then he should take the drug." A person on Level 3 might respond, "Heinz should take the drug because he will save the life of his wife, and life always has to be protected" or "Heinz should not take the drug because it is always wrong to steal, no matter what the circumstances." Kohlberg argued that there is hierarchical progression up these levels, so that Level 2 moral thinking is more advanced than Level 1. However, not everyone reaches higher levels of moral development; some individuals remain at lower levels.

On the basis of analyzing responses to his moral dilemmas, Kohlberg concluded that "stages form an invariant sequence. Under all conditions except extreme trauma, movement is always forward, never backward. Individuals never skip stages, and movement is always to the next stage up. This is true in all cultures" (Kohlberg & Hersh, 1977, p. 54). Kohlberg claimed that his model is universal and that a person who has achieved a certain level of moral thinking will remain consistently at that level. For example, the select individuals who reach the highest level of moral development would be expected to act on principles applied consistently across contexts: "Right is defined by the decision of conscience in accord with self-chosen ethical principles appealing to logical comprehensiveness, universality, and consistency. . . . At heart, these are universal principles of justice" (Kohlberg & Hersh, 1977, p. 55).

According to Kohlberg's model of moral reasoning, then, individuals who reach the highest level of principled moral reasoning make moral judgments consistently across contexts based on universal principles of justice. If this is true, then these individuals are not influenced in their decisions by the characteristics of the context.

Consistency, Ideology, and Context

An alternative to Kohlberg's (1963, 1973) model of moral development is that, rather than principled thinking being exclusive to an elite group, it is a capacity shared by most people, but its application depends on other factors. Indeed, most people can make moral decisions that fall into the preconventional, conventional, or postconventional (principled) level of Kohlberg's model (Emler, Renwick, & Malone, 1983; Moghaddam & Vuksanovic, 1990). Which particular level of moral decision making they adopt, some research has suggested, will depend on how the issues and decisions line up with their political ideologies, among other things. For example, Margaret Thatcher (1925–2013), U.K. prime minister from 1979 to 1990, and Ronald Reagan (1911–2004), U.S. president from 1981 to 1989, acted to severely limit the influence of labor unions in their home countries but strongly supported labor unions (e.g., Solidarity led by Lech Walesa in Poland) that worked against communist rule in the former communist Eastern Europe. The "freedoms" that Thatcher and Reagan advocated for labor unions in communist states on the basis of principled reasoning, they denied to labor unions in the United Kingdom and the United States. As this example suggests, a person who makes decisions at Level 3, according to Kohlberg's model, in context A could then shift to making decisions that would be classified according to Kohlberg's model as Level 2 or even Level 1 in context B. The particular level of moral reasoning a person will adopt in a particular context depends on that person's ideology. In line with this alternative view, evidence has shown that individuals of different political orientations shift their positions on moral issues depending on the circumstances (Emler et al., 1983; Emler & St. James, 2004; Sparks & Durkin, 1987).

Of course, this position-shifting is well known in politics. Politicians routinely espouse one set of views when they are in opposition and in circumstances in which they do not have the rights and responsibilities of political office, but shift position and make decisions in a different way when they win power and come into political office. The same is true for revolutionaries before and after they topple a government and seize power (Moghaddam, 2004). Politicians also shift positions depending on whether they are discussing an issue at home or abroad: Many Western politicians who support the rights of workers in China, Russia, Cuba, and other communist countries fail to support similar ideas in their own societies. In this, they are adopting the tactic "the enemy of my enemy is my friend" and changing their views across contexts to suit their ideological goals (Dufour, Goldberg, & Moghaddam, 2013). They are not applying a general principle consistently across contexts, such as a human rights principle regarding trade unions (Section 4 of Article 23 of the United Nations [1948] Universal Declaration of Human Rights states, "Everyone has the right to form and to join trade unions").

An extreme example of such opportunistic shifting comes from Iran after the 1979 revolution, when Islamic extremists routinely used religious "revelations" to condone whatever practices they felt necessary at the moment to achieve and maintain their monopoly on power. They used religious texts as Rorschach inkblots to conjure whatever interpretations were necessary for the moment and the situation.

Years later, I had the opportunity in North America to demonstrate such shifts experimentally (Moghaddam & Vuksanovic, 1990). The studies we undertook involved asking participants to make decisions, in the Kohlbergian tradition, about different moral dilemmas. The first moral dilemma we presented involved a mother who was caught shoplifting. In her defense, the mother explained that she had stolen food to feed her hungry children. A second moral dilemma involved a television anchorwoman who refused to change her hairstyle and clothing as demanded by her employers; she claimed her freedom of speech was being violated. Each moral dilemma was developed and pretested to be difficult to decide. After all, is it understandable to steal to feed your hungry children? One could present strong arguments for and against stealing in such a situation. These moral dilemmas were presented to Canadian participants in a study with three conditions in which the context of the event described in the moral dilemma was changed: Context 1, Canada; Context 2, Russia (communist at that time); Context 3, India. The name of the character in each scenario also was changed in line with context; for example, in the case of the moral dilemma about a woman who is caught stealing food, she was named Mrs. Lambert in context Canada, Mrs. Borzov in context Russia, and Mrs. Singh in context India.

According to Kohlberg's (1963) model, people should not be influenced by the context in which the event has occurred. For example, if they judge stealing to be wrong, then their moral judgment about stealing should remain consistent across contexts. However, we found that the context did influence moral judgments (Moghaddam & Vuksanovic, 1990). For example, in exactly the same scenario, Mrs. Singh was judged less harshly when she stole food in India than when Mrs. Lambert stole food in Canada.

Again, examples of this phenomenon are found in politics. Consider, for instance, politicians who emphatically declare "no new taxes" and make this issue the centerpiece of their political campaigns—only to go back on their word when circumstances change. This is what famously happened to George H. W. Bush, 41st president of the United States, who, at the 1988 Republican National Convention made the phrase "read my lips, no new taxes" famous. However, faced with the constraints and responsibilities of being in the White House, President Bush approved raising taxes.

In some important respects, moral dilemmas research has continued to be influenced by Kohlberg. For example, the Kohlbergian tradition of presenting participants with scenarios involving moral dilemmas continues. However, research on moral decision making has taken on some new, post-Kohlberg characteristics. I begin this section by reviewing a variety of explanations for how people make moral judgments. Next, I discuss recent studies on moral decision making: first, those conducted with participants not involved in the judicial system and then studies conducted with judges as participants.

Explanations of Moral Judgments

Kohlberg is part of a rationalist tradition that assumes that humans consciously think through moral dilemmas, such as a scientist solving a puzzle. In psychological research, Kohlberg built on the cognitive approach of Jean Piaget (1896–1980), who viewed moral thinking as a form of conscious problem solving that is integral to stagewise progression in cognitive development (Piaget, 1932/1965). In a broader context, this approach was influenced by German philosopher Immanuel Kant (1724–1804), as reflected in his famous categorical imperative: "Act only in accordance with that maxim through which you can at the same time will that it become universal law" (Kant, 1785/2002, G 4:421). In other words, act according to principles that you would want to see applied to everyone, including yourself, irrespective of circumstances. Another version of this deontological approach is found in John Rawls's (1971) thought experiment that adopted the so-called veil of ignorance (as discussed in Chapters 6 and 9 of this volume). We are asked to consider a society in which roles are revised and reassigned, but we do not know what our role will be—whether we will be a male or female, Black or White, rich or poor, young or old, and so on. In such a society, Rawls argued, we are more likely to choose fair rules. The assumption in this rationalist tradition is that people will consciously think things through and arrive at the best, most logical solutions. However, as previously discussed, a series of studies that used methodology similar to Kohlberg's showed that ideology and other factors influence moral judgment. Parallel to these developments, an alternative explanation for moral thinking has evolved: one that emphasizes intuition, unconscious fast thinking, and emotions (Haidt, 2007; Ham & van den Bos, 2010).

The idea that moral decisions are influenced by factors other than conscious cognition is in line with another intriguing explanation: that self-control depends on a limited kind of energy or resource (Baumeister, Bratslavsky, Muraven, & Tice, 1998). Self-control plays a central role in moral life; taking morally correct actions invariably involves refraining from taking an alternative action that also could have resulted in rewarding outcomes. Consider, for example, a situation in which 10-year-old John has been given two cookies: one for himself and one for his younger sister. John is aware that he could eat both cookies and nobody would find out. Should he go ahead and eat both cookies? Research has suggested that factors such as John's blood glucose level will influence the self-control he shows in this situation (Gailliot & Baumeister, 2007): At a time of day when his glucose level is low, John will show less self-control. The effect of blood glucose on his self-control is likely to remain hidden from John, but it influences his moral decisions. As a limited resource, self-control is depleted each time it is used (without being replenished, see Hagger, Wood, Stiff, & Chatzisarantis, 2010), and thus our moral decision making tends to change over time, often unconsciously, depending on the level of ego depletion experienced.

Studies With Laypersons and With Judges as Participants

Following the Kohlbergian tradition, 21st-century research on moral thinking has continued to present participants with moral dilemmas. The most influential moral dilemma used has been the so-called footbridge dilemma (Greene, Sommerville, Nystrom, Darley, & Cohen, 2001) in which you, the participant, are asked to imagine standing next to a large stranger on a footbridge that spans a railroad track. You look up and are horrified to see an out-of-control trolley thundering down the track and headed toward five people who are walking along the track and unaware that they are going to be hit and killed. You realize that the only way to save the five people is by pushing the large stranger in front of you off the footbridge onto the railroad track below. This will kill the large stranger you push but save the other five people. A utilitarian approach, intended to maximize the benefit for everyone involved, would lead you to push the stranger off the footbridge. However, a deontological approach, which in a Kantian way would apply the same principle (e.g., thou shalt not kill) irrespective of context, would result in your not pushing the stranger in front of the trolley because, no matter what the circumstance, it would be wrong to kill.

In the footbridge dilemma, participants have to choose between two different rules for behavior—maximizing benefits for everyone (by killing a person) versus the moral duty not to kill under any circumstance (and allowing five people to die)—and typically experience some level of uncertainty in doing so (Greene et al., 2001). Research has suggested that the alternative chosen by individuals faced with this dilemma depends on which of the rules, save lives versus do not kill, is more cognitively accessible at the time of decision making (Broeders, van den Bos, Müller, & Ham, 2011). By priming (and thus making more cognitively accessible) either the save-lives or do-not-kill rules, researchers were able to increase the probability that participants would apply a particular rule and make the corresponding choice: pushing the stranger off the bridge when the save-lives rule was primed and letting the trolley kill five people when the do-not-kill rule was primed.

But the traditional distinction between making moral judgments by relying on conscious, deliberate, controlled cognition versus unconscious, intuitive, fast, automatic cognition is too simplistic. In practice, both types of processes are involved in moral decision making: The immediate intuitive reaction often is revised by a more deliberate, controlled assessment (Greene, Morelli, Lowenberg, Nystrom, & Cohen, 2008; Ham & van den Bos, 2010).

Although the studies discussed so far have involved moral decision making by participants who are not legal professionals, another set of studies has focused on decision making by judges (e.g., Danziger, Levav, & Avnaim-Pessoa, 2011; Englich, Mussweiler, & Strack, 2006; Guthrie, Rachlinski, & Wistrich, 2007; Porter & ten Brinke, 2009; Steffensmeier & Britt, 2001). Are judges' decisions made in a rational and conscious manner based solely on relevant facts and the law, as claimed by legal formalists? Or, do psychological, social, political, and other factors also influence decision making by judges, as claimed by legal realists? The empirical evidence has tended to endorse the descriptive self-reports from judges themselves on this topic (e.g., Posner, 2008), which suggests that judges often are influenced by factors other than facts and the law, as legal realists claim (see the review by Vidmar, 2011).

Danziger et al. (2011) reported a study that endorses the depletion model of self-control discussed earlier in this chapter. In an analysis of 1,112 judicial rulings, they found that judges were more likely to give favorable rulings immediately after a meal break, a finding that suggests that factors such as level of blood glucose and mental fatigue do influence judicial decision making. Englich et al. (2006) demonstrated the influence of an *anchoring effect*, a tendency to be influenced by a first piece of information that acts as a base or anchor, on decisions by judges and legal prosecutors. The first piece of information (e.g., the defendant should get 3 months in jail, rather than 9 months of probation) could be introduced through a question by a journalist, a prosecutor's sentencing demand, or the participants' throwing the dice, but irrespective of the anchor source, it will influence the decisions made by experienced legal professionals. Guthrie et al. (2007) also discussed evidence suggesting that judges are influenced by the *representative heuristic*, the assumption that an item that looks similar to members of a category also belongs to that category. For example, if a defendant looks like a typical criminal, then he or she must be a criminal. The representative heuristic leads to an overreliance on intuition rather than factual statistical information. Judges also were influenced by the *hindsight bias*, a tendency to reconstruct our memory of the past to fit how events actually turned out; hindsight bias leads to the overestimation of the predictability of past events. An assessment of judges' beliefs about how to assess the credibility of individuals in court revealed major disagreements and, thus, suggested a lack of consensus. For example, although some judges said that dishonest witnesses give more details, other judges said that honest witnesses give more details (Porter & ten Brinke, 2009). Also, the race of the judge has been shown to make a difference; Black judges tend to give harsher sentences (Steffensmeier & Britt, 2001). Decision making by judges is influenced by psychological, demographic, and related factors other than the facts and law.

Research findings about how judges actually make decisions can be used to help develop programs that limit judicial biases. For example, Guthrie et al. (2007) used that research to suggest reforms to achieve less biased decisions. These reforms included that judges be given more time to make decisions, be required to write opinions more often, be provided with in-depth continuing legal education, and be supported with scripts, checklists, and other tools to lessen reliance on memory. Unfortunately, this approach still will not solve the problem facing the U.S. Supreme Court, particularly in the 21st-century: politicians purposely selecting judges for their political ideology rather than judicial acumen.

CONCLUSION

I have proposed that judicial independence is a necessary step toward actualized democracy, but we need to be realistic about the limitations imposed on judicial independence by psychological factors. A first step is to develop the institutional context that enables judicial independence, such as lifetime tenure for all judges and financial stability and independence for the judiciary. A second step is to acknowledge that psychological, social, political, and other factors can and often do influence how judges make decisions, and develop programs that help judges overcome such biases(as suggested by Guthrie et al., 2007). The relationship between judicial independence and national development is complex, particularly because of the institutional instability that often characterizes developing nations (Helmke & Rosenbluth, 2009). Although it is not yet clear why, research has suggested that political competition, which is assumed to be a sign of a healthy democracy, often can result in a less independent judiciary in developing societies (Aydin, 2013). Political competition can even add to political, economic, and social instability of the entire developing society. On the other hand, in a study of 163 countries from 1960 to 2000, Gibler and Randazzo (2011) demonstrated that a more independent judiciary is a safeguard against regime instability and backsliding toward authoritarianism. This is of the greatest importance, given that there is no guarantee that societal change is always toward greater democracy (Moghaddam, 2013).

10

UNIVERSAL SUFFRAGE

Men in general judge more by the eyes than by the hands, for every one can see, but very few have to feel. Everybody sees what you appear to be, few feel what you are, and those few will not dare oppose themselves to the many. . . . The vulgar is always taken by appearances and the issue of the event; and the world consists only of the vulgar, and the few who are not vulgar are isolated when the many have a rallying point.

—Niccolò Machiavelli (1532/1950, p. 66)

This judgment by Machiavelli seems to be too harsh for our 21st-century democratic sentiments. The dismissal of the majority as being "taken by appearances" does not sit well with most of us. After all, we are used to ideas such as majority rule and elections in which voters make decisions freely and every vote counts. The rational model of the voter also has been extremely influential in research (Edlin, Gelman, & Kaplan, 2007; Geys, 2006) on the assumption that voters make rational decisions both in deciding to vote and who to vote for. However, before dismissing Machiavelli's writings as irrelevant to our era, consider closely the following findings from 21st-century research on the characteristics of people as voters in contemporary political elections:

- In a study on the influence of "irrelevant events" on how voters evaluate the performance of governments, Healy, Malhotra, and Mo (2010) demonstrated that a win within the last 10 days

http://dx.doi.org/10.1037/14806-011
The Psychology of Democracy, by F. M. Moghaddam

by a local college football team can boost votes for the incumbent by 1.61 percentage points in U.S. Senate, gubernatorial, and presidential elections. The effect increases for teams with a broader fan support. Presidential approval ratings also were shown to be influenced by surprise wins and losses in NCAA men's basketball tournament.

- The percentage of votes that candidates received in actual U.S. Senate and House of Representatives elections was predicted above chance by study participants' split-second impressions of competence based solely on the candidates' faces (Todorov, Mandisodza, Goren, & Hall, 2005). "Elected in 100 Milliseconds" is the title of another research paper that demonstrated the same trend (Olivola & Todorov, 2010a). Physical appearance has been shown to influence our evaluations of others in important ways (Mueller & Mazur, 1996; Olivola & Todorov, 2010b).

- Assessments made by U.S. participants of the competence, dominance, and facial maturity of faces that, unbeknownst to them, belonged to Canadian politicians significantly predicted the success of these politicians in actual elections in Canada (Rule & Ambady, 2010).

- Conservative voters were shown to prefer candidates who are closer in appearance to the stereotypic Republican candidate (Olivola, Sussman, Tsetsos, Kang, & Todorov, 2012). Thus, "looking the part" is an advantage in elections.

- Studies that have explored neural correlates of trustworthiness have suggested an important role for the amygdala and for automatic implicit processes in judgments of the trustworthiness of faces (Baron, Gobbini, Engell, & Todorov, 2011). Greater amygdala response to the faces of CEOs was associated with a CEO's leadership success (Rule et al., 2011). Neural responses of a small group of individuals, but not their self-reports, predicted the success of wide-scale advertising campaigns in a population (Falk, Berkman, & Lieberman, 2012). These findings seem to suggest aspects of behavior that are outside conscious awareness but are tracked by neural signals.

- By wrapping political messages in enthusiasm-eliciting images and music, researchers have influenced voters to be less vigilant and questioning about political issues and to vote more on preexisting political preferences (Brader, 2005). This appeal to emotions through music and images a routine part of 21st-century political campaigns.

These findings of psychological science seem to dispel the myth of the rational voter. They remind one of the words of Marcius, a noble Roman in Shakespeare's play *Coriolanus*; Marcius accuses the rabble protesting in the streets of being fickle and irrational:

> Who deserves greatness
> Deserves your hate; and your affections are
> A sick man's appetite, who desires most that
> Which would increase his evil. He that depends
> Upon your favours swims with fins of lead
> And hews down oaks with rushes. Hang ye! Trust Ye?
> With every minute you do change a mind,
> And call him noble that was now your hate,
> Him vile that was your garland. (I.i.179–187; see Evans, 1997)

In *Coriolanus*, Shakespeare explored the relationship between leaders and their subjects. When a talented leader refuses to adapt his self-presentation to please the people, we see them turn against him. Indeed, a central theme of the play is the irrationality of the people. This same theme is underlined by well-received books in the modern era, such as Caplan's (2007) *The Myth of the Rational Voter*, in which he argued that the ills of democracy have arisen largely from the irrationality and ignorance of voters. He gave less attention to the antidemocratic motivations and role of the super-rich in making sure democracy does not meet the needs of the majority.

In the 21st century, the attack on the rational voter has been coupled with what Rancière (2014) described as a hatred of democracy:

> The "government of anybody and everybody" is bound to attract the hatred of all those who are entitled to govern men by their birth, wealth, or science. Today it is bound to attract this hatred more radically than ever, since the social power of wealth no longer tolerates any restrictions on its limitless growth. (p. 95)

In line with these trends is research that has examined how advanced social and political science techniques are being used to manipulate democracy (see papers in Le Cheminant & Parrish, 2011). For example, Druckman and Jacobs (2015) argued that politicians are using opinion polls in ways that betray democracy. Instead of using those polls to better understand public sentiments and needs, politicians have selectively used information from polls to shape and manipulate public opinion. President Lyndon B. Johnson, for example, used polling data to support his Vietnam policy, and President George W. Bush did so to support his invasion of Iraq. The manipulative use of survey research has been coupled with a strong tendency for politicians to be responsive to the highest income elites and narrow economic interests (Druckman & Jacobs, 2015).

What should we make of these research trends, which seem to undermine the ideal of politicians who respond to the people's needs and of voters who are rational and informed? In the journey toward actualized democracy, we are confronted by enormous challenges in voter behavior. Universal suffrage and the active, informed participation of all adults in elections and in the political process is a requirement for actualized democracy. However, as we have just seen, the research literature presents a picture of manipulative politicians, voters who are persuaded by emotional messages and looks, and political candidates elected in 100 milliseconds (Olivola & Todorov, 2010a). Can we get to actualized democracy from where we are presently? My resounding answer to this question is, Yes we can! However, we must meet certain conditions.

I begin by discussing the idea of universal suffrage and its slow historical development to the present, and then examine two lines of thinking that strongly argue that the rational voter model itself has shortcomings. I next discuss the kind of education needed to help develop actualized democracy and how we might arrive at actualized democracy starting from where we are today. We have already made some progress, particularly in the United States and other Western societies, but we still have a long way to go before achieving actualized democracy.

THE PSYCHOLOGY OF WHO VOTES AND WHY IT MATTERS

It matters a great deal who among the eligible electorate votes. The kind of leadership achieved is in important respects determined by the characteristics of "followership" in society (Kellerman, 2008; Tee, Paulsen, & Ashkanasy, 2013), and it is the people who vote who determine political leadership among those who run for office. Those who vote are using the opportunity to give emphasis to their rights. We are now in an age of rights rather than duties (Finkel & Moghaddam, 2005), but the rights of certain interest groups have priority over the rights of others—in part through the exercise of voting rights.

Getting the Vote

The history of how and why voting rights were gradually extended is best summed up by the phrase "reform to preserve" that is associated with the aristocratic reformer Earl Grey (1764–1845), who played a vital role in passage of the 1832 British Parliamentary Reform Act (Derry, 1992). This act extended the vote to a greater number of propertied men, increased the power of men with capital in newly expanding urban areas, and decreased the influence of the traditional landed gentry. Over the course of centuries, the power elites in different societies have responded to revolutionary threats by extending the right to vote (Przeworski, 2009) in a way that has helped to preserve the group-based inequalities that characterize major societies. The spreading around the world the idea that democracy is good means that even modern dictators have incorporated "voting" as a regular social practice (Gellately, 2013) to create what I have termed *democratic dictatorships*, regimes that fake legitimacy by coercing their populations through election rituals to "approve" of government actions (Moghaddam, 2013).

The spread of voting as a right that all adults should have has been interpreted as part of a larger trend involving the Europeanization of the world from the colonial era onward (Headley, 2008). But adopting this viewpoint may lead to overlooking important local cultural roots and traditions. As the concept of contextualized democracy discussed in Chapter 1 suggests, democracy has developed in different ways in different European countries. For example, the way in which voting influences the selection of political leadership is different in French democracy, in which voters elect a president, compared with British democracy, in which voters elect members of Parliament and the head of the political party with the most seats in Parliament becomes prime minister. Even though the diffusion of European ideas is integral to the spread of democracy, local cultural traditions play an important role in how democracy evolves in non-European societies. For example, in India, local cultural traditions involving language, religion, gender, caste, and family affiliation are highly influential in politics (Gilmartin, 2012).

From the end of the 18th century until the early 20th century, an increasing number of countries extended franchise to more males based on property qualifications. These franchise extensions came as a result of revolutionary movements, such as occurred throughout Europe in 1848, when the lower classes challenged the ruling power elites (Przeworski, 2009). By the early 20th century, the right to vote was extended in democracies to all men. New Zealand (in 1893) and Australia (in 1901) were the first countries to grant women the right to vote on the same basis as men. By 1950, half of those countries that allowed voting rights of any kind enfranchised women and men on the same basis.

The main opposition to extended voting rights was the fear that the poor population would use the vote to redistribute wealth through taxation and various other wealth transfer policies. This danger to property was highlighted by politicians throughout the reform period of the 19th century (Przeworski, 2009). Meltzer and Richard (1981) proposed that the motivation shown by the median voter for wealth redistribution would be positively associated with higher wealth inequality. The logic is as follows: Given that voters will act on narrow self-interest and given that, in their urge for electoral support, politicians will respond to demands from voters, the outcome will be higher wealth redistribution where there initially was greater wealth inequality. But empirical tests have not found support for the idea that more unequal societies redistribute more (Luebker, 2014). This lack of support for the Meltzer-Richard hypothesis also has been demonstrated by the trend of increasing income inequalities in the United States and other major societies (Piketty, 2014).

Who Votes

> Political inequality in voter turnout is not new. . . . Since 1972, the wealthy have always voted more than the poor, and hence have always been overrepresented at the polls (in both presidential and congressional elections). But now the income and wealth gap between the wealthy and the poor is much greater than it was in 1972. (Leighley & Nagler, 2014, p. 6)

Far from everyone who has the right to vote in the United States, European Union member states, and other countries with relatively open elections takes advantage of the opportunity. In their extensive analysis of "Who Votes Now?" Leighley and Nagler (2014) demonstrated systematic differences in the characteristics of voters versus nonvoters in the United States. More affluent people are more likely to vote (Leighley & Nagler, 2014, pp. 27–34), and this trend has been confirmed in cross-national studies (e.g., Nevitte, Blais, Gidengil, & Nadeau, 2000). Older people are more likely to vote than younger, and, in recent years, women have been more likely to vote than men. Earlier studies have focused on how voter turnout is influenced by institutional characteristics, such as nationally competitive districts and strong linkages between political parties and local groups (Jackman, 1987). However, in their cross-national study, Nevitte et al. (2000) confirmed the important role of socioeconomic status (SES): "SES indicators are significantly related to non-voting in every country regardless of substantial variations in economic performance and political and institutional arrangements" (p. 12).

What explains this lower turnout among poorer people? From a psychological perspective, voter turnout can be interpreted as a habit, a repeated response under similar conditions so that the same response becomes automatic when the similar conditions arise (Aldrich, Montgomery, & Wood, 2011). But this interpretation does not explain why low socioeconomic status people should be less inclined to form a voting habit. An important factor related to basic interests is that poorer people do not vote because the competing political parties and representatives do not offer policies that reflect their interests. More specifically, the Meltzer–Richard hypothesis has not really been tested because poorer people do not have a realistic opportunity to vote for wealth redistribution; none of the viable political candidates from major parties seriously offers wealth redistribution as a policy. Poor people can vote for the next-best-candidate, but this strategy does not lead them to major changes in wealth parity.

Thus, from this perspective, the lack of wealth redistribution is not so much because of low voter turnout among poorer people but a consequence of the lack of viable political candidates who accurately represent the interests of the poorer voters regarding wealth distribution. This becomes clear when considering countries, such as Australia, where voting is a duty rather than a right and results in a 10- to 15-point increase in turnout (Blais, 2006). However, although making voting compulsory increases turnout, in countries such as Australia, it does not increase wealth redistribution—again, partly because poorer voters do not have the option of voting for viable political candidates who are advocating major wealth redistribution.

THE PSYCHOLOGY OF THE RATIONAL VOTER

The rational model of human behavior dominant in the social and psychological sciences has been criticized as inaccurate and as contradicted by evidence about how humans actually behave—such as, in the economic sphere, emotional decisions driven by fear of loss and distortions of financial risk (Kahneman, 2011; Sen, 1977). In response to various criticisms, the *omniscient* or *unbounded rationality model*, which assumes perfect rationality, has given way to a *bounded rationality model*, which assumes that limitations to rationality exist and people are rational to different degrees in varying situations (Chong, 2013). But there is now a danger that through cognitive neuroscience, a new, equally distorted model is emerging of the human being as *cognitive autonom*, a being who is making instantaneous decisions and actions without conscious awareness and explicit motivation (Harré & Moghaddam, 2012).

Humans as cognitive autonoms seems to arise, for example, from the tradition established by Tversky and Kahneman's (1974) now classic research on *cognitive heuristics*, automatic, instantaneous decision-making strategies that save time and effort but can result in errors. Most famously, the *availability heuristic* occurs when one falsely judges the frequency and probability of an event by how easily examples are brought to mind. In the months following the 9/11 terrorist attacks, people in the United States traveled less by air and more by roads mainly because they (wrongly) judged air travel to be more dangerous, although more fatalities occur from road accidents every year than in accidents involving air travel. The availability heuristic meant that deaths associated with air travel came to mind far more easily than deaths in road travel. The result was that, in the months after 9/11, fatalities in car accidents rose even higher.

The autonom model seems to be endorsed by research on both cognitive automaticity among voters and supposed biological factors that influence political behavior (Fowler & Schreiber, 2008). For example, Dodd et al. (2012) showed that those to the political right automatically show more physiological responsiveness to aversive stimuli (e.g., a spider on a man's face; an open wound with maggots in it) and direct greater attention to such stimuli. The findings seem to reflect the right-wing tendency to attend to phenomena that show the world as a dangerous, threatening place. Such tendencies are outside conscious awareness and apparently influenced by individuals' inherited characteristics (Fowler & Dawes, 2008).

Is there an alternative to the opposite extremes of rational and autonom models? One such alternative is to recognize the importance of motivation and to view voting and other political behavior from the perspective of research on motivated reasoning.

Motivated Reasoning and the Voter

> In September 2004, Charles Duelfer, advisor to the Director of the Central Intelligence Agency, filed the final report of the Iraq Survey Group, saying that Iraq's WMD [weapons of mass destruction] programs had ended by 1996. . . . Soon thereafter, the Bush administration conceded that large weapons caches probably would never be found. With such politically loaded facts, did interpretations vary? In a word: yes. Once it was evident that the United States would not find WMD, the question became, why not? . . . Democrats concluded that the WMDs had not existed. . . . Republicans gave one of the following reasons: Iraq moved the WMDs; it destroyed them; or, they had not yet been found. Republicans thus opted for interpretations that maintained rationales for the invasion. (Gaines, Kuklinski, Quirk, Peyton, & Verkuilen, 2007, p. 965)

The invasion of Iraq by United States–led forces in 2003 was one of the most politically divisive events of recent American history. The original reason given for the invasion by the George W. Bush administration was to put an end to the threat of weapons of mass destruction (WMDs) that, the administration claimed, the Iraqi regime had been developing to attack the United States and its allies. After it became clear that WMDs would not be found in Iraq, this "fact" did not substantially change support among Republicans for the war. The research of Gaines et al. (2007) suggested that "weak" Republicans did change their positions as new facts about the Iraq war became available. However, "strong" Republicans did not change their opinions as they learned new facts; they simply changed their interpretations of the facts.

The key factor in this situation is identification with an ingroup such as "Republican" or "Democrat." Through identification, individual interpretations of factual information become shaped by group interpretation. G. L. Cohen (2003) showed that liberal and conservative individuals changed their assessment of a welfare policy to be consistent with that of their party and shifted away from the position they would have taken without knowledge of party positions. Interestingly, participants assumed they had come to their positions independently and denied the influence of their parties. This is in line with long-established findings that have shown the subtle but powerful effect of groups on individual behavior. Examples are Sherif's (1936) studies on conformity to group-established norms that are both arbitrary and objectively wrong, and Asch's (1948) studies of group influence on how favorably or unfavorably politicians are perceived.

The Rational Voter and New Information

Another blow against the rational voter has been dealt by research showing that exposure to new scientific information does not change the positions of individuals who strongly identify with political parties. The deficit model of science assumes that a lack of (deficit in) scientific knowledge leads people to have incorrect opinions. People will correct their opinions when they are provided with accurate information about scientific issues. As a result, public opinion will move to the position of scientists. This deficit model has been shown to be correct for individuals who moderately or weakly identify with a group. However, for strong identifiers, more information and education does not necessarily change their views in the direction of becoming more scientifically attuned. For example, when Sol Hart and Nisbet (2012) exposed adults to simulated news stories that presented scientifically accurate information about the effect of climate change, they found that the partisan divide among strong believers and nonbelievers grew larger. The result was what the authors called a boomerang effect. Levendusky (2013) exposed participants to partisan or neutral media messages about the Barack Obama presidency, and found that partisan messages further polarized those who already identified strongly with a party. Thus, rather than influencing moderates, partisan messages made extremists more extreme. Nyhan, Reifler, and Ubel (2013) also showed that communicating corrective information about the Obama health care reform failed to dissuade politically committed Sarah Palin supporters from believing in the veracity of death panels and other myths associated with Obamacare. This trend was confirmed by T. A. Myers, Maibach, Roser-Renouf, Akerlof, and Leiserowitz (2012), who showed that Americans with strong beliefs (for and against) climate change interpret their personal experiences with the weather in a manner that further endorses their personal beliefs.

Research on motivated reasoning has provided a counterintuitive picture of how people interpret negative information about political candidates and positions they support. Taber and Lodge (2006) presented U.S. participants with arguments about gun control and affirmative action. They found that arguments that were congruent with the participant's prior position were assessed less critically, whereas incongruent arguments were given more critical and closer attention. The outcome was polarization of attitudes and a tendency for incongruent information to strengthen, rather than weaken, support for prior positions. Similarly, Redlawsk (2002) showed that strongly motivated voters might increase, rather than decrease, their support for a political candidate after receiving negative information about the candidate. This implies, Redlawsk (2002) concluded, that "political scientists who prefer voters as affect-free calculators who coolly consider candidates and make even-handed evaluations if simply given enough information miss a critical piece of the puzzle. Affect counts" (p. 1041).

BEYOND THE RATIONALITY–AFFECT–MOTIVATION TRIANGLE: EDUCATION AND REACHING THE IDEAL VOTER

The traditional debates and research that have focused on franchise and voting behavior have been situated within the confines of the rationality–affect–motivation triangle (see Figure 10.1). A first perspective emphasizes rationality: The voter is depicted as a cold calculating machine. A second perspective focuses on affect and incorporates emotions and motivation to correct the exaggeration of rationality in the traditional economic model. A third perspective highlights political motivations. However, the focus on the numerous ways in which affect and biased motivation enter political decision making has reinforced the historically dominant view of voters as not to be trusted.

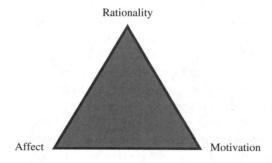

Figure 10.1. The rationality–affect–motivation triangle

The picture of the voter derived from psychological research implies that it is not necessarily detrimental that much of the population is disengaged from politics and fails to vote in elections. Whereas in early 19th century, Earl Grey and other members of the elite viewed it as expedient to limit franchise through ownership qualifications, in the 21st century, it is seen as expedient to limit franchise simply through a political, educational, economic, and cultural system that ensures a lack of engagement and information among much of the population, particularly poor people. Interestingly, the lack of political engagement among the poor populations in contemporary Western countries partly goes back to the reasons originally used to not extend franchise to poor people: that the working poor lack the time and resources to become informed voters. How can an individual with a low level of education and who works long hours at a poorly paid job find the time and resources to engage in politics? It would be far more efficient, according to this thinking, to allow such poorly educated individuals to remain apathetic toward politics so that the better-educated people could make the important decisions. This assumes that the better-educated and more affluent groups are more rational and more interested in the public good than the masses—an assumption not validated by biases in favor of the rich in government policies.

Associated with a focus on the deficits of voters is the proposition that politics has become personalized, so that politicians' personalities rather than ideologies more often make the difference in political campaigns (Caprara, 2007). Political persuasion increasingly is taking place through the *peripheral route*, how a message makes people feel, and less through the *central route*, a message engaging cognitive and critical thinking (see Chapter 4, with reference to Petty & Cacioppo, 1986). Effective leadership in this context means being able to influence people to feel good about a future with Person/Party X leading the country, but to feel anxious about a future with Person/Party Y leading the country. The epitome of this style is President Reagan, the so-called great communicator who moved voters to feel good that "it's morning in America."

However, researchers have disagreed strongly about whether there has been an end to ideology, the thesis put forward by American social theorist Daniel Bell (1919–2011) in his highly influential book *The End of Ideology* (Bell, 1960) that major political ideologies, particularly Marxism, have become exhausted and ideological disagreement has declined (see Jost, 2006, for a critical reassessment from a psychological perspective). It may be that major political parties, such as the Republicans and Democrats in the United States and the Conservatives and Labour Party in the United Kingdom, have become more similar in ideology. But that does not necessarily mean that this shift in the positions of political parties reflects real shifts in the ideologies of populations. It may well be that political parties are led by elites who fail to represent most people ideologically, which also might help explain the disengagement of so many voters because the candidates they have the option to vote for do not represent their own ideologies. In particular, it might be that poor people are less inclined to vote in elections because candidates for political office fail to represent their interests. It may be that if and when there emerged viable candidates who support using taxation and other means to achieve major wealth redistribution, the more than 50% of the American adult population who do not participate in elections would then become motivated to do so.

Despite the mainly impoverished and detrimental picture of the voter, and political behavior that emerges from research, there is nevertheless evidence that investments in appropriate education can help all societies become stronger democracies.

The Difference the Right Kind of Education Can Make

In making the case that education moves societies toward actualized democracy, I am not proposing that the link between education and democracy is a direct causal one. Advances in education in the larger society do not necessarily cause movement toward greater democracy; we can hope for such movement, but change toward democracy may very well be long term. This is particularly the case when a society is in the grip of a brutal dictatorship. For example, educational and scientific advancement in the Soviet Union was highly impressive (Graham, 1993), but this did not translate to greater democracy within the Soviet system. Eventually, the USSR (Union of Soviet Socialist Republics) collapsed, but the outcome was Vladimir Putin's regime—not an open society. Thus, it would be invalid to claim that advances in education and science freed Russia from the grip of dictatorship.

Similarly, the educational advances in China, particularly in higher education (B. Wu & Zheng, 2008), have not resulted in a more democratic political system, despite the 2014 prodemocracy demonstrations in Hong Kong. Total enrollment in higher education in China was 3.5 times higher in 2006 than in 1997, with a gross enrollment rate reaching 22% (2006). Higher education is now something for the masses and not just for the elite in China. Despite these enormous changes, political decision making remains in the hands of a small and private elite: "The leaders of the most powerful organization in the world today, the Chinese Communist Party, are almost as mysterious to most of their 1.3 billion fellow citizens as the emperors of old" (Callick, 2013, p. 171). Interestingly, members of this privately selected ruling clique like to give the impression of being democratically elected, which they obviously are not:

> During a tour of Japan in 2008, Hu Jintao visited a school and was asked by eight-year-old Songtan Haoji, "Grandpa Hu, why do you want to be president?" After the laughter subsided, Hu replied, "I want to tell you,

I myself did not want to be president. It was the people in the whole country who voted me in and wanted me to be the president. I should not let the people throughout the whole country down." (Callick, 2013, pp. 171–172)

Obviously, the claim that "Grandpa Hu" was elected by "the people in the whole country" is utterly false; but it is fascinating that Grandpa Hu feels he needs to make such a claim at all.

Iran is another country where it has become clear that more education is not necessarily translating to greater democracy, at least in the short and medium term. The expansion of education in Iran began in the 1960s. The growth of women in higher education occurred at the same time as a dramatic drop in fertility rate from 7.0% in the early 1980s to 1.9% in 2006 (Lutz, Cuaresma, & Abbasi-Shavazi, 2010). Changes in the educational achievements of women in Iran have been extraordinary. At the lower level, literacy among 20- to 24-year-old rural women went from 10% in 1976 to 91% in 2006. At the higher level, the percentage of students who were female and admitted to government-run universities shot up to 65% by 2007. However, educational advances for women have not, as yet, resulted in increased political power or equal rights for women in Iran, nor has there been a serious move toward democracy in Iran. Lutz et al. (2010) predicted that such a shift toward democracy will come about in Iran, but they may well be underestimating the influence of two key factors in the continuation of dictatorial regimes.

A first factor is the willingness of the regime to use extreme violence to crush opposition and all forms of dissent (Moghaddam, 2013). Dictatorships rely on strict ideological conformity to keep the ruling elite cohesive and, through absolute obedience and tight discipline, the elite uses the state's security apparatus to brutalize and keep the masses under control. The masses do not necessarily have to accept and adopt the ideology propagated by the state; it is the elite who must absorb and apply this ideology to maintain strict cohesion in the face of possible mass uprising. From this realist perspective, the optimistic view of Lutz et al. (2010) that educational gains in Iran will result in democracy seems questionable, at least in the short and medium term.

A second factor in the relationship between education and democracy is the kind of education being expanded. The proposition that expansions in education will undermine and end dictatorship assumes that education is a standard commodity that brings about standard experiences and changes, and that more is necessarily better irrespective of the type of education. However, education that nurtures critical thinking, tolerance for ambiguity and complexity, and the information and skills to become politically engaged is very different from the education available in dictatorships, such as Iran and Russia. Evidence has suggested that democracy is improved through educational projects that better inform citizens about political processes, as well as about specific issues, such as corruption among politicians. For example, a program that educated citizens about corruption among local politicians in Brazil resulted in a lower probability of corrupt politicians' being reelected (Ferraz & Finan, 2008). In reviewing evidence from field experiments in African elections, Vicente and Wantchekon (2009) found that information campaigns do limit *clientelism*, "transactions between politicians and citizens whereby material favors are offered in return for political support at the polls" (Wantchekon, 2003, p. 400).

Countries such as the United States also have yet to fully achieve a democracy-nurturing education (Shaker & Hellman, 2008). Even at the elite level there are enormous gaps in American education, which results in narrowly trained elite experts who are capable of being productive along increasingly specialized professional and research lines (Moghaddam, 1997). American education for the masses results in a population that lacks basic knowledge and skills necessary for becoming critically engaged citizens. In books such as *Excellent Sheep* (Deresiewicz, 2014), critics have attacked the U.S. education system for the conformity it instills in students. But the main critical focus should be on the university administrations and faculty because they hold power over the students and are the source of the conformity and obedience that characterizes American universities. Reform in this education system is a prerequisite for America to progress toward actualized democracy.

The evidence also has suggested that there are benefits, such as reduced clientelism, to supporting women's greater involvement in political processes (Vicente & Wantchekon, 2009). One strategy for increasing the participation of women is to introduce temporary electoral quotas for women, so that they are better represented at local, state, and national leadership levels. Field experiments in India have shown that even after electoral quotas have been withdrawn, the benefit of their initial implementation continues: The probability of a woman winning an election remains 5 times higher than if a quota had not once been temporarily introduced (Bhavnani, 2009).

Psychology and Educating for Democracy

> Conceptions of democracy and citizenship have been and will likely always be debated. . . . The work of John Dewey, for example, which probably has done the most to shape dialogues on education and democracy, has not led to resolution. Rather, scholars and practitioners interpret his ideas in multiple ways, so no single conception emerges. In large part, discussion and debate regarding these different perspectives continue because the stakes are so high. Conceptions of "good citizenship" imply conceptions of the good society. (Westheimer & Kahne, 2004, p. 238)

Educating for "good citizenship" is politically controversial and sensitive because it is at the heart of the kind of a society those of us interested in actualized democracy should be trying to develop. A false dichotomy has been set up, pitting education for jobs against education for critical thinking and citizenship. Particularly during difficult economic times, this false dichotomy has led to a focus on how curricula need to be designed to help students find jobs. Should there be so many humanities students when there are fewer openings for graduates with humanities concentrations? This sort of question has dominated debates about education together with discussions about the need to use new technologies and introduce MOOCS (massive open online courses) and other such innovations to try to make education less costly. There has been far less debate directly on the role of education in the political system and specifically on the question of how education can socialize citizens for a fuller, more developed democracy.

It could be argued that people are motivated to arrive at a particular worldview, and providing them with more information through education will not change their perceptions. The image of the voter that has arisen from motivated cognition research (e.g., Taber & Lodge, 2006) suggests that political behavior is driven by "hot" emotions, and no amount of information will lead a voter to abandon his or her original political biases. From this perspective, education has limited influence because voters are motivated to interpret all information through their biased political lenses. But strong evidence (see Redlawsk, Civettini, & Emmerson, 2010) suggests that the accumulation of information does make a difference, and individuals do abandon their original political positions when they receive more and more information showing their original positions are incorrect. Consequently, except for those individuals who hold extreme positions, additional information results in a tipping point, after which individuals change their minds. This is a hopeful sign about the larger potential effect of education. Thus, the education of the young to develop critical thinking skills in the wider social and political arena is of the highest importance for the future of actualized democracy.

CONCLUSION

The vote has, on paper, become a right that all adults have in many societies. In practice, however, as far as the interests of the masses of people in many societies are concerned, this right has little influence on political outcomes. For example, in the United States—for a whole host of factors even in the most important national elections—about half of the population, mostly members of the poorer half, does not vote. Factors that limit voting include roadblocks to voting set up by certain entrenched elites who do not want the masses to participate in politics, and apathy and cynicism among the poor and minority populations. Many of the citizens who do vote have little information about candidates' policies and, most important, the likely actual effect of these policies on their own collective and personal interests. Psychological research has highlighted the poverty of knowledge among voters and nonvoters, and the role of implicit processes in political decision making.

A number of possible solutions are available to improve this situation and move societies toward actualized democracy. First, voting must be treated as a duty rather than a right so that citizens are obligated by law to vote in elections (as already happens in a number of countries, such as Australia). We must abandon the false dichotomy between education for jobs and education for critical thinking and citizenship. Engaged and informed citizens are better employees. The education system needs to be redesigned to adopt as its primary goal the training of engaged, knowledgeable democratic citizens with the characteristics discussed in Chapter 2, including the ability to take the following positions: I could be wrong; I must critically question everything, including the sacred beliefs of my society; I must revise my opinions as the evidence requires; I must seek to better understand those who are different from me; I can learn from those who are different from me; I must seek information and opinions from different sources; I should be actively open to new experiences; I should be open to creating new experiences for others; there are principles of right and wrong; and I should actively seek out experiences of higher value (see Figure 2.1). The current state of affairs, that is, citizens failing to act as informed and engaged voters, reflects the poverty of the education and political systems as far as the needs of democracy are concerned.

11

MERITOCRACY

Actualized democracy is meritocratic in the sense that individuals are selected for positions on the basis of their personal merit. This means that, for example, politicians gain political office because, as individuals—irrespective of their wealth, investments, group affiliations, connections, and other such factors—they are the best people for the job. By applying the criteria appropriate for selecting political leaders, the voters in an actualized democracy accurately recognize the best political candidates as such. These criteria are not necessarily the same as the best criteria for selecting leaders in industry, education, health, or any other sector, although they might overlap to some degree.

Meritocracy goes hand in hand with actualized democracy, but meritocracy and democracy seem contradictory when one critically assesses practices in democratic societies today, such as the United States and the United Kingdom. For example, in contemporary democracies, a premium has been placed on

http://dx.doi.org/10.1037/14806-012
The Psychology of Democracy, by F. M. Moghaddam

popular choice. It might be argued that popular choice does not result in victory for the most meritorious candidates. However, this shortcoming reflects the current state of affairs and highlights the difference between where we are today and the distance we have to travel to reach actualized democracy. The ideal of actualized democracy involves an informed, fully engaged electorate that chooses political leaders based on personal merit. In an actualized democracy, popular choice results in the most meritorious political candidates' winning elections. This is an ideal worth striving for.

Empirical evidence has supported a distinction between *descriptive meritocracy* (a meritocracy in which the present sociopolitical system actually *is* meritocratic) and *prescriptive meritocracy* (the ideal of meritocracy, which dictates that outcomes in society *should be*, but currently are not, distributed on the basis of merit; Son Hing, Bobocel, Zanna, Garcia, Gee, & Orazietti, 2011). Son Hing et al. (2011) argued that although belief in descriptive meritocracy serves to justify group-based inequalities, belief in prescriptive meritocracy presents a goal that society should strive toward with the recognition that rewards currently are not on the basis of merit. In essence, belief in descriptive meritocracy endorses a false view of society being a meritocracy, but belief in prescriptive meritocracy does not.

PSYCHOLOGY UNDERLYING THE CURRENT SITUATION

> What a change there has been! The distribution of rewards has become far more unequal and yet with less strife than before. How has such a happy state arisen? (Young, 1958/1994, p. 142)

Michael Young, the originator of the term *meritocracy* (see Chapter 6, this volume) raised this interesting question that is applicable to Western societies: How is it that group-based inequalities have increased (Dorling, 2014; Piketty, 2014), yet class-based conflicts seem to have declined? His answer was that people have been persuaded to live with greater group-based inequalities because of widespread belief that inequalities now are based on merit. In essence, the American Dream has become popularly accepted, at least in capitalist societies, on the assumption that society is open and mobility in the social hierarchy depends largely on individual characteristics. Anyone can make it if they work hard enough and have sufficient talent, so the myth goes. And if you do not make it, the hidden feeling is that you did not deserve to.

Young (1958/1994) saw meritocracy as complex, and his book intended to "present two sides of the case—the case against as well as the case for a meritocracy" (p. xvii). It is in the same spirit that I approach this topic. I argue that it important to distinguish between belief in a *false meritocracy* in which one mistakenly believes that meritocracy is being practiced when it is not, and belief in a *true meritocracy* in which one recognizes it accurately as being practiced when it is. The vast bulk of social sciences literature on meritocracy has been highly critical and controversial—with a focus on false meritocracy. In essence, this literature has tried to show that meritocracy is a myth because it does not exist and that it is false ideology propagated by the ruling elite to perpetuate their own power and resource monopolies. Thus, the bulk of the literature has highlighted the rift between descriptive meritocracy and prescriptive meritocracy. A smaller literature has implied that no rift exists between descriptive and prescriptive meritocracy: As discussed in Chapter 6, this literature has assumed that meritocracy is based mainly on IQ and does exist in contemporary America.

PSYCHOLOGICAL RESEARCH AND FALSE MERITOCRACY

How many goodly creatures are there here!
How beauteous mankind is! O brave new world
That hath such people in't! (William Shakespeare, *The Tempest*, V.ii, 204–206; see Evans, 1997)

The progressive, Left-liberal hope that the tension between equality and excellence gets solved easily through meritocratic equality of opportunity has been a myth from its inception. (LaVaque-Manty, 2009, p. 189)

Integral to the rise of capitalist industrialization in the West for more than 400 years from the 15th to the 19th centuries was the rise of a culture of individualism and eventually the development of a self-help ideology: The fate of each person in the social hierarchy of this brave new world was explained as depending on that person's individual talents and efforts. This self-help, personal-responsibility ideology that had bloomed by the 19th century provided a convenient justification for the unequal distribution of resources. Individuals earned rewards on the basis of personal merits rather than inheriting them because of their family, race, gender, and other group characteristics. The spread of equality of opportunity would ensure that those who achieved excellence would rise to the top, so the argument went.

Shakespeare's play *The Tempest* reflects the beginnings of this major transformation in Western societies from feudalism to capitalism. Themes, such as colonization by Europe and the use of science to gain power over primitive indigenous peoples, underlie *The Tempest*, which was written in the Elizabethan era when Britain was starting her march toward becoming the preeminent imperial power.

Psychological research has played at least two important roles in this concern with increasing efficiency. First, it has served as the foundation for the testing movement, including the creation of tests thought to measure intelligence and that have been used as avowed "objective" measures of abilities. In that way, psychology has been used to support the claim that a meritocracy currently is in place in the United States, United Kingdom, and rest of the Western world, and that the most talented individuals have been identified and promoted. This role of psychological science was discussed in Chapter 6. We now turn to the second, critical role of psychological research: showing that meritocracy is a myth (i.e., that today's sociopolitical system is not a meritocracy and that group-based inequalities remain large and camouflaged; Billig, 1976; Moghaddam, 1987).

MERITOCRACY AS A MYTH

We have not suggested that merit itself is irrelevant or that merit has no effect on who ends up with what. We have suggested that, despite the pervasive rhetoric of meritocracy in America, merit is in reality only one factor among many that influence who ends up with what. Nonmerit factors are also at work. These nonmerit factors not only coexist with merit, blunting its effects, but also act to suppress merit, preventing individuals from realizing their full potential based on merit alone. Chief among the nonmerit factors is inheritance. (McNamee & Miller, Jr., 2014, p. 215)

Although inheritance plays a larger role in an individual's life course than their natural ability and hard work, the public has yet to fully accept the implications of that fact. (Longoria, 2009, p. 83)

Influential books, such as McNamee and Miller's (2014) *The Meritocracy Myth*, have argued that the present sociopolitical system gives unfair advantages to elite individuals—that the present system is not meritocratic. McNamee and Miller presented a detailed case for how the effect of merit on life outcomes is blunted by the family one is born into; social, political, professional, and other connections; possession of money to buy the best education; and inheritance. This last factor is particularly complex: Surveys have demonstrated a fundamental contradiction that involves a belief that rewards should be based on hard work and talents, and a belief that people should inherit wealth and be able to use it to their children's advantage.

The generally held view that offspring should inherit their parents' wealth favors a nonmeritocratic system, as can be seen through a simple example: When Susan inherits $10 million from her parents and Joan inherits nothing because her parents were in debt when they died, Susan has not earned a $10 million head start through hard work and talent. Susan and Joan are not competing on a level playing field, and the conditions they create for their children also will be extremely uneven. Susan's children will attend the best-resourced kindergartens and private schools and will be in an excellent position to compete to enter top private universities and to graduate free of college debt. Joan's children will attend underresourced day care centers (or no day care) and schools in poor neighborhoods. If they go on to higher education, it will probably be at community colleges or state schools, where they graduate with tens of thousands of dollars of debt. In every way, Susan's inherited wealth will help her children stay ahead of Joan's children, and this will be independent of how hard Susan's children and Joan's children work and how talented they are.

Empirical research has shown that our society has group-based inequalities (i.e., that society is *not* a meritocracy). Furthermore, it has shown that when we mistakenly believe that society is a meritocracy, we also believe that group-based inequalities are justified.

FALSE MERITOCRACY AND GROUP-BASED INEQUALITIES

> High-stakes, standardized testing, once adopted within the United States . . . took on a dual role of both legitimating and masking structural race and class inequalities. (Au, 2013, p. 16)

> Existing research has shown that believing in meritocracy can make members of low-status groups more likely to accept inequality. . . . Our study adds to this research, showing that rejecting meritocracy can make people more likely to . . . identify with their ethnic group and to support efforts to change its position in society. (Wiley, Deaux, & Hagelskamp, 2012, p. 177)

If we accept that descriptive meritocracy is a myth, as McNamee and Miller (2014) and others have argued, several questions arise: Why do people believe that society is a meritocracy when the evidence has shown otherwise? What purpose does the myth serve? How is the myth sustained?

A variety of psychological theories that, in modern times, can be traced back to Karl Marx (1818–1883) can help address the question of what purpose is served by the myth. Marx (1852/1979; Marx & Engels, 1848/1967) famously argued that the capitalist class controls not only the means of economic production but also ideological production. Through its control of mass media, entertainment industry, educational institutions, religious institutions, and other means of manufacturing and influencing ideology, the capitalist class can shape the beliefs that dominate society, namely, those who serve to uphold the existing class structure and justify the inequalities that pervade the system. As a consequence, most people fail to accurately recognize ramifications of the existing inequalities in society, including their own class membership and the incompatible interests of their own class with the capitalist class.

Marx (Marx, 1852/1979; Marx & Engels, 1848/1967) termed this misperception *false consciousness* (see Chapter 4).

The idea that, to mobilize collectively a group must first perceive itself as a group with distinct interests that are different and sometimes opposed to that of other groups, became particularly influential in social psychology starting in the 1960s (Billig, 1976). In the wider society, this idea was associated with collective mobilization and the struggle for equal rights for various minorities. Consciousness raising and group consciousness became central to the collective mobilization of women, gays, ethnic minorities, green (i.e., environmental), animal rights activists, and other minority groups. A goal of consciousness raising is to help minority group members see through the dominant ideology in society. In this way, groups can escape false consciousness and take action to serve the true ingroup interests.

Empirical research on the nature of false consciousness has focused on the gap between descriptive and prescriptive meritocracy—that is, the gap between what is and what should be (e.g., Au, 2013; Ledgerwood, Mandisodza, Jost, & Pohl, 2011; Wiley et al., 2012). Belief in descriptive meritocracy results in explanations of success and failure that come back to the characteristics of individuals, rather than groups. For example, if we believe in descriptive meritocracy, then we attribute John's low score on the SAT (the university entrance examination used in North America) to low intelligence or poor work ethic. However, an alternative interpretation is that John lacked the resources to adequately prepare for the exam. He suffers distress from living in a crime-ridden neighborhood with high unemployment; he has a one-parent family that lives from paycheck to paycheck; and he cannot afford school supplies, SAT prep courses, or any other kinds of educational support. Similarly, if we believe in descriptive meritocracy, then we attribute David's high SAT score to high intelligence and strong work ethic. However, an alternative interpretation is that David's success resulted from the extensive and expensive private tutoring he received, the well-resourced school he attends, and the strong academic culture in his successful and well-connected family.

The dominant tendency in the United States and many other countries is to adopt meritocracy descriptively, and thereby endorse false meritocracy. People widely acknowledge that the system is imperfect but view instances of imperfection as aberrations, not the norm, and thus discount them. The belief in descriptive meritocracy can be so strong that people in a disadvantaged position often deny the existence of discrimination against them, even when objective evidence of discrimination exists (McCoy & Major, 2007). However, the consequences of believing in descriptive meritocracy also depend on one's group membership. Women who were the target of discrimination reported greater well-being when they believed descriptive meritocracy to be false—that is, when they believed that the system unfairly discriminated against women

(Foster & Tsarfati, 2005). To experience discrimination while believing that society is a meritocracy can raise anxiety and negatively affect self-esteem because the implication of this belief is that one deserves one's disadvantaged position (Foster, Sloto, & Ruby, 2006). From the point of view of the dominant group, belief in descriptive meritocracy justifies one's superior position, so Whites who endorse descriptive meritocracy deny that Whites, as a racial group, are in a privileged position vis-à-vis Blacks (Knowles & Lowery, 2012).

Given that descriptive meritocracy does not exist in major contemporary societies and that the belief in descriptive meritocracy justifies the advantages of elites, it is deeply puzzling as to how and why large numbers of nonelites continue to believe the system is basically meritocratic. Why should those who do not benefit continue to believe in descriptive meritocracy? Research has suggested answers to this puzzle. First, the power of the media is enormous, and evidence has suggested that television viewing, particularly reality television programs of competitions that result in winners and losers, helps strengthen belief in descriptive meritocracy (Stavrositu, 2014). Second, research has demonstrated that children as young as 3 years have learned to use merit as a basis for resource distribution (Hamann, Bender, & Tomasello, 2014). Given the increasing role of television in the lives of children around the world (see Pecora, Murray, & Wartella, 2007), belief in descriptive meritocracy undoubtedly is being socialized early through television. As discussed in Chapter 6, the education system and the IQ testing industry also have helped propagate the myth of descriptive meritocracy in the 21st century (Au, 2013).

Another line of research has suggested that members of disadvantaged groups endorse descriptive meritocracy, even though this ideology stigmatizes them as failures because they benefit in what might, on the surface, seem a paradoxical way (McCoy, Wellman, Cosley, Saslow, & Epel, 2013). Even though descriptive meritocracy suggests that disadvantaged group members have failed, it strongly implies that the path upward is still open and that people have some control over their own destinies. The feeling of having control is a psychological benefit (McCoy et al., 2013). This trend is probably most evident among first-generation immigrants when they first arrive in their adopted land. A study of visible minority first-generation women immigrants found that the longer they remained in the adopted land, the less they saw themselves as belonging to the new country (Moghaddam & Taylor, 1987). Another study showed that first-generation immigrants endorsed descriptive meritocracy more than did second-generation immigrants (Wiley et al., 2012). As an immigrant and a researcher who has studied immigrants, I have been struck by how strongly immigrants cling to the American Dream when they first arrive in the adopted land, even though most of them start at the bottom of the ladder and never rise up much higher than where they started.

THE PSYCHOLOGY OF INDIVIDUALISM AND MERITOCRACY

An assumption that is implicit in discussions about descriptive and prescriptive meritocracy is that a truly meritocratic system only can exist in a society that is, to a high degree, individualistic, meaning that people emphasize independence rather than interdependence, loose rather than strong group ties, and geographical mobility and decision making based on personal motives and interests. The traditional literature on individualism–collectivism has depicted Western societies as more individualistic and non-Western societies as less so, and has posited a picture of individualism that is increasing around the world—in some respects, with globalization (Hamamura, 2012). Associated with this picture is the idea that communal ties and social capital are declining as people invest less in collective activities and do more things by themselves (Putnam, 2001).

At the same time that individualism has been depicted as a hallmark of advanced Western societies, a belief has taken root that individuals exert more effort when they work by themselves than when they work as part of a group. Economists have referred to the phenomenon of *free riding*; psychologists call it *social loafing* (Comer, 1995). Social loafing has been demonstrated on a variety of physical, cognitive, and judgment tasks (see Karau & Williams, 1993, for a review). An examination of the role of culture in social loafing has suggested that, in so-called collectivistic cultures, such as China, social loafing that was tested under standard experimental procedures was lower and was not found under the same conditions as it occurs in the United States and other individualistic cultures (Earley, 1989).

The standard discussions concerning individualism–collectivism and social loafing are, in important respects misguided, however. With respect to individualism–collectivism, the misguided discussions are based on measures that get at narrative conventions in each culture and then assume those conventions depict objective reality (Harré & Moghaddam, 2012). In other words, the research has assumed that how Americans, Chinese, and other nationalities talk about themselves, complete surveys, and report their own behavior provides an accurate measure of individualism–collectivism rather than reflects certain conventions of communications in each culture. Just because surveys follow the conventional American narrative—that is, Americans are "rugged individualists" and "nonconformists"—does not mean that this is the objective reality of American social life. This is rather like the contrast between rhetoric about the American Dream and high social mobility in America, and the actual fact of relatively low social mobility in America.

Thus, in assessing the relationship between meritocracy (descriptive and prescriptive) and individualism, we must avoid accepting the simplistic assumptions that underlie the traditional research on individualism–collectivism and endorse flimsy national stereotypes. Similarly, we must critically scrutinize the belief that individuals generally exert less effort when they are working as part of a group compared with when they work by themselves. Surely, we have all been part of, or at least witnessed, group performances in which all group members put in a superior performance because they were motivated to do their very best as a member of the group. For example, consider a rowing team with members who push as hard as they possibly can in the race: That team is an example of *social laboring*, in which individual team members try their utmost, even though only the collective effort is recognized.

SOCIAL LABORING IN CONTRAST TO SOCIAL LOAFING

The term *social laboring* has been used to describe the increased effort that arises from a motivation to improve collective outcome (Haslam, 2004). That is, under certain conditions individuals will increase, rather than decrease, their efforts when working in a group. A number of earlier studies that have provided evidence for social laboring have suggested that it comes about when individuals are undertaking a personally engaging task (Brickner, Harkins, & Ostrom, 1986) and when they expect that other team members will not expend sufficient effort to complete a task that is personally meaningful to them as individuals (Williams & Karau, 1991).

The increased influence of social identity theory (Tajfel & Turner, 1979) has resulted in a more systematic conceptual reassessment of social loafing (Haslam, 2004; van Dick, Tissington, & Hertel, 2009). This comes as part of a broader reassessment of *Taylorism* (Moghaddam, 1987), a movement pioneered by industrial engineer Frederick Taylor (1856–1915). Taylorism was an early theory of management that attempted to improve worker efficiency (F. W. Taylor, 1911). Underlying this theory is the assumption that workers are lazy and generally will tend to work less when they are given the opportunity to hide in a group so their individual effort is not identified. Related to this is the view that personal greed is the main motivation for hard work and entrepreneurship.

Underlying debates about the relationship between democracy and the financial sector are different assumptions about what people are naturally like psychologically. In some respects, this is an ongoing debate. For example, when the Securities and Exchange Commission was first created to try to regulate the chaotic financial markets of the 1930s in the United States, a member of the fabulously rich Du Pont family retorted, "Men are by nature speculators, and Nature enforces the necessity of speculation on all of us" (quoted in Phillips-Fein, 2009, p. 3). Many psychologists have adopted this individualistic, personal-greed-is-good line of thinking in their research on economic development and have focused on individual entrepreneurship (Collins, Hanges, & Locke, 2004) rather than economic development as a collective process (Hirschman, 1984). This free-market view stands in contrast to a view that depicts human beings as communal by nature, a view that depicts group loyalty, group cohesion, and dedication to collective efforts as enormously important in motivating people to work hard. This view relates to democracy, which also depends on collective effort, community priorities, and collective wisdom.

As van Dick et al. (2009) argued, "Team success depends on the meaning the team has for its members" (p. 236). The vast majority of traditional social loafing studies have been conducted by bringing together a bunch of strangers in a study that typically lasts an hour. These strangers do not have the opportunity to form relationships or develop allegiances, loyalties, and a group culture. When group members have the opportunity to interact, make group life meaningful, and forge their group into a strong functional unit, the result typically is social laboring instead of social loafing (Haslam, 2004).

PSYCHOLOGY, MERITOCRACY, AND ACTUALIZED DEMOCRACY

I have argued that, in examining descriptive and prescriptive meritocracy, we must first abandon certain aspects of received wisdom from traditional psychological research. This received wisdom tells us that individuals are self-interested, that they will loaf when they can hide in a group and will share in group rewards without an effort, that increasing individualism is integral to economic developments, and that individual entrepreneurship is the basis of a nation's economic success. A more balanced view surely is needed: one in which collective processes are given more importance. When people are engaged in tasks that are meaningful to them, as part of groups with which they have developed affiliations, allegiances, and loyalties, they often work even harder than when they are working by themselves. The family is a good example: We may see the group as extensions of, and more important than, ourselves.

A balanced view is one in which importance is given to the desire for personal gain and for success through group achievement. People are motivated to gain wealth and success as individuals. But people also are motivated to exert effort as part of a group with which they have developed group loyalties and allegiances. The challenge is to create conditions in which there is a balance between these two tendencies.

Societal failures of the past often have arisen out of an imbalance. Consider, for example, the Soviet Union, North Korea, Cuba, China before the 1980s, and other states that have attempted to establish collectivist societies in which private property is prohibited or limited to a large degree and that publicly frown on individual motivation for personal gain. These societies have experienced economic stagnation in addition to corruption and despotism (Moghaddam, 2013). It was only from the 1980s, when the communist leadership in China changed government policies and opened up the economy to allow for personal entrepreneurial activity, that the Chinese economy advanced and achieved high growth rates. With this economic growth came larger and larger wealth differences between the staggeringly rich and poor in China, an imbalance of a different kind.

The United States and some other Western countries also suffer from serious imbalances, in which the view that personal greed is good often is allowed to shape the economic landscape and results in, or at least exacerbates, severe boom-and-bust cycles. Influencing this swing toward greed is good is the premise that individual effort and motivation requires an unregulated market. This view assumes that government regulations result in all kinds of ills, such as loafing and free riding, and in entrepreneurs' being unable to develop their talents. According to this viewpoint, a meritocracy can come about only if the government does not intervene; however, the economic crash of 2008 and the destructive boom–bust cycles of the past few decades have shown that markets that do not have appropriate regulation result in monopolies, inefficiencies, and biases that prevent rather than nurture meritocracy.

Thus, for a healthy meritocracy to come about, a balanced approach in government policy is necessary. On the one hand, individuals must enjoy a large enough degree of freedom to develop their talents and follow entrepreneurial instincts. Competition must be free and open enough, with sufficient personal incentives, so that the best ideas, projects, and people rise to the top. On the other hand, appropriate regulation must exist to ensure that there really is open competition and that inherited wealth, monopolies, and other such factors do not lead to unjust outcomes. In an actualized democracy, there is room for individual effort and profit within a community that avoids enormous imbalances of poverty and wealth. At present, the Scandinavian countries have come closer to this ideal than have the United States and the United Kingdom.

CONCLUSION

The United States and other major societies are not fully meritocratic. To create the conditions for actual meritocracy, as part of the movement toward actualized democracy, government policy must achieve a balance between two extremes. The first gives priority to personal property, individual liberty, and the free market. The second extreme gives priority to public ownership, collective rights, and the regulated market. Underlying these two extremes are different models of human behavior: Humans as motivated by personal greed and profit, and humans are motivated by the collective good. Psychological research has demonstrated that, under certain conditions, humans can behave in ways that fit both of these models: Humans can show social loafing and social laboring. We make best progress toward actualized democracy through balanced policies to gain from the advantages of both models of human behavior.

In present conditions, it can be difficult for us to see the connection between democracy and meritocracy—both descriptive and prescriptive—because current democracies, such as the United States, are seriously flawed; they are neither fully democratic nor meritocratic. An actualized democracy is meritocratic: The best individuals are elected for political leadership based on their personal characteristics and independent of the influence of wealth and group sponsors. Even in current elections in Western societies, we instinctively feel the importance of this ideal when, as voters, we sometimes say, "I am going to vote for the best candidate, irrespective of the party, race, or religion he or she belongs to." Such a sentiment is a start toward the kind of thinking achieved in actualized democracy. But it is only a start because, at present, vast amounts of money from the rich and special interest groups pour in to shape election results, and the majority of citizens remain uninformed and unengaged—largely because no candidates are representing their true interests.

12

JUSTICE

> Democracy should be defined as a set of institutions and practices whose
> intention is to implement a certain kind of equal participation of citizens
> in the political process. Justice, on the other hand, consists in a set of
> relations among persons, and between persons and goods, in a society.
> —John E. Roemer (1999, p. 57)

What is the relationship between democracy and justice? In the post–
World War II era, the influence of the Austro American economist and
political theorist Joseph Schumpeter's (1942/2010) interpretation of democracy is evident. He highlighted the ignorance and gullibility of the masses
and saw politicians as manipulating rather than representing mass interests.
Schumpeter's influence led many scholars to support a weak or minimal form
of democracy and to see the ideal or strong form of democracy—rule for
the people by the people—as unrealistic. Reflecting this trend, Shapiro and
Hacker-Cordón (1999) viewed democracy as "not fundamentally about representation; it is about selling a product" (p. 4), and Roemer (1999) represented
democracy and justice as independent of one another, so that democracy
need not result in or require justice.

This tendency to minimize democracy's scope has been enhanced by
arguments from the social-choice literature (Arrow, 1963) to the effect that

http://dx.doi.org/10.1037/14806-013
The Psychology of Democracy, by F. M. Moghaddam

there is no "correct" way of aggregating the choices of voters into sensible outcomes (see Mackie, 2003). Criticisms of democracy have a long history, going back to Plato (trans. 1987), but population size has created a new challenge for democracy. As the populations of democracies have grown much larger compared with the size of Athens, where a form of democracy was first attempted 2,500 years ago—today, India has reached a population estimated at 1.3 billion and the United States, 330 million—the distance between citizens and their representatives has increased in important respects, and trust in government institutions and politicians has declined (Americans reporting that they trust the government to do what is right just about always or most of the time declined from 73% in 1958 to 24% in 2014; see Pew Research Center, 2014b). The result has been an increased appeal for weak, minimal democracy. However, I believe that the solution is to move in the opposite direction: to support robust, justice-based democracy.

My argument in this chapter is that democracy *does* require justice, and movement toward actualized democracy requires that fairness become normative in society. In an actualized democracy, all people feel they are in a just society in the sense that they are full and equal participants in the political process; their voice matters equally, irrespective of their wealth and group membership. But the interplay between democracy and justice is not straightforward. Rorty (1997) highlighted this point by asking us to

> consider . . . the plausible hypothesis that democratic institutions and freedoms are viable only when supported by an economic affluence that is achievable regionally but impossible globally. If this hypothesis is correct, democracy and freedom in the First World will not be able to survive a thoroughgoing globalization of the labor market. So the rich democracies face a choice between perpetuating their own democratic institutions and traditions and dealing justly with the Third World. (p. 10)

Although I do not accept the zero-sum assumption underlying Rorty's hypothesis because globalization does not necessarily involve advances in the Third World at the expense of the First World, he does highlight an important challenge: how to ensure that justice and democracy remain compatible in changing economic conditions. My position is that under all conditions, justice is a prerequisite for democratic actualization.

A society that is seen to be just is more likely to have citizens who are loyal and trusting. Breakwell (2014) argued that "there is a, perhaps routinized, battle going on to harvest optimal measures of distinctiveness, continuity, self-esteem and self-efficacy in the context of the changing social and emotional circumstances surrounding the individual" (p. 34). At present, what pass as democratic societies in some ways fail to provide a rich context for this harvesting. At the root of the lack of participation and low trust in these contemporary democracies is a sense of injustice among large segments of the population, particularly minorities and poor people who feel that those like themselves are powerless. The electoral system forces the two major political parties in America to cater to the rich rather than to the party of nonvoters who, according to surveys, are economically at the bottom:

> Fully 45% of nonvoters say they have had trouble paying bills in the past year, compared with 30% of likely voters. Nonvoters are also much more likely than voters to borrow money from family or friends (41% vs. 21%) and to receive a means-tested government benefit (33% vs. 18%). (Pew Research Center, 2014a)

Democracy is not working well when most poor people remain disengaged from political processes.

In the first part of this chapter, I distinguish between varieties of justice and argue that the perception of fair procedures in decision making often is more important than the outcomes of decision making. In the second part, I discuss equality of opportunity and the idea of measuring happiness. My argument is that for citizens to be able to participate fully in democratic procedures, a minimum level of equality in resources and opportunities must be guaranteed for everyone.

PSYCHOLOGY AND VARIETIES OF JUSTICE

> The quality of mercy is not strain'd,
> It droppeth as the gentle rain from heaven
> Upon the place beneath. It is twice blest—
> It blesseth him that gives, and him that takes.
> 'Tis mightiest in the mightiest. It becomes
> The thronèd monarch better than his crown.
> His sceptre shows the force of temporal power,
> The attribute to awe and majesty,
> Wherein doth sit the dread and fear of kings;
> But mercy is above this sceptred sway,
> It is enthronèd in the hearts of kings,
> It is an attribute to God himself;
> And earthly power doth then show likest God's
> When mercy seasons justice. (William Shakespeare, *The Merchant of Venice*, IV.i.189–202; see Evans, 1997)

Shakespeare took pains to show how justice as represented by formal law, law as it is on the books, does not ensure arriving at a fair outcome. In *The Merchant of Venice*, fairness is arrived at by showing mercy rather than insisting that the law be strictly implemented. Similarly, in *Measure for Measure*, the law is shown to be a necessity, but not something that should necessarily be hammered down on the heads of the people:

> O, it is excellent
> To have a giant's strength; but it is tyrannous
> To use it like a giant. (II.ii.108–110; see Evans, 1997)

Psychologists have conceptualized varieties of justice, starting with the simple distinction between *black-letter law*, the formal law that is on the books, and *subjective justice*, what people believe to be fair. Considerable evidence has shown that what the formal legal system takes as the law differs from what people have in their heads as fairness (Finkel & Moghaddam, 2005). Beyond this, the most important distinction psychologists have made is one between distributive and procedural justice, a distinction I review next (following a tradition set in the inaugural issue of *Social Justice Research* through articles by R. L. Cohen, 1987, and Tyler, 1987).

Distributive Justice

> Every . . . description of the concept of distributive justice entails four central dimensions. There are (i) things allotted . . . to (ii) persons— or recipient units—whose relative shares can be described (iii) by some functional rule and judged (iv) by some standard. (Cohen, 1987, pp. 20–21)

Distributive justice concerns what recipients get out of (or is distributed by) a process, such as a guilty or not guilty verdict at the end of a legal trial or the pay increase employees can receive each year. Social sciences research has a long tradition of viewing distributive justice in terms of social exchanges and with the assumption that individuals want to arrive at a fair exchange (Moghaddam, 2008b). What makes relationships complex and interesting is that fairness, and what people believe they get out of a relationship, is based on subjective interpretations.

The role of subjective interpretations in distributive justice is the central focus of a number of highly influential social psychological theories, including equity theory and relative deprivation theory (Moghaddam, 2008b). *Equity theory* argues that for a relationship between two parties to be perceived as fair, the ratio of inputs (i.e., what each individual/group puts into a relationship) to outcomes (i.e., what each individual/group gets out of a relationship), but not necessarily the objectively measured levels of inputs and outcomes, must be similar for both. For example, from the outside, John and Jane seem to have an unfair husband–wife relationship because she earns more money than he does outside the home and does more of the housework in their home. However, John is a handsome, outgoing, charming man who is loved by, and extremely popular among, their children, family, and friends. His low income and lack of work at home are compensated by his social success in the family and among friends. Jane, who is extremely shy and introverted, sees John's charisma and flair as a huge input in their relationships. Besides, both Jane and John see his outcome in the form of sense of happiness satisfaction as mediocre, and her outcome in the same sense as high; he says he is "fairly happy," whereas she reports herself as "extremely happy." So, according to their subjective perceptions, John's self-reported input is 5 and his outcome is also 5, whereas Jane's self-reported input is 10 and her outcome is also 10, resulting in a ratio of 1 to 1, an equitable relationship when seen from the perspective of subjective justice.

Relative deprivation theory also heavily emphasizes subjective interpretations. Both individual and collective feelings of deprivation are assumed to arise out of social comparison processes that result in people's feeling they are worse off than others (Moghaddam, 2008b). By changing the comparison target, the outcomes of social comparison processes can be manipulated: Compared with Bill Gates, I feel extremely deprived, but compared with homeless people, I feel well off. Systematic patterns have been identified in such manipulations. For example, before revolutions, revolutionaries attempt to focus on human rights violations to get people to feel deprived and to mobilize. However, after a successful revolution, the government that has come to power attempts to focus on duties among the people and influence people to make downward comparisons to highlight how much worse the situation could be for them; the new government takes this approach to influence the people to feel relatively satisfied so they will not to seek further changes (Moghaddam, 2004).

In addition to the subjective biases that influence everyday justice judgments in the present, Thompson (2011) argued that another bias exists with respect to the future:

> Conceptions of justice do not work well when extended to future generations. . . . The basic problem is that future citizens cannot be parties to the actual or hypothetical agreement that is typically assumed to be necessary to generate the principles of justice. (p. 23)

The same point can be made with respect to the logical social contract (discussed in Chapter 6) and the assumption that, sometime in the past, our ancestors came to an agreement to give up certain rights to a central authority in exchange for the benefits of life in a more secure and stable society. It could be argued that the original social contract agreement is unfair to future generations because the "basic problem is that future citizens cannot be parties to the actual or hypothetical agreement" (Thompson, 2011, p. 23) reached by our ancestors.

The criticisms raised by Thompson (2011) bring us to a major challenge: how to calibrate and regulate change while balancing the need for continuity and tradition, on the one hand, and the need for innovation and novelty, on the other. This tension is symbolized in many societies by competition between those who support staying with original texts of sacred documents that regulate behavior (e.g., the Constitution, Bible, Koran, Torah) and those who argue for reinterpretations or even the setting aside of and replacement of traditional, sacred documents in the light of contemporary needs. Thomas Jefferson (1743–1826), the third president of the United States and the principal author of the Declaration of Independence, was for setting aside traditional documents. He argued that the U.S. Constitution should be rewritten by the next generation every 19 years because

> by the European tables of mortality, of the adults living at any one moment of time, a majority will be dead in about nineteen years. At the end of that period then, a new majority is come into place; or, in other words, a new generation. Each generation is as independent of the one preceding them, as that was of all which had gone before. (Jefferson, quoted in Achenbaum, 1993, p. 30)

This is in sharp contrast to those who argue for strict adherence to the U.S. Constitution in its original form—as ratified in 1790.

Procedural Justice

> One of the central virtues of fair social cooperation is civility. Civility is a willingness to listen to others, a commitment to resolve our disagreements via deliberation and a democratic process rather than through deception, manipulation or appeal to violence. . . . The democratic process is a transformative process, one that requires citizens, legislatures and courts to participate in authentic deliberation with others. (Farrelly, 2007, p. 206)

From a materialist perspective, a focus on what people think they get out of a justice system makes sense. Do employees think their salaries are fair? Does Mike think the guilty verdict given at the end of the legal trial is fair? Surely, the instrumental result of justice processes is all that matters? But, particularly from the 1970s, research has strongly suggested that adjudication procedures, and not only instrumental outcomes, influence perceptions of fairness (Sunshine & Tyler, 2003). For example, consider the case of a driver who is pulled over by a police officer and fined $120 for speeding. The driver is asked, "Did the police officer treat you fairly?" and he responds, "Well, he treated me with respect and he was courteous. I was driving 40 miles per hour in a 30-mile-per-hour zone, so I guess the ticket is fair." But now consider another situation in which the driver is not given a ticket by the police officer; in response to the same questions about fair treatment, he responds, "Not fair at all! He was rude and disrespectful. He didn't end up fining me, but the way he treated me was outrageous. Completely unfair!"

If a sense of justice is based in part on factors other than instrumental outcomes, such as whether an employee receives a pay raise, what are these other factors? The most important of such factors I believe is *identity needs*, such as a need for favorable evaluations by others. From this perspective, a pay increase represents not just more money but also a reflection of how much a person or group is valued and how positively their identity is viewed. This perspective is in line with the central role given to identity in social life by Henri Tajfel (1919–1982) and his associates, and by researchers who have explored identity transformations in democratic contexts (Davis & Marin, 2009; Gutmann, 2003; Schmidt, 2009). Tom Tyler (Blader & Tyler, 2009; Lind & Tyler, 1988) specifically researched the role of procedural justice in group life:

> Given their role in regulating much of the interaction within groups, procedures and evaluations of them assume massive importance in our social life. . . . When procedures are in accord with fundamental values of the group and the individual, a sense of procedural justice results. . . . To the extent that group procedures are fair, evaluation of the group and commitment and loyalty to the group will increase. (Lind & Tyler, 1988, pp. 231–232)

Perceptions of fairness in procedures influence the extent to which individuals, first, identify as group members and believe they are included and, second, participate and invest in group activities. As to why fairness is of particular concern in the democratic arena, the simple answer is in no small part that electoral procedures in politics often are unfair. Fraud has played a role in elections both in industrialized societies, such as the United States, and in developing countries, such as Mexico (Lehoucq, 2003). Since the 1980s, international standards and procedures have had greater influence, so that, for example, observers have been used to monitor some elections, to varying effect. Because of the large geographical areas involved relative to the number of observers, in countries such as Ghana, the introduction of observers can result in fraud moving to a part of the country that lacks observers (Ichino & Schündeln, 2012). However, the introduction of politically neutral observers does reduce fraud overall.

Cross-national studies have shown that electoral procedures influence voter behavior (Karp & Banducci, 2008). Important, fraud results in lower voter participation. In what are probably the most extensive studies on this topic to date, Birch (2010) reviewed trends across 31 countries, and Stockemer, LaMontagne, and Scruggs (2013) did the same across 72 countries; both showed that perceptions of higher electoral fraud led to a lower tendency to participate in elections.

I interpret confidence in the integrity of elections to be part of the social capital Putnam (1993) highlighted in his seminal study *Making Democracy Work*. His conception of social capital centered on social networks, values, norms, and obligations. Societies with stronger social capital make more progress. Putnam used a multimethods approach to study the performance of 20 regional governments in Italy. He found that the key factor that explains the wide differences in the performances of the regional governments, from terrible to very good, probably is the level of community and associative activity. The more effective regional governments are in northern Italy, where there is higher participation of citizens in various community activities, from sports associations, to guilds, musical groups, and so on. In southern Italy, community associations are weak, and the local governments, relative to those in the north, tend to be corrupt and inept.

The perception that procedures are fair is part of the social capital that makes for stronger, healthier democracies. Identification with and loyalty to the government, and society generally, is enhanced when people feel that the procedures for making decisions are fair and inclusive. Instrumental outcomes also are important, but particularly since the publication of Thibaut and Walker's (1975) book *Procedural Justice*, research has shown the central role that perceptions of procedures play in determining the perceived fairness of a justice system.

Given the importance of procedures, one is struck by the poverty of participation in political processes in the major democracies, particularly the United States (Macedo et al., 2005). Patterson (2003) pointed out that

> the period from 1960 to 2000 marks the longest ebb in turnout in U.S. history. Turnout was 63 percent of the adult population in the 1960 presidential election and stood at only 51 percent in 2000. . . . In 1960, 60 percent of the nation's television households had their sets on and tuned to the October presidential debates. In 2000, fewer than 30 percent were tuned in. (p. 13)

In *The Disappearing American Voter*, Teixeira (1992) reported a longer history of decline that began in the 19th century.

This decline has been discussed in terms of weakened social capital and a decline in civic engagement generally (Putnam, 2001). But another interpretation is that weakened participation in traditional political activities is compensated by increased participation in newly emerging ways to be politically engaged, particularly among young people who use electronic communications. This alternative interpretation reflects changing norms of citizenry—transformations in patterns of citizen activities rather than a straightforward decline. The new citizenry relies on *Internet activism*, political engagement through the electronic communications (discussed further in

Chapter 13). Great potential exists for local, regional, and national governments to use the Internet to further strengthen citizen activism.

OTHER INTERPRETATIONS OF JUSTICE

I do not address here the many varieties of justice, such as retributive and restorative justice, which focus on proportional punishment and repair after harm-doing, respectively (see Wenzel, Okimoto, Feather, & Platow, 2008). But I do discuss two interpretations of justice that are particularly important for democracy and are related to equality of opportunity and happiness. I focus on these interpretations because equality of opportunity often is discussed as a basis for justice, particularly in contemporary capitalist democracies. Happiness has become an alternative focus for some countries that have argued that the traditional criteria for progress, such as gross domestic product (GDP), are too materialistic and do not reflect justice as well as measures of happiness reflect progress.

Justice as Equality of Opportunity

Particularly since the publication of *A Theory of Justice* by John Rawls (1971), questions about justice and equality have been seen as falling within the disciplinary territory of political philosophers. But there are highly important ways in which psychological processes underlie the relationship between justice and equality and, more specifically, the opportunity for equality of opportunity—an essential component of actualized democracy.

For equality of opportunity to come about, at least two psychological conditions need to be met. First, individuals must feel that they have a realistic chance of making a difference by voting, running for office, and participating in the political process more generally. This requirement of seeing oneself as an effective participant in the democratic process is even integral to the minimalist or weak definition of democracy (see the quote by Roemer, 1999, at the beginning of this chapter). Psychologically, the vitally important issue is whether people feel they are equal participants. Second, citizens must identify with their society and perceive themselves as members with the rights and duties of membership so that they are ready to take advantage of opportunities to participate in democratic processes. Again, it is the subjective element of identification that takes precedence.

Perceptions and identifications, though, do not come about in a vacuum; they are influenced by "institutions and practices" in the larger society (Roemer, 1999, p. 57). A fascinating example can be found in research pioneered by British epidemiologist Michael Marmot (Marmot, 2004; Marmot

& Wilkinson, 2006). Our understanding of the relationship between inequality and physical and mental health took a leap forward with an analysis of Great Britain's Whitehall study, the first phase of which monitored the health of 18,000 British male civil servants over a 10-year period starting in 1967 (Marmot, Rose, Shipley, & Hamilton, 1978). The follow-up Whitehall II study included male and female participants (Marmot et al., 1991). The findings shattered common assumptions about how much people in "stressful high-status positions" suffer from cardiovascular disease relative to "those with less responsibility" in lower status positions. Against received wisdom, Marmot and his colleagues (Marmot et al., 1978, 1991) discovered a strong social health gradient: Those in higher positions enjoyed far better health.

Marmot (2004) brought to life the relationship between health and inequality by asking us to consider a famous tragedy: the *Titanic* disaster in which

> drowning rates varied with the class of passenger: highest in the third class, lower in the second class, lowest in the first. There are at least two reasons why we should care: personal and moral. The personal is that "there, but for the grace of God, go I." Most of us, although we don't travel through life in steerage, don't travel first class either. It could have been me going down with the *Titanic*. If we generalize from the *Titanic* to the health problems that plague us, the personal concern is that most of us are not in the top social group. The status syndrome therefore applies to us: we are suffering from a higher risk of worse health than those who travel through life in luxury class. (p. 244)

From the first phase of the Whitehall study, researchers moved on to explore broader issues of societal inequality and health (R. Wilkinson & Pickett, 2009). The basic point they demonstrated was that resource inequalities in societies have health consequences: the greater the inequalities, the more detrimental the health consequences, particularly for everyone who is not at the top of the status hierarchy. Just as resource inequalities have been increasing (Hacker & Pierson, 2010; Piketty, 2014), so have health inequalities (Marmot, 2004). To explain this relationship, Marmot (2006) adopted a psychosocial approach that "emphasizes subjective experience and emotions that produce acute and chronic stress which, in turn, affect biology and, hence, physical and mental illness" (p. 3).

In particular, Marmot (2004) emphasized two features of personal experience, control and participation:

> The lower in the hierarchy you are, the less likely it is that you will have full control over your life and opportunities for full social participation. Autonomy and social participation are so important for health that their lack leads to deterioration in health. (pp. 240–241)

Perceptions of control and how much one participates arise out of making social comparisons with others, recognizing disparities, and feeling deprived relative to the situation others enjoy higher up in the hierarchy. R. G. Wilkinson (2005) expanded this line of analysis by arguing that societies with greater inequalities also suffer in ways other than health, for example by people having less trust. Some critics of R. G. Wilkinson (e.g., Runciman, 2009) have argued that the evidence is not strong enough to show that resource inequalities are bad for all of society—just those who are worse off. Even if this is the case, those who are worse off are the numerical majority, and their suffering poor health is of great consequence.

Justice as Happiness

Received wisdom tells us that an important way to assess justice in society is according to traditional economic criteria: How is wealth in society distributed? How great is the difference between the richest group and the poorest group? Do the members of society receive the material rewards they deserve? Such questions are addressed through an economic lens, with reference to statistics on GDP, per capita income, income distribution, and various indicators of how purchasing power is distributed in society. But a new trend has emerged in the 21st century that involves the measurement of happiness, which also may tell us something about societal fairness. There is even an attempt to replace GDP with a happiness index.

So far, Bhutan is the only nation to have replaced GDP with a gross national happiness index as a measure of shifts in the health of a society. However, the movement to give happiness a central place in national development is growing stronger. This movement benefits from the weight of tradition: For example, in the United States, the inalienable right to the pursuit of happiness was given priority by the founding fathers. Jeremy Bentham (1748–1832) and others in the British utilitarianism movement emphasized the greatest good for the greatest number (Bentham, 1780/1874). More recently, it has been argued that happiness research contributes to public policy: "(1) It helps to identify which institutions enable individuals to best meet their preferences, and which therefore contribute most to their personal happiness; (2) It provides important informational inputs for the political process" (Frey & Stutzer, 2010, p. 569). But critics have pointed out that happiness divorced from material progress might be used to camouflage group-based inequalities. After all, countries such as Bhutan can direct attention away from extreme poverty, corruption, and the mistreatment of minorities by celebrating happiness.

Despite criticisms, research on happiness and related concepts (e.g., subjective well-being and satisfaction) has expanded considerably in the

21st century (see the *World Happiness Report*, edited by Helliwell, Layard, & Sachs, 2013). A launching pad for this kind of research was a pioneering study by Cantril (1965), which examined what people want out of life in 14 Western and non-Western countries. That study introduced the Cantril Self-Anchoring Scale, which asks study participants to imagine a ladder with steps numbered from 0 to 10. The bottom of the ladder represents the worst possible life for the participant; the top, the best possible life for the participant. Participants were asked to locate where they were on the ladder at present, where they were in the past, and where they will be in the future. The surprising finding was that large-scale national and international issues, such as political rights and major conflicts, were less likely to be reported by people as determining their location on the ladder. What mattered more were basic issues of standard of living, family life, and employment (although those issues ultimately are deeply affected by larger political and economic conditions). Moreover, in a finding that highlighted the subjective nature of happiness, Cantril (1965) found that people reported themselves to be happier than they had been in the past, but not as happy as they expected to be in the future. A series of studies also were conducted more specifically on the relationship between money and happiness—a topic that continues to generate psychological research (Oishi, Kesebir, & Diener, 2011).

Richard Easterlin (2001), probably the leading expert on happiness research, summed up the relationship between income and happiness: "As far as I am aware, in every representative national survey ever done a significant positive bivariate relationship between happiness and income has been found" (p. 468) and "to discount the happiness–income relationship is to discount the personal testimony of individuals in country after country who mention economic circumstances most frequently as a source of happiness" (p. 469). But the frequently expressed generalization that richer people report being happier, as reflected in world surveys (Deaton, 2008), has to be qualified in a number of ways.

First, self-reported happiness change over the life cycle is not just related to income. For most people, income increases with age until retirement, but there is only a slight increase in life satisfaction over the same period (Easterlin, 2006). Factors other than income, such as health, also play an important role in happiness over the life cycle.

Second, research has shown that happiness can be separated into different types, each with a different relationship to material resources. For example, Bhattacharya (2010) developed material, mental, and spiritual indexes of happiness, and found that material happiness is associated with mental happiness but not with spiritual happiness. That finding is in line with a general research trend that has shown a positive relationship between religiosity and happiness, and between happiness and income, but no association between religiosity and income (Gundlach & Opfinger, 2013). In another study that distinguished between types of happiness, Kahneman and Deaton (2010) found income to be positively associated with happiness as measured by the Cantril Self-Anchoring Scale, the traditional measure of life-evaluation used in happiness research, but not with happiness as indicated by emotional well-being, being aware of one's own emotions, experiencing balanced and appropriate emotions, and communicating well emotionally.

A third qualifier with respect to the positive association between income and happiness concerns societal context. Because feelings of happiness arise out of psychological processes that underlie social comparison and relative deprivation, societal context is highly influential in shaping personal perceptions of happiness. We have seen that rich people typically enjoy better health and poor people, in particular, suffer more in societies characterized by greater resource inequalities. Related to this trend in health and inequality, evidence has indicated that rank of income in society, not absolute income, influences happiness: Higher rank correlates with greater happiness (Boyce, Brown, & Moore, 2010). In addition, research has shown that greater income inequality leads to a fall in happiness in society (Oishi et al., 2011). However, raising the income of everyone will not result in a rise in the happiness of everyone (Easterlin, 1995), presumably because, comparatively, one's own situation will not have changed. These findings highlight the role of context and the influence of social comparison and relative deprivation processes in shaping subjective happiness.

In addition to the preceding qualifications to the generalization that money and happiness are positively related, consider that happiness has been shown to be greater in societies that enjoy more economic freedom (Gropper, Lawson, & Thorne, 2011) and stronger human rights safeguards (DiPietro, 2011). These links remind us of the role of happiness in actualized democracy: Societies that are freer and have stronger safeguards for human rights have happier citizens.

Trust and Justice

Since the last decades of the 20th century, extensive discussions have occurred about evidence that trust has been declining in the United States and other parts of the Western world (Llewellyn, Brookes, & Mahon, 2013). These discussions have extended to concerns that trust in authorities is essential for the progress of developing societies (Cheema & Popovski, 2010). A balance must exist between unquestioning trust and absolute distrust. Andrain and Smith (2006) proposed that "democracies retain their vitality by promoting a skeptical distrust toward government leaders, policies, and performance" (p. 5); but such distrust must not reach destructively high levels. As Putnam (2001) pointed out, trust is integral to the social capital that enables dense social interconnections to develop and a healthy democracy to function. Institutions and various mechanisms can be developed to enable some levels and forms of cooperation to take place without trust (Cook, Hardin, & Levi, 2005), but low trust in authorities with no sense of effective recourse is a major factor in disengagement and cynicism among large numbers of citizens in democracies, such as the United States. Back in the early 1960s, about three quarters of Americans trusted the federal government to do the right thing most of the time; by the 1990s, only about one third did, and the decline in trust continues (Llewellyn et al., 2013). Thus, trust must be of a kind and degree that enables citizens to become engaged in political processes.

In the United States, United Kingdom, and other countries, the decline in trust has coincided with rising resource inequalities. A causal relationship has been argued in studies that have shown that U.S. states with smaller income differences have a greater trust of government (Kawachi & Kennedy, 1997). Countries with lower income differences enjoy higher trust (Uslaner, 2002). In a more direct test of this hypothesized causal relationship, Gustavsson and Jordahl (2008) showed that counties in Sweden with lower differences in disposable income have more trust. One explanation for this trend is that greater resource disparities results in people with lower income feeling particularly distrustful and disengaged—an interpretation that is in line with evidence that people with higher income are more trusting (Saltkjel & Malmberg-Heimonen, 2014).

CONCLUSION

Some form and some level of justice are prerequisites for democracy to come about and are a necessary outcome of democracy. All citizens must enjoy a minimum level of material resources to be able to participate effectively in democracy. Also, resource inequalities must be limited because greater inequalities result in increased health problems, less happiness, and less trust—particularly for the bottom half of the income distribution. This point is important because improvements in the living conditions and political participation of this bottom half are essential for progress toward actualized democracy. In turn, each of these outcomes has consequences, such as a lower compliance with the law among those with less trust in government (Marien & Hooghe, 2011).

III

LOOKING FORWARD

In Parts I and II of this book, we saw that psychological science suggests certain characteristics necessary to achieve the democratic citizen, as well as certain conditions required to arrive at a democratic society. Perhaps the most valuable contribution of psychological research has been to explore the malleability of human behavior in different domains and to demonstrate how culture can influence thinking and action (Harré & Moghaddam, 2012). Our future is not fixed or predetermined, although there are certain structures that guide future development; psychological research shows how and in what domains we can influence and re-direct our individual and collective progress. In Part III, I explore future progress toward full democracy.

I set out six principles of democratic actualization, keeping in mind reasons to be optimistic but also factors that serve as limitations to future change. Macrolevel economic, political and legal changes can often come about far more rapidly than microlevel psychological changes (Moghaddam, 2002, 2008b). People become particularly aware of this (as I was) after a revolution, when economic, political, and legal changes are made rapidly (often by "revolutionary" governments), but how people think and act often fails to change as fast. Many revolutionary governments and idealists throughout

191

history have found that economic, political and legal changes can be made through a vote or a stroke of a pen, but changing actual behavior is far more difficult.

An example from the context of Western societies is race relations. In the United States and the European Union (EU), legal reforms have banned racial discrimination, but in practice many majority group members still show prejudice against ethnic minorities. One explanation for this faster speed of change at the macro-level of economic, political, and legal decision-making is that macrolevel changes are a result of Type 2 thinking, involving deliberate, explicit, and logical decision making, whereas micro-level changes are a result of Type 1 thinking, which is rapid, implicit, and emotional (Kahneman, 2011). Type 2 thinking is more open to scrutiny and easier to change through education; Type 1 thinking is more hidden and more difficult to identify, target, and influence in training programs. The different speed of change in macro versus micro processes is an important factor to consider in the long-term goal of moving toward actualized democracy. In the final chapter, I look ahead to possibilities in democratic actualization.

13

DEMOCRATIC ACTUALIZATION

It should be possible for the members of a social collective to envisage a form of life different from that which they currently live, and they must be able to conceive of a programme by which they take to be the most desirable form could be brought into being.

—Rom Harré (1993, p. 268)

Contemporary societies fall short of being fully developed democracies. Even in North America and the European Union, where societies are more open relative to dictatorships, such as China, Iran, Saudi Arabia, North Korea, and Russia, democracy is still more like a spectator sport for the masses and has little influence on governance. We can do a lot better in making real progress toward full democracy. Toward this end, I have set out the psychological changes that are essential to achieve actualized democracy, one in which all citizens enjoy full, informed, equal participation in wide aspects of political, economic, and cultural decision making independent of financial investment and resources.

We must act in the belief that humans can conceive of more desirable forms of societies that are better than their current forms, and they can organize themselves through inspired, constructive leadership to move their societies forward collectively to achieve actualized democracy. Inspiration

http://dx.doi.org/10.1037/14806-014
The Psychology of Democracy, by F. M. Moghaddam

can arise from leaders, such as Nelson Mandela, as well as from artists, poets, and writers. Buddhist leader Daisaku Ikeda (2010) pointed to such an opening as being related to "the greater self":

> I am firmly convinced that a large-scale awakening to the greater self will lead to a world of creative coexistence in the coming century. . . . The greater self of Mahayana Buddhism is another way of expressing the openness and expansiveness of character that embraces the sufferings of all people as one's own. (p. 175)

Writing of the poetry of William Wordsworth, Samuel Taylor Coleridge, George Gordon Byron (commonly known as Lord Byron), Percy Bysshe Shelley, and other leaders of the Romantic movement, D. Wu (2012) noted their faith "not in formalized religion, but in the redemptive potential of the mind" (p. xxxix) and of the possibility that through their experience of and with nature, humans can be transformed. In their different ways, the Romantics conceived of humanity's becoming one, that is, of individuals merging into a greater whole. There is little distance between the Buddhist embrace of "the suffering of all people as one's own" (Ikeda, 2010, p. 175), and Wordsworth's view of humanity as "a chain of linked thought" (from *Prometheus Unbound*) and Byron's "I live not in myself, but I become/Portion of that around me" (from *Childe Harold's Pilgrimage*). The common theme here is the perception of the self as folded into and inseparable from a larger universe—a sense of self involving a larger humanity that allows for diversity.

In this final chapter, I explore the context in which the greater self can develop by setting out the basic principles of democratic actualization. Despite many setbacks—fanaticism, terrorism, wars, plagues, the persistence of dictatorships, the majority of people relating to political processes as spectators rather than active participants, some elites who reject mass participation in politics—there are still reasons to be optimistic about the prospects for making progress toward democratic actualization.

REASONS FOR OPTIMISM

The first reason for optimism is that the idea of fundamental human rights is increasingly becoming influential around the world (Finkel & Moghaddam, 2005), and direct physical violence has been declining (Pinker, 2011). At least on paper, and increasingly in practice, major societies are agreeing that rule of law should be implemented universally, and slavery, the persecution of minorities, and other human rights violations must end. In many countries, a wide gap still exists between theoretical agreement and implementation, but agreement in principle is a good start. At the same time, I acknowledge that we have seen the continuation of *structural violence* in which social structures and institutions impede the fulfillment of human needs, and also *cultural violence*, which are aspects of cultural expression (including those of religions and ideologies) that support and legitimize structural violence (Galtung, 1969, 1990).

Second, although resource inequality has increased in the United States, the United Kingdom, and other major societies (Dorling, 2014; Hacker & Pierson, 2010; Piketty, 2014), evidence has suggested that the living conditions of the poorest humans has improved at the global level in the post–World War II period (Lakner & Milanovic, 2013). Billions of extremely poor people in China, India, Brazil, and elsewhere have seen improvements in resources. At least at the global level and for the current situation, there is some truth to the idea that the rising tide lifts all boats, although the rise is stop-and-go ("The Headwinds Return," 2014).

A third reason for optimism is the potential, and sometimes actual, use of new technologies to strengthen participatory democracy. Although governments have used new technologies to illegally spy on ordinary citizens around the world, they also have used new technologies to involve ordinary citizens much more directly in political processes and in decision making. For example, the Obama administration has used electronic communications to mobilize its supporters behind health care reform and other progressive legislation. On reviewing trends in the use of new technologies to strengthen participatory democracy, Polleta (2013) concluded that "participatory democracy has gone mainstream. It is championed by businesspeople and political strategists, municipal bureaucrats and social workers" (p. 48).

Electronic communications present enormous opportunities for expanding participatory democracy. Citizens could be kept informed about policies and practices in an ongoing manner. Correspondingly, feedback from citizens about policies and practices could be provided to politicians in an ongoing manner. Critics will contend that the masses are apathetic and disengaged from policies and procedures, even when those policies and procedures affect citizens' everyday lives in important ways. But political engagement is not fixed and naturally low. It can be changed through media campaigns. Consider the enormous engagement of people everywhere in sports. This engagement in basketball, cricket, tennis, rugby, golf, camel racing, ice hockey, and other sports is culturally shaped. The application of resources could increase mass engagement in politics.

Interestingly, aspects of sports connect to democratic ideals. An individual who joins a sports team and participates in competitions against other teams invariably finds that the same rules apply to everyone and equality of opportunity is practiced. Ideas about fairness, cooperation, equality, and certain ideals of human behavior are universal on the sports field. This common ground for all humanity, coupled with the power of global electronic communications, can help in mass education in support of democratic actualization.

Fourth, accelerating globalization and rapid societal change have been associated with new patterns of civil engagement and social capital. Received wisdom tells us that traditional neighborhoods, communities, and extended families have been seriously weakened over recent decades. It seems that traditional forms of social capital, such as community organizations, have declined in the United States (Putnam, 2001), and where America goes, the rest of the world is likely to follow. However, new forms of communities and collective life—made possible through the Internet, Facebook, Twitter, and other electronic communications systems—are emerging. Twitter communities are taking over where traditional neighborhood communities have left off. Civic engagement could be greatly enhanced through new technologies, and democracy could be strengthened rather than weakened. The 2008 U.S. presidential race reflected a dramatic change in the use of electronic communications and social networking in democratic elections (C. C. Miller, 2008). New patterns of democratic identity formation also seem to be emerging with globalization. For example, the identities of young people are being influenced not just by local family and communities but also by Internet groups and connections in geographically distant places.

Fifth, there is reason for optimism in the indefatigable human will and determination to achieve freedom and openness. When in dictatorships, I have never failed to meet people desperate and hungry for just a small taste of freedom and even the slightest opportunity to be heard—to have a voice in the politics that affect their own cramped lives. The gnawing hunger for freedom and information is raw and palpable in dictatorships, such as Iran, Russia, and China. The same human drive for more open societies is present and must make us optimistic in countries of North America and the European Union, where democracy seems sometimes to be receding.

CAUTION AND REALISM

We must calibrate our assessment and moderate our expectations by keeping in mind that the road to actualized democracy is a long one, and we should not expect to achieve dramatic progress in the short term. The first serious experiments with democracy occurred about 2,500 years ago in Greece, and progress from that time has been exceedingly slow and painful. We can be hopeful that progress toward actualized democracy will be faster in the future, but this is a hope and not a guarantee. At the start of the 21st century, the United States, the democratic superpower, has been characterized by destructive wars abroad and increasing economic inequalities and the purchase of electoral power by the rich at home. Israel, still the only relatively open society in the Middle East, is stuck in a cycle of destructive conflicts and violent territorial expansion (Bregman, 2014).

Our optimism also must be tempered because the situation in Muslim societies remains precarious. Revolutions and power transfers in Islamic countries, such as those in Iran in 1979 and in Egypt in 2013, have resulted in one dictatorship's being replaced by another, without any real progress being made. Islamic fundamentalism is on the rise, in part as a reaction against the perceived invasion of Islamic societies by Western culture, liberal values, and women's rights (Moghaddam, 2008a). Islamic fundamentalism even is spreading in Indonesia, the largest Muslim society with 255 million people and with a limited form of democracy after the 31-year dictatorship of Suharto (1921–2008). A historic transition took place in 2014, when, with 135 million ballots cast, Joko Widodo was elected as president of Indonesia. However, Indonesia is in grave danger of being overwhelmed by a repressive form of Islam. Only in Turkey and Tunisia have there been signs of real progress in the Islamic world, but this progress also is fragile and in danger of being squashed by authoritarianism.

The situations of Asia, Africa, and Latin America also give supporters of democracy cause for concern. The rising power of Asia is China, a dictatorship, and the superpower of Africa is South Africa, a country gripped by increasing corruption and ineptitude at the top. The promise of a more democratic Latin America has remained just that, a promise. Progress toward a more open Latin America has been slow, and in Venezuela, Argentina, and other countries, the danger of backward movement exists.

These grave challenges make it even more essential that we move ahead energetically and with determination to map the path toward actualized democracy.

PRINCIPLES OF DEMOCRATIC ACTUALIZATION

As I see it, six principles of democratic actualization are key to the ongoing democratization struggle:

1. There is no end, limit, or inevitability in human cultural, political, economic, and moral growth and development; just as there is no end, limit, or inevitability in human history.

   The goal of the democratic journey is to reach a dynamic state in which both the collective and the individual enjoy the necessary support and freedom to achieve their optimal potentials. Democratic actualization is a dynamic process involving continuous change and growth without an end point or predetermined path. Our future is fluid, and we can intentionally make progress toward actualized democracy.

2. Democratic actualization sets the stage for human development; it is the necessary context for the journey to begin.

Human growth and development depend highly on context. The vast majority of individuals are unable to grow and develop beyond the limits set by the societal context in which they live. When a society limits freedom in particular directions, most individuals will remain stunted in their growth and development in those particular directions. For example, when poor people are neglected and disenfranchised, most individuals born into poor families will be unable to escape poverty and will remain excluded from political decision making. This is the state of affairs in the United States and most other advanced societies in which social mobility remains stagnant, and tens of millions of citizens remain mired in poverty and excluded from mainstream political processes.

3. The potential for democratic actualization increases when wealth and resource disparities are large enough to sufficiently motivate competitive entrepreneurship but not too great as to result in a *status syndrome*—that is, when those with relatively low status suffer poor health and those with higher status enjoy better health (Marmot, 2004)—and to damage society.

A balance must be reached in creating a context that motivates individuals to show initiative and creativity, but, at the same time, does not lead to outrageously large wealth disparities that result in widespread feelings of relative deprivation and stagnation. On the one hand, the extreme of Soviet-style collective farming and the prohibition of private property must be avoided because it results in collective demise, but, on the other hand, the greed is good extremism that often has pervaded and damaged American society should also be avoided. A golden mean between these two extremes is best achieved when democratic education flourishes and there is mass participation in political processes.

In their discussion of the quality of democracy, L. Diamond and Morlino (2004) rightly highlighted the role of political equality as a prerequisite for effective citizen participation:

> A good democracy must ensure that all citizens are in fact able to make use of . . . formal rights to influence the decision

making process: to vote, to organize, to assemble, to protest, and to lobby for their interests. . . . Democratic quality is high when we in fact observe extensive citizen participation not only through voting but in the life of political parties and civil society organizations, in the discussion of public policy issues, in communicating with and demanding accountability from elected representatives, in monitoring official conduct, and in direct engagement with public issues at the local level. Participation in these respects is intimately related to political equality. Even if everyone's formal rights of participation are upheld, inequalities in political resources can make it harder for lower-status individuals to exercise their rights. (pp. 23–24)

The authors also described political equality in terms of basic education, a minimum of knowledge about politics and public affairs, and tolerance for political and social differences. These are preliminary steps toward developing comprehensive education for democracy.

4. Each individual has a special and valuable contribution to make in society. It is the duty of society to provide conditions in which each individual is able to fulfill his or her unique potential and make his or her unique contribution.

Actualized democracy is a point of departure, and not an end, for individual growth and development. From this point of departure, individuals will change to become, in some ways, more similar and, in others, more different from one another. For example, beliefs and skills related to the understanding of others who are "different from me" will lead some individuals to better understand atheists and other individuals to better understand religiously devout people. However, common to both experiences is the belief that, for the self to develop, growth in the nature of relationships with others who are different must come first. At every stage, the growth of individuals is made possible through developments in social relationships and collective processes.

Similarly, development toward democratic actualization occurs in different directions for different societies. For example, these societies will differ with respect to the distribution of wealth, with some of them having greater disparity between the rich and the rest, and some of them having less disparity. However, what societies have in common is giving the highest priority to enabling informed citizens to be engaged in political processes as a duty of citizenship.

5. A role of scientific research is to identify limitations and potentials for human development, how humans can change collectively and individually, in what ways they are less able to change, and the time frame for change.

   Scientific research is needed to better clarify the plasticity of human behavior, how people can change, and how fast they can change. It is not enough for revolutionaries to want to bring about change from dictatorship to democracy; they must base their plans, policies, and actions on a scientific understanding of the kinds of change that are possible within specific time frames. Many revolutions have failed, not because revolutionaries did not have the desire to build democracy but because they did not appreciate limitations to how people can change and how fast. Such limitations themselves are in different ways fluid and can be influenced.

6. A major goal of democratic education must be to help all humans understand and give priority to human commonalities, and to identify first and foremost with humankind, and only secondarily with national, ethnic, racial, language, sexual orientation, gender, social class, religious, and other such groups.

   So that the duty to give priority to human commonalities may be fulfilled by everyone, all citizens must experience deep and broad education in democracy, and adequate health and economic security to enable them to put into effect their education. This is far from the current state of affairs in contemporary societies, including Western democracies in which socialization and education is influenced by multiculturalism ideology to highlight and exaggerate group-based differences. In countless ways, contemporary socialization and education systems result in categorization of people on the basis of race, ethnicity, religion, nationality, language, and other such criteria. Following categorization, all kinds of group-based differences are manufactured and propagated often with the collusion of minority group leaders who benefit from this process.

Democratic education involves first and foremost recognizing and highlighting human commonalities and the universal features of all humans. Growth and development along the path of actualized democracy involves recognizing that all humans are part of a larger whole, and all people share a common path and destiny. Democratic education is profoundly psychological because, in its foundation, it involves transformations of the self and identity, and results in a belief that one is part of all humanity and the whole is more than the sum of its parts.

CONCLUSION

The context of actualized democracy enables collectives and individuals to develop toward fulfilling their potential and to progress along paths that lead to greater similarities and differences. Democratic education leads to people interacting with others on the basis of the omnicultural imperative: "First give priority to the characteristics you share with other people as members of the human group" (Moghaddam, 2012, p. 318). Differences among ethnic, national, religious, and other such groups also are recognized, but as secondary.

Growth along the path of actualized democracy started in earnest with the Greeks around 2,500 years ago, and every step of progress has been enabled and accompanied by changes in the psychological characteristics of humankind. The direct and indirect connections that exist between psychological functioning and the political system indicate that those interested in fulfilling the promises of actualized democracy must attend to the relevant research emerging from psychological science. As I have discussed in this book, psychological research has pointed to the potentialities and limitations in democratic actualization—to how we can grow and the limitations we might face in our development. Hamlet described humans in the same speech as "the beauty of the world" and as "quintessence of dust" (Shakespeare, *Hamlet*, II.ii.293–310; see Evans, 1997). Psychological science can and should help our societies move closer to creating the context to realize that beauty for all.

REFERENCES

Achenbaum, W. A. (1993). Generational relations in historical context. In V. L. Bengtson & W. A. Achenbaum (Eds.), *The changing contract across generations* (pp. 25–42). New York, NY: Aldine de Gruyter.

Adida, C. L., Laitin, D. D., & Valfort, M. A. (2010). Identifying barriers to Muslim integration in France. *PNAS: Proceedings of the National Academy of Sciences of the United States of America, 107,* 22384–22390. http://dx.doi.org/10.1073/pnas.1015550107

Adorno, T. W., Frenkel-Brunswik, E., Levinson, D. J., & Sanford, B. W. (1950). *The authoritarian personality.* New York, NY: Harper & Row.

Ajzen, I., & Fishbein, M. (2005). The influence of attitudes on behavior. In D. Albarracin, B. T. Johnson & M. P. Zanna (Eds.), *The handbook of attitudes* (pp. 173–221). Mahwah, NJ: Erlbaum.

Alderfer, C. P. (1972). *Existence, relatedness and growth: Human needs in organizational settings.* New York, NY: Free Press.

Aldrich, J. H., Montgomery, J. M., & Wood, W. (2011). Turnout as habit. *Political Behavior, 33,* 535–563. http://dx.doi.org/10.1007/s11109-010-9148-3

Alford, J. R., Funk, C. L., & Hibbing, J. R. (2005). Are political orientations genetically transmitted? *American Political Science Review, 99,* 153–167. http://dx.doi.org/10.1017/S0003055405051579

Allport, G. W. (1954). *The nature of prejudice.* Cambridge, MA: Addison-Wesley.

Allport, G. W. (1955). *Becoming: Basic considerations for a psychology of personality.* New Haven, CT: Yale University Press.

Altemeyer, B. (1988). *Enemies of freedom: Understanding right-wing authoritarianism.* San Francisco, CA: Jossey-Bass.

Anderson, M. L. (2000). *Practicing democracy: Elections and political culture in imperial Germany.* Princeton, NJ: Princeton University Press.

Andrain, C. F., & Smith, J. T. (2006). *Political democracy, trust, and social justice: A comparative overview.* Boston, MA: Northeastern University Press.

Arjomand, S. A. (1988). *The turban for the crown: The Islamic revolution in Iran.* New York, NY: Oxford University Press.

Arkes, H. R., & Tetlock, P. E. (2004). Attributions of implicit prejudice, or "would Jesse Jackson 'fail' the Implicit Association Test?" *Psychological Inquiry, 15,* 257–278. http://dx.doi.org/10.1207/s15327965pli1504_01

Aristotle. (1943). *Aristotle's Politics* (B. Jowett, Trans.). New York, NY: The Modern Library.

Arrow, K. J. (1963). *Social choice and individual values* (2nd ed.). New Haven, CT: Yale University Press.

Asch, S. E. (1948). The doctrine of suggestion, prestige and imitation in social psychology. *Psychological Review, 55,* 250–276. http://dx.doi.org/10.1037/h0057270

Au, W. (2013). Hiding behind high-stakes testing: Meritocracy, objectivity and inequality in U.S. education. *International Education Journal, 12,* 7–19.

Aurelius, M. (1964). *Meditations* (M. Staniforth, Trans.). Harmondsworth, England: Penguin Books. (Original work published 180)

Aydin, A. (2013). Judicial independence across democratic regimes: Understanding the varying impact of political competition. *Law & Society Review, 47,* 105–134. http://dx.doi.org/10.1111/lasr.12003

Baehr, J. (2011). The structure of open-mindedness. *Canadian Journal of Philosophy, 41,* 191–213. http://dx.doi.org/10.1353/cjp.2011.0010

Baker, C. E. (2007). *Media concentration and democracy: Why ownership matters.* New York, NY: Cambridge University Press.

Balfour, S., & Quiroga, A. (2007). *The reinvention of Spain: Nation and identity since democracy.* Oxford, England: Oxford University Press. http://dx.doi.org/10.1093/acprof:oso/9780199206674.001.0001

Bardhan, P. (1997). Corruption and development: A review of issues. *Journal of Economic Literature, 35,* 1320–1346.

Baron, S. G., Gobbini, M. I., Engell, A. D., & Todorov, A. (2011). Amygdala and dorsomedial prefrontal cortex responses to appearance-based and behavior-based person impressions. *Social Cognitive and Affective Neuroscience, 6,* 572–581. http://dx.doi.org/10.1093/scan/nsq086

Barrett, A. N., Barile, J. P., Malm, E. K., & Weaver, S. R. (2012). English proficiency and peer interethnic relations as predictors of math achievement among Latino and Asian immigrant students. *Journal of Adolescence, 35,* 1619–1628.

Barth, J. R., Caprio, G., & Levine, R. (2012). *Guardians of finance.* Cambridge, MA: MIT Press.

Baumeister, R. F., Bratslavsky, E., Muraven, M., & Tice, D. M. (1998). Ego depletion: Is the active self a limited resource? *Journal of Personality and Social Psychology, 74,* 1252–1265. http://dx.doi.org/10.1037/0022-3514.74.5.1252

Bedford, O., & Kwang-Kuo, H. (2006). *Taiwanese identity and democracy: The social psychology of Taiwan's 2004 elections.* New York, NY: Palgrave Macmillan. http://dx.doi.org/10.1057/9781403983558

Beetham, D. (2009). The contradictions of democratization by force: The case of Iraq. *Democratization, 16,* 443–454. http://dx.doi.org/10.1080/13510340902914338

Bell, D. (1960). *The end of ideology: On the exhaustion of political ideas in the fifties.* Glencoe, IL: Free Press.

Bentham, J. (1874). *An introduction to the principles of morals and legislation.* Oxford, England: Clarendon Press. (Original work published in 1780)

Berns, G. S., Chappelow, J., Zink, C. F., Pagnoni, G., Martin-Skurski, M. E., & Richards, J. (2005). Neurobiological correlates of social conformity and independence during mental rotation. *Biological Psychiatry, 58*, 245–253. http://dx.doi.org/10.1016/j.biopsych.2005.04.012

Berry, J. W. (1998). Social and psychological costs and benefits of multiculturalism: A view from Canada. *Trames: A Journal of Humanities and Social Sciences, 3*, 209–233.

Berscheid, E., & Reis, H. T. (1998). Attraction and close relationships. In S. T. Fiske, D. T. Gilbert, & G. Lindzey (Eds.), *The handbook of social psychology* (4th ed., Vol. 2, pp. 193–281). New York, NY: Oxford University Press.

Besharov, D. J., Lopez, M. H., & Siegel, M. (2013). International conference news: Trends in migration and migration policy. *Journal of Policy Analysis and Management, 32*, 655–660. http://dx.doi.org/10.1002/pam.21700

Bhattacharya, S. (2010). Relationship between three indices of happiness: Material, mental and spiritual. *Journal of Human Values, 16*, 87–125. http://dx.doi.org/10.1177/097168581001600108

Bhavnani, R. R. (2009). Do electoral quotas work after they are withdrawn? Evidence from a natural experiment in India. *American Political Science Review, 103*, 23–35. http://dx.doi.org/10.1017/S0003055409090029

Billig, M. G. (1976). *Social psychology and intergroup relations*. London, England: Academic Press.

Binder, J., Zagefka, H., Brown, R., Funke, F., Kessler, T., Mummendey, A., et al. (2009). Does contact reduce prejudice or does prejudice reduce contact? A longitudinal test of the contact hypothesis among majority and minority groups in three European countries. *Journal of Personality and Social Psychology, 96*, 843–856. http://dx.doi.org/10.1037/a0013470

Birch, S. (2010). Perceptions of electoral fairness and voter turnout. *Comparative Political Studies, 43*, 1601–1622. http://dx.doi.org/10.1177/0010414010374021

Blader, S., & Tyler, T. (2003). What constitutes fairness in work settings? A four-component model of procedural justice. *Personality and Social Psychology Bulletin, 29*, 747–758. http://dx.doi.org/10.1177/0146167203029006007

Blader, S. L., & Tyler, T. R. (2009). A four-component model of procedural justice: Defining the meaning of a "fair" process. *Journal of Applied Psychology, 94*, 445–464. http://dx.doi.org/10.1037/a0013935

Blais, A. (2006). What affects voter turnout? *Annual Review of Political Science, 9*, 111–125. http://dx.doi.org/10.1146/annurev.polisci.9.070204.105121

Block, J., & Block, J. H. (2006). Nursery school personality and political orientation two decades later. *Journal of Research in Personality, 40*, 734–749. http://dx.doi.org/10.1016/j.jrp.2005.09.005

Bodie, G. D. (2011). The Active-Empathic Listening Scale (AILS): Conceptualization and evidence of validity within the interpersonal domain. *Communication Quarterly, 59*, 277–295. http://dx.doi.org/10.1080/01463373.2011.583495

Borgida, E., Federico, C. M., & Sullivan, J. L. (Eds.). (2009). *The political psychology of democratic citizenship*. New York, NY: Oxford University Press. http://dx.doi. org/10.1093/acprof:oso/9780195335453.001.0001

Boseovski, J. J. (2010). Evidence for "rose-colored glasses": An examination of the positivity bias in young children's personality judgments. *Child Development Perspectives, 4*, 212–218. http://dx.doi.org/10.1111/j.1750-8606.2010.00149.x

Bowlby, J. (1946). Psychology and democracy. *Political Quarterly, 17*, 61–75. http:// dx.doi.org/10.1111/j.1467-923X.1946.tb01028.x

Bowles, N., Hamilton, J. T., & Levy, D. A. L. (Eds.). (2014). *Transparency in politics and the media: Accountability and open government*. London, England: I. B. Tauris.

Bowles, S., & Gintis, H. (2011). *Schooling in capitalist America: Educational reform and the contradictions of economic life*. Chicago, IL: Haymarket Books. (Original work published 1977)

Boyce, C. J., Brown, G. D. A., & Moore, S. C. (2010). Money and happiness: Rank of income, not income, affects life satisfaction. *Psychological Science, 21*, 471–475. http://dx.doi.org/10.1177/0956797610362671

Brader, T. (2005). Striking a responsive chord: How political ads motivate and persuade voters by appealing to emotions. *American Journal of Political Science, 49*, 388–405. http://dx.doi.org/10.1111/j.0092-5853.2005.00130.x

Breakwell, G. M. (2014). Identity process theory: Clarifications and elaborations. In R. Jaspal & G. M. Breakwell (Eds.), *Identity process theory: Identity, social action, and social change* (pp. 20–38). Cambridge, England: Cambridge University Press. http://dx.doi.org/10.1017/CBO9781139136983.004

Bregman, A. (2014). *Cursed victory: A history of Israel and the occupied territories*. London, England: Allen Lane.

Brickner, M. A., Harkins, S. G., & Ostrom, T. M. (1986). Effects of personal involvement: Thought-provoking implications for social loafing. *Journal of Personality and Social Psychology, 51*, 763–769. http://dx.doi.org/10.1037/0022-3514.51.4.763

Briefing: Europe's populist insurgents. (2014, January 14). *The Economist*, pp. 16–18.

Brion, S., & Anderson, C. (2013). The loss of power: How illusions of alliance contribute to powerholders' downfall. *Organizational Behavior and Human Decision Processes, 121*, 129–139. http://dx.doi.org/10.1016/j.obhdp.2013.01.005

Brodkin, K. (2007). *Making democracy matter: Identity and activism in Los Angeles*. New Brunswick, NJ: Rutgers University Press.

Broeders, R., van den Bos, K., Müller, P. A., & Ham, J. (2011). Should I save or should I not kill? How people solve moral dilemmas depends on which rule is most accessible. *Journal of Experimental Social Psychology, 47*, 923–934. http://dx.doi. org/10.1016/j.jesp.2011.03.018

Burger, J. M. (2009). Replicating Milgram: Would people still obey today? *American Psychologist, 64*, 1–11. http://dx.doi.org/10.1037/a0010932

Burgess, G. (1992). The divine right of kings reconsidered. *English Historical Review, 107,* 837–861.

Buruma, I. (2007). *Murder in Amsterdam: The death of Theo van Gogh and the limits of tolerance.* London, England: Atlantic Books.

Byrne, D. E. (1971). *The attraction paradigm.* New York, NY: Academic Press.

Calhoun, C. (Ed.). (1994). *Social theory and the politics of identity.* Oxford, England: Basil Blackwell.

Callick, R. (2013). *The party forever: Inside China's modern communist elite.* New York, NY: Palgrave Macmillan.

Canadian Multiculturalism Act, R.S.C., 1985, c. 24 (4th Supp.).

Cantril, H. (1965). *The pattern of human concerns.* New Brunswick, NJ: Rutgers University Press.

Caplan, B. (2007). *The myth of the rational voter: Why democracies choose bad policies.* Princeton, NJ: Princeton University Press.

Caprara, G. V. (2007). The personalization of modern politics. *European Review, 15,* 151–164. http://dx.doi.org/10.1017/S1062798707000178

Carty, A. (1992a). Introduction. In A. Carty. (Ed.), *Law and development* (pp. xi–xxiii). New York: New York University Press.

Carty, A. (Ed.). (1992b). *Law and development.* New York: New York University Press.

Castles, S. (2011). Globalization, ethnic identity and the integration crisis. *Ethnicities, 11,* 23–26. http://dx.doi.org/10.1177/14687968110110010204

Chan, J. (2007). Democracy and meritocracy: Toward a Confucian perspective. *Journal of Chinese Philosophy, 34,* 179–193. http://dx.doi.org/10.1111/j.1540-6253.2007.00408.x

Cheema, G. S., & Popovski, V. (Eds.). (2010). *Building trust in government: Innovations in governance reform in Asia.* New York, NY: United Nations University Press.

Chloros, A. G. (1992). Common law, civil law and socialist law: Three leading systems in the world, three kinds of legal thought. In C. Varga (Ed.), *Comparative legal cultures* (pp. 83–98). New York: New York University Press. (Original work published 1978)

Chong, D. (2013). Degrees of rationality in politics. In L. Huddy, D. O. Sears, & J. S. Levy (Eds.), *The Oxford handbook of political psychology* (pp. 96–129). New York, NY: Oxford University Press.

Christens, B. D. (2012). Toward relational empowerment. *American Journal of Community Psychology, 50,* 114–128. http://dx.doi.org/10.1007/s10464-011-9483-5

Cicero, M. T. (2008). *Cicero: Selected letters: A new translation by P. G. Walsh* (P. G. Walsh, Trans.). Oxford, England: Oxford University Press.

Citizens United v. Federal Election Commission, 558 U.S. 310 (2010).

Clark, T. S. (2011). *The limits of judicial independence.* New York, NY: Cambridge University Press.

Clark, G. (2014). *The son also rises: Surnames and the history of social mobility.* Princeton, NJ: Princeton University Press.

Cohen, G. L. (2003). Party over policy: The dominating impact of group influence on political beliefs. *Journal of Personality and Social Psychology, 85,* 808–822. http://dx.doi.org/10.1037/0022-3514.85.5.808

Cohen, J. (1997). Deliberation and democratic legitimacy. In R. E. Goodin & P. Pettit (Eds.), *Contemporary political philosophy* (pp. 143–155). Oxford, England: Basil Blackwell. (Original work published 1989)

Cohen, R. L. (1987). Distributive justice: Theory and research. *Social Justice Research, 1,* 19–40. http://dx.doi.org/10.1007/BF01049382

Cohn, S. K. (2013). *Popular protest in late medieval English towns.* Cambridge, England: Cambridge University Press.

Coleman, S. (2005). Blogs and the new politics of listening. *Political Quarterly, 76,* 272–280. http://dx.doi.org/10.1111/j.1467-923X.2005.00679.x

Collins, C. J., Hanges, P. J., & Locke, E. A. (2004). The relationship of achievement motivation to entrepreneurial behavior: A meta-analysis. *Human Performance, 17,* 95–117. http://dx.doi.org/10.1207/S15327043HUP1701_5

Comer, D. R. (1995). A model of social loafing in real work groups. *Human Relations, 48,* 647–667. http://dx.doi.org/10.1177/001872679504800603

Conacher, J. B. (Ed.). (1971). *The emergence of British parliamentary democracy in the nineteenth century: The passing of the Reform Acts of 1832, 1867, and 1884–1885.* New York, NY: Wiley.

Conger, J. A. (1989). *The charismatic leader: Behind the mystique of exceptional leadership.* San Francisco, CA: Jossey-Bass.

Conrad, J. (1958). Heart of darkness. In J. Conrad, *Three great tales* (pp. 217–307). New York, NY: Random House. (Original work published 1899)

Conradt, L., & Roper, T. J. (2007). Democracy in animals: The evolution of shared group decisions. *Proceedings of the Royal Society: Biological Sciences, 274,* 2317–2326. http://dx.doi.org/10.1098/rspb.2007.0186

Cook, K. S., Hardin, R., & Levi, M. (2005). *Cooperation without trust?* New York, NY: Russell Sage Foundation.

Cooter, R. (2000). Do good laws make good citizens? An economic analysis of internalized norms. *Virginia Law Review, 86,* 1577–1601. http://dx.doi.org/10.2307/1073825

Cornelis, L., Van Hiel, A., & De Cremer, D. (2012). The effect of followers' belongingness needs on leaders' procedural fairness enactment: Mediation Through Interpersonal and Team Attraction. *Journal of Personnel Psychology, 11,* 31–39. http://dx.doi.org/10.1027/1866-5888/a000053

Crick, B. (1962). *In defense of politics.* London, England: Weidenfeld and Nicholson.

Dahl, R. A. (1971). *Who governs? Democracy and power in an American city.* New Haven, CT: Yale University Press.

Dahl, R. A. (1989). *Democracy and its critics*. New Haven, CT: Yale University Press.

Danziger, S., Levav, J., & Avnaim-Pessoa, L. (2011). Extraneous factors in judicial decisions. *PNAS: Proceedings of the National Academy of Sciences of the United States of America, 108*, 6889–6892. http://dx.doi.org/10.1073/pnas.1018033108

Dardanelli, P., & Stojanovic, N. (2011). The acid test? Competing theses on the nationality-democracy nexus and the case of Switzerland. *Nations and Nationalism, 17*, 357–376. http://dx.doi.org/10.1111/j.1469-8129.2010.00453.x

Davis, J. B., & Marin, S. R. (2009). Identity and democracy: Linking individual and social reasoning. *Development, 52*, 500–508. http://dx.doi.org/10.1057/dev.2009.77

Davis-Kean, P. E. (2005). The influence of parent education and family income on child achievement: The indirect role of parental expectations and the home environment. *Journal of Family Psychology, 19*, 294–304. http://dx.doi.org/10.1037/0893-3200.19.2.294

Deaton, A. (2008). Income, health, and well-being around the world: Evidence from the Gallup World Poll. *Journal of Economic Perspectives, 22*, 53–72. http://dx.doi.org/10.1257/jep.22.2.53

De Cremer, D., & Tyler, T. R. (2005). Managing group behavior: The interplay between procedural fairness, sense of self, and cooperation. In M. Zanna (Ed.), *Advances in experimental social psychology* (Vol. 37, pp. 151–218). New York, NY: Academic Press.

Delli Caprini, M. X., & Keeter, S. (1996). *What Americans know about politics and why it matters*. New Haven, CT: Yale University Press.

DelReal, J. A. (2014, November 10). Voter turnout in 2014 was the lowest since WWII. *The Washington Post*. Retrieved from http://www.washingtonpost.com/blogs/post-politics/wp/2014/11/10/voter-turnout-in-2014-was-the-lowest-since-wwii/

Dench, G. (Ed.). (2006). *The rise and rise of the meritocracy*. Oxford, England: Basil Blackwell.

Deresiewicz, W. (2014). *Excellent sheep: The miseducation of the American elite and the way to a meaningful life*. New York, NY: Free Press.

Derry, J. W. (1992). *Charles, Earl Grey: Aristocratic reformer*. Oxford, England: Basil Blackwell.

Dershowitz, A. (2004). *Rights from wrongs: A secular theory of the origin of rights*. New York, NY: Basic Books.

Devlin, B., Fienberg, S. E., Resnick, D. P., & Roeder, K. (Eds.). (1997). *Intelligence, genes, and success: Scientists respond to* The Bell Curve. New York, NY: Springer. http://dx.doi.org/10.1007/978-1-4612-0669-9

Dhont, K., Van Hiel, A., & Hewstone, M. (2014). Changing the ideological roots of prejudice: Longitudinal effects of ethnic intergroup contact on social dominance orientation. *Group Processes & Intergroup Relations, 17*, 27–44. http://dx.doi.org/10.1177/1368430213497064

Diamond, J. M. (2005). *Guns, germs, and steel: The fates of human societies*. New York, NY: Norton.

Diamond, L. (2010). Why are there no Arab democracies? *Journal of Democracy, 21*, 93–112. http://dx.doi.org/10.1353/jod.0.0150

Diamond, L., & Plattner, M. F. (Eds.). (2001). *The global divergence of democracy*. Baltimore, MD: Johns Hopkins University Press.

Diamond, L. J., & Morlino, L. (2004). The quality of democracy: An overview. *Journal of Democracy, 15*, 20–31. http://dx.doi.org/10.1353/jod.2004.0060

DiPietro, W. R. (2011). Happiness and human rights. *Journal of Global Business Issues, 5*, 67–71.

Dodd, M. D., Balzer, A., Jacobs, C. M., Gruszczynski, M. W., Smith, K. B., & Hibbing, J. R. (2012). The political left rolls with the good and the political right confronts the bad: Connecting physiology and cognition to preferences. *Philosophical Transactions of the Royal Society of London, Series B, Biological Sciences, 367*, 640–649. http://dx.doi.org/10.1098/rstb.2011.0268

Doise, W. (2002). *Human rights as social representations*. New York, NY: Routledge. http://dx.doi.org/10.4324/9780203219676

Dollar, D., & Kraay, A. (2004). Trade, growth, and poverty. *Economic Journal, 114* (February), F22–F49. http://dx.doi.org/10.1111/j.0013-0133.2004.00186.x

Doniger, W. (1991). *The laws of Manu*. New York, NY: Penguin Books.

Dorling, D. (2014). *Inequality and the 1%*. London, England: VersoBooks.

Dostoevsky, F. (1951). *Crime and punishment* (D. Magarshack, Trans.). Harmondsworth, England: Penguin Books. (Original work published 1866)

Druckman, J. N., & Jacobs, L. R. (2015). *Who governs? Presidents, public opinion, and manipulation*. Chicago, IL: University of Chicago Press.

Duckitt, J. (2005). Personality and prejudice. In J. F. Dovidio, P. Glick, & L. A. Rudman (Eds.), *On the nature of prejudice: Fifty years after Allport* (pp. 395–412). Malden, MA: Blackwell. http://dx.doi.org/10.1002/9780470773963.ch24

Dufour, D. J., Goldberg, R., & Moghaddam, F. M. (2013). The enemy of my enemy is my friend. In R. Harré & F. M. Moghaddam (Eds.), *The psychology of friendship and enmity: Relationships in love, work, politics and war* (Vol. 2, pp. 37–52). Santa Barbara, CA: Praeger.

Dukerich, J. M., Golden, B. R., & Shortell, S. M. (2002). Beauty is in the eye of the beholder: The impact of organizational identification, identity, and image on the cooperative behaviors of physicians. *Administrative Science Quarterly, 47*, 507–533. http://dx.doi.org/10.2307/3094849

Dyer, J. R. G., Johansson, A., Helbing, D., Couzin, I. D., & Krause, J. (2009). Leadership, consensus decision making and collective behaviour in humans. *Philosophical Transactions of the Royal Society of London. Series B, Biological Sciences, 364*, 781–789. http://dx.doi.org/10.1098/rstb.2008.0233

Earle, T. (Ed.). (1991). *Chiefdoms: Power, economy, ideology*. Cambridge, England: Cambridge University Press.

Earley, P. C. (1989). Social loafing and collectivism: A comparison of the United States and the People's Republic of China. *Administrative Science Quarterly, 34*, 565–581. http://dx.doi.org/10.2307/2393567

Easterlin, R. A. (1995). Will raising the income of all increase the happiness of all? *Journal of Economic Behavior & Organization, 27*, 35–47. http://dx.doi.org/10.1016/0167-2681(95)00003-B

Easterlin, R. A. (2001). Income and happiness: Toward a unified theory. *Economic Journal, 111*, 465–484. http://dx.doi.org/10.1111/1468-0297.00646

Easterlin, R. A. (2006). Life cycle happiness and its sources: Intersections of psychology, economics, and demography. *Journal of Economic Psychology, 27*, 463–482. http://dx.doi.org/10.1016/j.joep.2006.05.002

Edlin, A., Gelman, A., & Kaplan, N. (2007). Voting as a rational choice: Why and how people vote to improve the well being of others. *Rationality and Society, 19*, 293–314. http://dx.doi.org/10.1177/1043463107077384

Eichengreen, B., & Leblang, D. (2006). *Democracy and globalization* (National Bureau of Economic Research Working Paper No. 12450). Retrieved from http://www.nber.org/papers/w12450

Eliot, G. (1964). *Middlemarch: A study of provincial life*. New York, NY: Signet Classic/New American Library. (Original work published 1872)

Ellickson, R. C. (1991). *Order without law: How neighbors settle disputes*. Cambridge, MA: Harvard University Press.

Emler, N., Renwick, S., & Malone, B. (1983). The relationship between moral reasoning and political orientation. *Journal of Personality and Social Psychology, 45*, 1073–1080. http://dx.doi.org/10.1037/0022-3514.45.5.1073

Emler, N., & St. James, A. (2004). Moral judgment and reasoning: A social psychological perspective. *New Review of Social Psychology, 3*, 112–120.

Englich, B., Mussweiler, T., & Strack, F. (2006). Playing dice with criminal sentences: The influence of irrelevant anchors on experts' judicial decision making. *Personality and Social Psychology Bulletin, 32*, 188–200. http://dx.doi.org/10.1177/0146167205282152

Esposito, J. L. (1996). *Islam and democracy*. New York, NY: Oxford University Press.

Esposito, J. L. (2011). The saga of Islam and democracy in the Middle East. In A. Paya & J. L. Esposito (Eds.), *Iraq, democracy and the future of the Muslim world* (pp. 159–171). New York, NY: Routledge.

Esser, J. K. (1998). Alive and well after 25 years: A review of groupthink research. *Organizational Behavior and Human Decision Processes, 73*, 116–141. http://dx.doi.org/10.1006/obhd.1998.2758

Evans, G. B. (Ed.). (1997). *The riverside Shakespeare: The complete works* (2nd ed.). Boston, MA: Houghton Mifflin.

Falk, E. B., Berkman, E. T., & Lieberman, M. D. (2012). From neural responses to population behavior: Neural focus group predicts population-level media effects. *Psychological Science, 23*, 439–445. http://dx.doi.org/10.1177/0956797611434964

Falomir-Pichastor, J. M., & Frederic, N. S. (2013). The dark side of heterogeneous ingroup identities: National identification, perceived threat, and prejudice against immigrants. *Journal of Experimental Social Psychology, 49*, 72–79. http://dx.doi.org/10.1016/j.jesp.2012.08.016

Farrelly, C. (2007). *Justice, democracy and reasonable agreement.* New York, NY: Palgrave Macmillan. http://dx.doi.org/10.1057/9780230596870

Ferraz, C., & Finan, F. (2008). Exposing corrupt politicians: The effects of Brazil's publicly released audits on electoral outcomes. *Quarterly Journal of Economics, 123*, 703–745. http://dx.doi.org/10.1162/qjec.2008.123.2.703

Finkel, N., & Moghaddam, F. M. (Eds.). (2005). *The psychology of rights and duties: Empirical contributions and normative commentaries.* Washington, DC: American Psychological Association. http://dx.doi.org/10.1037/10872-000

Fish, M. S. (2009). Encountering culture. In Z. Barany & R. G. Moser (Eds.), *Is democracy exportable?* (pp. 57–84). New York, NY: Cambridge University Press. http://dx.doi.org/10.1017/CBO9780511809262.004

Fish, M. S., & Brooks, R. S. (2004). Does diversity hurt democracy? *Journal of Democracy, 15*, 154–166. http://dx.doi.org/10.1353/jod.2004.0009

Fiske, S. T., & Markus, H. R. (Eds.). (2012). *Facing social class: How societal rank influences interaction.* New York, NY: Russell Sage Foundation.

Flynn, J. R. (2007). *What is intelligence? Beyond the Flynn effect.* Cambridge, England: Cambridge University Press. http://dx.doi.org/10.1017/CBO9780511605253

Foster, M. D., Sloto, L., & Ruby, R. (2006). Responding to discrimination as a function of meritocracy beliefs and personal experiences: Testing the model of shattered assumptions. *Group Processes & Intergroup Relations, 9*, 401–411. http://dx.doi.org/10.1177/1368430206064641

Foster, M. D., & Tsarfati, E. M. (2005). The effects of meritocracy beliefs on women's well-being after first-time gender discrimination. *Personality and Social Psychology Bulletin, 31*, 1730–1738. http://dx.doi.org/10.1177/0146167205278709

Fowler, J. H., & Dawes, C. T. (2008). Two genes predict voter turnout. *Journal of Politics, 70*, 579–594. http://dx.doi.org/10.1017/S0022381608080638

Fowler, J. H., & Schreiber, D. (2008). Biology, politics, and the emerging science of human nature. *Science, 322*, 912–914. http://dx.doi.org/10.1126/science.1158188

Frank, T. (2004). *What's the matter with Kansas? How conservatives won the heart of America.* New York, NY: Metropolitan Books.

Frenkel-Brunswik, E. (1949). Intolerance of ambiguity as an emotional and perceptual personality variable. *Journal of Personality, 18*, 108–143. http://dx.doi.org/10.1111/j.1467-6494.1949.tb01236.x

Freud, S. (1950). Project for a scientific psychology. Part II: Psychopathology. In J. Strachey (Ed. & Trans.), *The standard edition of the complete psychological works of Sigmund Freud* (Vol. 1, pp. 281–392). London, England: Hogarth and Institute of Psycho-Analysis. (Original work published 1895)

Freud, S. (1953). A case of hysteria, three essays on sexuality and other works. In J. Strachey (Ed. & Trans.), *The standard edition of the complete psychological works of Sigmund Freud* (Vol. 7, pp. 135–243). London, England: Hogarth Press. (Original work published 1901–1905)

Freud, S. (1955). Group psychology and the analysis of the ego. In J. Strachey (Ed. & Trans.), *The standard edition of the complete psychological works of Sigmund Freud* (Vol. 18, pp. 67–143). London, England: Hogarth Press. (Original work published 1921)

Freud, S. (1961). Civilization and its discontents. In J. Strachey (Trans. & Ed.), *The standard edition of the complete psychological works of Sigmund Freud* (Vol. 21, pp. 64–145). London, England: Hogarth Press. (Original work published 1930)

Frey, B. S., & Stutzer, A. (2010). Happiness and public choice. *Public Choice, 144,* 557–573. http://dx.doi.org/10.1007/s11127-010-9681-y

Fukuyama, F. (2006). *The end of history and the last man.* New York, NY: Free Press.

Furnham, A., & Marks, J. (2013). Tolerance of ambiguity: A review of the recent literature. *Psychology, 4,* 717–728.

Furnham, A., & Ribchester, T. (1995). Tolerance of ambiguity: A review of the concept, its measurement and applications. *Current Psychology: A Journal for Diverse Perspectives on Diverse Psychological Issues, 14,* 179–199. http://dx.doi.org/10.1007/BF02686907

Gailliot, M. T., & Baumeister, R. F. (2007). The physiology of willpower: Linking blood glucose to self-control. *Personality and Social Psychology Review, 11,* 303–327. http://dx.doi.org/10.1177/1088868307303030

Gaines, B. J., Kuklinski, J. H., Quirk, P. J., Peyton, B., & Verkuilen, J. (2007). Same facts, different interpretations: Partisan motivation and opinion on Iraq. *Journal of Politics, 69,* 957–974. http://dx.doi.org/10.1111/j.1468-2508.2007.00601.x

Galinsky, A. D., Magee, J. C., Ena Inesi, M. & Gruenfeld, D. H. (2006). Power and perspectives not taken. *Psychological Science, 17,* 1068–1074. http://dx.doi.org/10.1111/j.1467-9280.2006.01824.x

Galton, F. (1907). Vox populi. *Nature, 75,* 450–451. http://dx.doi.org/10.1038/075450a0

Galtung, J. (1969). Violence, peace, and peace research. *Journal of Peace Research, 6,* 167–191. http://dx.doi.org/10.1177/002234336900600301

Galtung, J. (1990). Cultural violence. *Journal of Peace Research, 27,* 291–305. http://dx.doi.org/10.1177/0022343390027003005

Garzia, D. (2011). The personalization of politics in Western democracies: Causes and consequences on leader-follower relationships. *Leadership Quarterly, 22,* 697–709. http://dx.doi.org/10.1016/j.leaqua.2011.05.010

Gellately, R. (2013). Voting for Hitler and Stalin: Elections under 20th century dictatorships. *Social History, 38,* 276–277. http://dx.doi.org/10.1080/03071022.2013.786262

Geys, B. (2006). "Rational" theories of voter turnout: A review. *Political Studies Review, 4,* 16–35. http://dx.doi.org/10.1111/j.1478-9299.2006.00034.x

Gibler, D. M., & Randazzo, K. A. (2011). Testing the effects of independent judiciaries on the likelihood of democratic backsliding. *American Journal of Political Science*, *55*, 696–709. http://dx.doi.org/10.1111/j.1540-5907.2010.00504.x

Gibson, J., & Gouws, A. (2003). *Overcoming intolerance in South Africa: Experiments in democratic persuasion.* New York, NY: Cambridge University Press.

Gilens, M., & Page, B. I. (2014). Testing theories of American politics: Elites, interest groups, and average citizens. *Perspectives on Politics*, *12*, 564–581.

Gilmartin, D. (2012). Towards a global history of voting: Sovereignty, the diffusion of ideas, and the enchanted individual. *Religions*, *3*, 407–423. http://dx.doi.org/10.3390/rel3020407

Glasius, M. (2006). *The International Criminal Court: A global civil society achievement.* London, England: Routledge. http://dx.doi.org/10.4324/9780203414514

Gneezy, A., & Fessler, D. M. T. (2012). Conflict, sticks and carrots: War increases prosocial punishments and rewards. *Proceedings of the Royal Society, Biological Sciences*, *279*, 219–223. http://dx.doi.org/10.1098/rspb.2011.0805

Goidel, R. K. (2014). *America's failing experiment: How we the people have become the problem.* Lanham, MD: Rowman & Littlefield.

Graham, L. R. (1993). *Science in Russia and the Soviet Union: A short history.* Cambridge, England: Cambridge University Press.

Granick, J. S., & Sprigman, C. J. (2013, June 27). The criminal N.S.A. *The New York Times*. Retrieved from www.nytimes.com/2013/06/28/opinion/the-criminal-nsa.html?_r=0

Greenberg, D. F. (1992). Law and development in light of dependency theory. In A. Carty (Ed.), *Law and development* (pp. 89–119). New York: New York University Press.

Greene, J. D., Morelli, S. A., Lowenberg, K., Nystrom, L. E., & Cohen, J. D. (2008). Cognitive load selectively interferes with utilitarian moral judgment. *Cognition*, *107*, 1144–1154. http://dx.doi.org/10.1016/j.cognition.2007.11.004

Greene, J. D., Sommerville, R. B., Nystrom, L. E., Darley, J. M., & Cohen, J. D. (2001). An fMRI investigation of emotional engagement in moral judgment. *Science*, *293*, 2105–2108. http://dx.doi.org/10.1126/science.1062872

Greenleaf, R. K. (2002). *Servant leadership: A journey into the nature of legitimate power and greatness.* Mahwah, NJ: Paulist Press. (Original work published 1977)

Greenwald, A. G., Poehlman, T. A., Uhlmann, E. L., & Banaji, M. R. (2009). Understanding and using the Implicit Association Test: III. Meta-analysis of predictive validity. *Journal of Personality and Social Psychology*, *97*, 17–41. http://dx.doi.org/10.1037/a0015575

Greenwald, G. (2014). *No place to hide: Edward Snowden, the NSA and the surveillance state.* New York, NY: Metropolitan Books.

Gropper, D. M., Lawson, R. A., & Thorne, J. T. (2011). Economic freedom and happiness. *Cato Journal*, *31*, 237–255.

Gross, B. (1980). *Friendly fascism: The new face of power in America*. New York, NY: M. Evans.

Gundlach, E., & Opfinger, M. (2013). Religiosity as a determinant of happiness. *Review of Development Economics, 17*, 523–539. http://dx.doi.org/10.1111/rode.12047

Gustavsson, M., & Jordahl, H. (2008). Inequality and trust in Sweden: Some inequalities are more harmful than others. *Journal of Public Economics, 92*, 348–365. http://dx.doi.org/10.1016/j.jpubeco.2007.06.010

Guthrie, C., Rachlinski, J. J., & Wistrich, A. J. (2007). Blinking on the bench: How judges decide cases. *Cornell Law Review, 93*, 1–43.

Gutmann, A. (2003). *Identity in democracy*. Princeton, NJ: Princeton University Press.

Gutmann, A., & Dennis, T. (1996). *Democracy and disagreement*. Cambridge, MA: Harvard University Press.

Haas, P. M. (2004). When does power listen to truth? A constructionist approach to the policy process. *Journal of European Public Policy, 11*, 569–592. http://dx.doi.org/10.1080/1350176042000248034

Hacker, J. S., & Pierson, P. (2010). *Winner-takes-all politics: How Washington made the rich richer—and turned its back on the middle class*. New York, NY: Simon & Schuster.

Hafner, G. (2005). An attempt to explain the position of the United States toward the ICC. *Journal of International Criminal Justice, 3*, 323–332. http://dx.doi.org/10.1093/jicj/mqi033

Hagger, M. S., Wood, C., Stiff, C., & Chatzisarantis, N. L. D. (2010). Ego depletion and the strength model of self-control: A meta-analysis. *Psychological Bulletin, 136*, 495–525. http://dx.doi.org/10.1037/a0019486

Haidt, J. (2007). The new synthesis in moral psychology. *Science, 316*, 998–1002. http://dx.doi.org/10.1126/science.1137651

Hall, R. E., & Jones, C. I. (1999). Why do some countries produce so much more output per worker than others? *Quarterly Journal of Economics, 114*, 83–116. http://dx.doi.org/10.1162/003355399555954

Ham, J., & van den Bos, K. (2010). On unconscious morality: The effects of unconscious thinking on moral decision making. *Social Cognition, 28*, 74–83. http://dx.doi.org/10.1521/soco.2010.28.1.74

Hamamura, T. (2012). Are cultures becoming individualistic? A cross-temporal comparison of individualism–collectivism in the United States and Japan. *Personality and Social Psychology Review, 16*, 3–24. http://dx.doi.org/10.1177/1088868311411587

Hamann, K., Bender, J., & Tomasello, M. (2014). Meritocratic sharing is based on collaboration in 3-year-olds. *Developmental Psychology, 50*, 121–128. http://dx.doi.org/10.1037/a0032965

Hamilton, A., Madison, J., & Jay, J. (1996). *The Federalist: The famous papers on the principles of American government* (B. F. Wright, Ed.). New York, NY: Barnes & Noble Books. (Original work published 1787 under pen name "Publius")

Hare, W. (1979). *Open-mindedness and education*. Kingston, Canada: McGill-Queen's University Press.

Hare, W., & Portelli, J. P. (Eds.). (2007). *Key questions for educators*. San Francisco, CA: Caddo Gap Press.

Harell, A., & Stolle, D. (2010). Diversity and democratic politics. *Canadian Journal of Political Science, 43*, 235–256. http://dx.doi.org/10.1017/S000842391000003X

Harré, R. (1993). *Social being* (2nd ed.). Oxford, England: Basil Blackwell.

Harré, R. (2003). Forward. In P. Weinreich & W. Saunderson (Eds.), *Analysing identity* (pp. xvii–xxii). London, England: Routledge.

Harré, R., & Moghaddam, F. M. (2012). *Psychology for the third millennium: Integrating cultural and neuroscience perspectives*. London, England: Sage. http://dx.doi.org/10.4135/9781446288542

Harris, D. A. (2003). *Profiles in injustice: Why racial profiling cannot work*. New York, NY: New Press.

Hasen, R. L. (2012). *The fraudulent fraud squad: A sneak preview from the voting wars, from Florida 2000 to the next election meltdown*. New Haven, CT: Yale University Press.

Haslam, S. A. (2004). *Psychology in organizations: The social identity approach*. London, England: Sage.

Hayek, F. A. (1969). *The road to serfdom*. Chicago, IL: The University of Chicago Press. (Original work published 1944)

Headley, J. M. (2008). *The Europeanization of the world: On the origin of human rights and democracy*. Princeton, NJ: Princeton University Press.

The headwinds return. (2014, September 13). *The Economist*, pp. 29–31.

Healy, A. J., Malhotra, N., & Mo, C. H. (2010). Irrelevant events affect voters' evaluations of government performance. *PNAS: Proceedings of the National Academy of Sciences of the United States of America, 107*, 12804–12809. http://dx.doi.org/10.1073/pnas.1007420107

Held, D. (1997). Democracy: From city-states to a cosmopolitan order? In R. E. Goodin & P. Pettit (Eds.), *Contemporary political philosophy* (pp. 78–101). Oxford, England: Basil Blackwell.

Helliwell, J., Layard, R., & Sachs, J. (2013). *World happiness report*. Retrieved from http://unsdsn.org/resources/publications/world-happiness-report-2013/

Helmke, G., & Rosenbluth, F. (2009). Regimes and the rule of law: Judicial independence in comparative perspective. *Annual Review of Political Science, 12*, 345–366. http://dx.doi.org/10.1146/annurev.polisci.12.040907.121521

Herman, J. L., Stevens, M. J., Bird, A., Mendenhall, M., & Oddou, G. (2010). The tolerance of ambiguity scale: Towards a more refined measure for international management research. *International Journal of Intercultural Relations, 34*, 58–65. http://dx.doi.org/10.1016/j.ijintrel.2009.09.004

Herrnstein, R. J., & Murray, C. (1994). *The bell curve: Intelligence and class structure in American life*. New York, NY: Free Press.

Herodotus. (1954). *The histories* (A. de Sèlincourt, Trans.). Harmondsworth, England: Penguin Books. (Original work published 5th century BC)

Hill, C. (1991). *The world turned upside down: Radical ideas during the English Revolution*. London, England: Penguin Books.

Hill, C. (1997). *Puritanism and revolution: Studies in the interpretation of the English Revolution of the 17th century*. New York, NY: Palgrave Macmillan. (Original work published 1958)

Hirschman, A. O. (1984). *Getting ahead collectively: Grassroots experiences in Latin America*. New York, NY: Pergamon Press.

Hobbes, T. (1991). *Leviathan* (R. Tuck, Ed.). Cambridge, England: Cambridge University Press. (Original work published 1651)

Hobhouse, L. T. (1904). *Democracy and reaction*. London, England: T. Fisher Unwin.

Hochschild, A. (1999). *King Leopold's ghost: A story of greed, terror, and heroism in Colonial Africa*. Boston, MA: Houghton Mifflin.

Hodson, G., & Hewstone, M. (Eds.). (2012). *Advances in intergroup contact*. New York, NY: Psychology Press.

Holt, J. C. (1992). *Magna Carta* (2nd ed.). Cambridge, England: Cambridge University Press.

Holvino, E., & Kamp, A. (2009). Diversity management: Are we moving in the right direction? Reflections on both sides of the North Atlantic. *Scandinavian Journal of Management, 25*, 395–403.

Hoppe, H. H. (2001). *Democracy: The God that failed*. London, England: Transaction.

Horowitz, D. L. (1993). Democracy in divided societies. *Journal of Democracy, 4*, 18–38.

Howard, A. E. D. (1997). *Magna Carta: Text and commentary*. Charlottesville: University Press of Virginia.

Huddy, L. (2013). From group identity to political cohesion and commitment. In L. Huddy, D. O. Sears, & J. S. Levy (Eds.), *The Oxford handbook of political psychology* (pp. 737–773). New York, NY: Oxford University Press. http://dx.doi.org/10.1093/oxfordhb/9780199760107.013.0023

Hume, D. (1948). Of the original contract. In E. Barker (Ed.), *Social contract: Essays by Locke, Hume and Rousseau* (pp. 147–166). London, England: Oxford University Press. (Original work published 1748)

Iceland, J., & Wilkes, R. (2006). Does socioeconomic status matter? Race, class, and residential segregation. *Social Problems, 53*, 248–273. http://dx.doi.org/10.1525/sp.2006.53.2.248

Ichino, H., & Schündeln, M. (2012). Deterring or displacing electoral irregularities? Spillover effects of observers in a randomized field experiment in Ghana. *Journal of Politics, 74*, 292–307. http://dx.doi.org/10.1017/S0022381611001368

Ikeda, D. (2010). *A new humanism*. New York, NY: I. B. Tauris.

Inglehart, R. (2003). How solid is mass support for democracy—and how can we measure it? *Political Science and Politics*, 51–57. http://dx.doi.org/10.1017/S1049096503001689

Iranian cleric blames quakes on promiscuous women. (2010, April). *BBC News*. Retrieved from http://news.bbc.co.uk/2/hi/middle_east/8631775.stm

Islam, S. (2012). Demographic changes in Europe's Muslim communities: Implications and challenges. In H. Groth & A. Sousa-Poza (Eds.), *Population dynamics in Muslim countries: Assembling the jigsaw* (pp. 279–292). New York, NY: Springer-Verlag Berlin Heidelberg. http://dx.doi.org/10.1007/978-3-642-27881-5_17

Iyer, R., Graham, J., Koleva, S., Ditto, P., & Haidt, J. (2010). Beyond identity politics: Moral psychology and the 2008 Democratic primary. *Analyses of Social Issues and Public Policy*, 10, 293–306. http://dx.doi.org/10.1111/j.1530-2415.2010.01203.x

Jackman, R. W. (1987). Political institutions and voter turnout in the industrial democracies. *American Political Science Review*, 81, 404–423.

Jain, A. K. (2001). Corruption: A review. *Journal of Economic Surveys*, 15, 71–121. http://dx.doi.org/10.1111/1467-6419.00133

Janis, I. L. (1972). *Victims of groupthink: A psychological study of foreign-policy decisions and fiascoes*. Oxford, England: Houghton Mifflin.

Jendrysik, M. S. (2002). *Explaining the English revolution: Hobbes and his contemporaries*. New York, NY: Lexington Books.

Johnson, M. K., Rowatt, W. C., & La Bouff, J. P. (2012). Religiosity and prejudice revisited: In-group favoritism, out-group derogation, or both? *Psychology of Religion and Spirituality*, 4, 154–168. http://dx.doi.org/10.1037/a0025107

Jones, K. (2009). *Swiss democracy*. Suffolk, England: Arena Books.

Jost, J. T. (2006). The end of the end of ideology. *American Psychologist*, 61, 651–670. http://dx.doi.org/10.1037/0003-066X.61.7.651

Kahneman, D. (2011). *Thinking fast and slow*. New York, NY: Farrar, Straus and Giroux.

Kahneman, D., & Deaton, A. (2010). High income improves evaluation of life but not emotional well-being. *PNAS: Proceedings of the National Academy of Sciences of the United States of America*, 107, 16489–16493. http://dx.doi.org/10.1073/pnas.1011492107

Kalb, M. (2013). *The road to war: Presidential commitments honored and betrayed*. Washington, DC: Brookings Institution Press.

Kallen, H. M. (1924). *Culture and democracy in the United States: Studies in the group psychology of the American people*. New York, NY: Boni and Liveright.

Kamenica, E. (2012). Behavioral economics and psychology of incentives. *Annual Review of Economics*, 4, 13.1–13.26.

Kant, E. (2002). *Groundwork for the metaphysics of morals* (A. W. Wood, Ed. & Trans.). New Haven, CT: Yale University Press. (Original work published 1785)

Karau, S. J., & Williams, K. D. (1993). Social loafing: A meta-analytic review and theoretical integration. *Journal of Personality and Social Psychology, 65*, 681–706. http://dx.doi.org/10.1037/0022-3514.65.4.681

Karp, J. A., & Banducci, S. A. (2008). Political efficacy and participation in twenty-seven democracies: How electoral systems shape political behaviour. *British Journal of Political Science, 38*, 311–334. http://dx.doi.org/10.1017/S0007123408000161

Kawachi, I., & Kennedy, B. P. (1997). The relationship of income inequality to mortality: Does the choice of indicator matter? *Social Science & Medicine, 45*, 1121–1127. http://dx.doi.org/10.1016/S0277-9536(97)00044-0

Keane, J. (2009). *The life and death of democracy.* New York, NY: Norton.

Kellerman, B. (2008). *Followership: How followers are creating change and changing leaders.* Boston, MA: Harvard Business Review Press.

Kelley, R. D. G. (1999). The people in me. *Utne Reader, 95*, 79–81.

Keltner, D., Gruenfeld, D. H., & Anderson, C. (2003). Power, approach, and inhibition. *Psychological Review, 110*, 265–284. http://dx.doi.org/10.1037/0033-295X.110.2.265

Kerr, N. L., & Bruun, S. E. (1983). Dispensability of member effort and group motivation losses: Free-rider effects. *Journal of Personality and Social Psychology, 44*, 78–94. http://dx.doi.org/10.1037/0022-3514.44.1.78

Ketchum, D. (n.d.). Why did John Adams say that "democracy never lasts long"? Retrieved May 15, 2015, from http://classroom.synonym.com/did-john-adams-say-democracy-never-lasts-long-7843.html

Kim, Y. M. (1997). "Asian-style democracy": A critique from East Asia. *Asian Survey, 37*, 1119–1134. http://dx.doi.org/10.2307/2645761

Knowles, E. D., & Lowery, B. S. (2012). Meritocracy, self-concerns, and Whites' denial of racial inequality. *Self and Identity, 11*, 202–222. http://dx.doi.org/10.1080/15298868.2010.542015

Kohlberg, L. (1963). The development of children's orientations toward a moral order. I. Sequence in the development of moral thought. *Vita Humana, 6*, 11–33.

Kohlberg, L. (1973). The claim to moral adequacy of a highest level of moral judgment. *Journal of Philosophy, 70*, 630–646. http://dx.doi.org/10.2307/2025030

Kohlberg, L., & Hersh, R. H. (1977). Moral development: A review of the theory. *Theory Into Practice, 16*, 53–59. http://dx.doi.org/10.1080/00405847709542675

Kozinski, A. (1993). What I ate for breakfast and other mysteries of judicial decision making. *Loyola of Los Angeles Law Review, 26*, 993–999.

Kraus, P. A. (2011). Neither united nor diverse? The language issue and political legitimization in the European Union. In A. L. Kjær & S. Adamo (Eds.), *Linguistic diversity and European democracy* (pp. 17–33). Furnham, England: Ashgate.

Krause, J., Ruxton, G. D., & Krause, S. (2010). Swarm intelligence in animals and humans. *Trends in Ecology & Evolution, 25*, 28–34. http://dx.doi.org/10.1016/j.tree.2009.06.016

Kriesi, H., & Trechsel, A. H. (2008). *The politics of Switzerland: Continuity and change in a consensus democracy.* Cambridge, England: Cambridge University Press. http://dx.doi.org/10.1017/CBO9780511790676

Kruglanski, A. W. (2004). *The psychology of closed mindedness.* New York, NY: Psychology Press.

Kruglanski, A. W., & Boyatzi, L. M. (2012). The psychology of closed and open mindedness, rationality, and democracy. *Critical Review: A Journal of Politics and Society, 24,* 217–232.

Kuhn, D. (1999). A developmental model of critical thinking. *Educational Researcher, 28,* 16–46. http://dx.doi.org/10.3102/0013189X028002016

Ladner, A., & Fiechter, J. (2012). The influence of direct democracy on political interest, electoral turnout and other forms of citizens' participation in Swiss municipalities. *Local Government Studies, 38,* 437–459. http://dx.doi.org/10.1080/03003930.2012.698242

Laing, R. D., & Esterson, A. (1964). *Sanity, madness and the family.* Harmondsworth, England: Penguin Book.

Lakner, C., & Milanovic, B. (2013, December). *Global income distribution: From the fall of the Berlin Wall to the Great Recession* (Working Paper No. 6719). Washington, DC: World Bank. http://dx.doi.org/10.1596/1813-9450-6719

Lalonde, R. N. (in press). Are we really different from each other? The difficulties of focusing on similarities in psychological research. *Peace and Conflict.*

Lamiell, J. T. (2004). *Beyond individual and group differences.* London, England: Sage.

Lammers, J., Galinsky, A. D., Gordijn, E. H., & Otten, S. (2008). Illegitimacy moderates the effects of power on approach. *Psychological Science, 19,* 558–564. http://dx.doi.org/10.1111/j.1467-9280.2008.02123.x

Lammers, J., Gordijn, E. H., & Otten, S. (2008). Looking through the eyes of the powerful. *Journal of Experimental Social Psychology, 44,* 1229–1238. http://dx.doi.org/10.1016/j.jesp.2008.03.015

Lammers, J., Stapel, D. A., & Galinsky, A. D. (2010). Power increases hypocrisy: Moralizing in reasoning, immorality in behavior. *Psychological Science, 21,* 737–744. http://dx.doi.org/10.1177/0956797610368810

Lareau, A. (2011). *Unequal childhoods: Class, race, and family life* (2nd ed.). Berkeley: University of California Press.

Latané, B., Williams, K., & Harkins, S. (1979). Many hands make light the work: The causes and consequences of social loafing. *Journal of Personality and Social Psychology, 37,* 822–832. http://dx.doi.org/10.1037/0022-3514.37.6.822

LaVaque-Manty, M. (2009). *The playing fields of Eton.* Ann Arbor: University of Michigan Press.

Le Cheminant, W., & Parrish, J. M. (Eds.). (2011). *Manipulating democracy: Democratic theory, political psychology, and mess media.* New York, NY: Routledge.

Ledgerwood, A., Mandisodza, A. N., Jost, J. T., & Pohl, J. (2011). Working for the system: Motivated defense of meritocratic beliefs. *Social Cognition, 29*, 322–340. http://dx.doi.org/10.1521/soco.2011.29.3.322

Lee, R. (2011). The outlook for population growth. *Science, 333*, 569–573. http://dx.doi.org/10.1126/science.1208859

Lehoucq, F. (2003). Electoral fraud: Causes, types, and consequences. *Annual Review of Political Science, 6*, 233–256. http://dx.doi.org/10.1146/annurev.polisci.6.121901.085655

Leighley, J. E., & Nagler, J. (2014). *Who votes now? Demographics, issues, inequality, and turnout in the United States*. Princeton, NJ: Princeton University Press.

Levendusky, M. S. (2013). Why do partisan media polarize viewers? *American Journal of Political Science, 57*, 611–623. http://dx.doi.org/10.1111/ajps.12008

Levitt, P., & Jaworsky, B. N. (2007). Transnational migration studies: Past developments and future trends. *Annual Review of Sociology, 33*, 129–156. http://dx.doi.org/10.1146/annurev.soc.33.040406.131816

Lincoln, A. (1863). *The Gettysburg address*. Retrieved from http://www.abrahamlincolnonline.org/lincoln/speeches/gettysburg.htm

Lind, E. A. (2001). Fairness heuristic theory: Justice judgments as pivotal cognitions in organizational relations. In J. Greenberg & Cropanzano (Eds.), *Advances in organizational justice* (pp. 56–88). Stanford, CA: Stanford University Press.

Lind, E. A., & Tyler, T. (1988). *The social psychology of procedural justice*. New York, NY: Plenum Press. http://dx.doi.org/10.1007/978-1-4899-2115-4

Linder, W. (1994). *Swiss democracy: Possible solutions to conflict in multicultural societies*. London, England: Macmillan.

Linebaugh, P. (2008). *The Magna Carta manifesto: Liberties and commons for all*. Berkeley: University of California Press.

Lintott, A. W. (1999). *The constitution of the Roman Republic*. Oxford, England: Clarenden Press.

Lipman, M. (2003). *Thinking in education* (2nd ed.). New York, NY: Cambridge University Press. http://dx.doi.org/10.1017/CBO9780511840272

Lipset, S. M. (1998). George Washington and the founding of democracy. *Journal of Democracy, 9*, 24–38.

Longoria, R. T. (2009). *Meritocracy and Americans' views on distributive justice*. New York, NY: Lexington Books.

Liptak, A. (2010, January 22). Justices, 5–4, reject corporate spending limit [Electronic version]. *New York Times*, p. A1. Retrieved from http://www.nytimes.com/2010/01/22/us/politics/22scotus.html?pagewanted=all&_r=1

Llewellyn, S., Brookes, S., & Mahon, A. (2013). *Trust and confidence in government and public services*. New York, NY: Routledge.

Lord, R. G., & Brown, D. J. (2004). *Leadership processes and follower self-identity*. Mahwah, NJ: Erlbaum.

Luebker, M. (2014). Income inequality, redistribution, and poverty: Contrasting rational choice and behavioral perspectives. *Review of Income and Wealth, 60,* 133–154. http://dx.doi.org/10.1111/roiw.12100

Luo, Y., & Waite, L. J. (2005). The impact of childhood and adult SES on physical, mental, and cognitive well-being in later life. *Journals of Gerontology. Series B, Psychological Sciences and Social Sciences, 60,* S93–S101. http://dx.doi.org/10.1093/geronb/60.2.S93

Lutz, W., Cuaresma, J. C., & Abbasi-Shavazi, M. J. (2010). Demography, Education, and Democracy: Global trends and the case of Iran. *Population and Development Review, 36,* 253–281. http://dx.doi.org/10.1111/j.1728-4457.2010.00329.x

Ma, D., & van Zanden, J. L. (Eds.). (2011). *Law and long-term economic change.* Stanford, CA: Stanford University Press. http://dx.doi.org/10.11126/stanford/9780804772730.001.0001

MacDonald, K., Schug, M., Chase, E., & Barth, H. (2013). My people, right or wrong? Minimal group membership disrupts preschoolers' select trust. *Cognitive Development, 28,* 247–259. http://dx.doi.org/10.1016/j.cogdev.2012.11.001

Macedo, S., Alex-Assensoh, Y., Berry, J. M., Brintnall, M., Campbell, D. E., Fraga, L. R., et al. (2005). *Democracy at risk: How political choices undermine citizen participation, and what we can do about it.* Washington, DC: Brookings Institution Press.

Machiavelli, N. (1950). *The prince and the discourses* (L. Ricci, Trans.). New York, NY: Modern Library. (Original work published 1532)

Machiavelli, N. (2003). *The discourses* (B. Crick, Ed., & L. J. Walker, Trans.). London, England: Penguin Books. (Original work published 1531)

Mackie, G. (2003). *Democracy defended.* Cambridge, England: Cambridge University Press. http://dx.doi.org/10.1017/CBO9780511490293

Malik, I. H. (2002). *Religious minorities in Pakistan.* London, England: Minority Rights Group International.

Mandela, N. (1994). *Long walk to freedom.* New York, NY: Little, Brown.

Manza, J., & Uggen, C. (2006). *Locked out: Felon disenfranchisement and American society.* New York, NY: Oxford University press. http://dx.doi.org/10.1093/acprof:oso/9780195149326.001.0001

Marcus, G., Sullivan, J. L., Theiss-Morse, E., & Wood, S. L. (1995). *With malice toward some: How people make civil liberties judgments.* New York, NY: Cambridge University Press. http://dx.doi.org/10.1017/CBO9781139174046

Marcus, L. J., McNulty, E., Dorn, B. C., & Goralnick, E. (2014). *Crisis meta-leadership lessons from the Boston Marathon bombings response: The ingenuity of swarm intelligence* [White Paper, initial findings]. Boston, MA: National Preparedness Leadership Initiative, Center for Public Leadership, Harvard University.

Marien, S., & Hooghe, M. (2011). Does political trust matter? An empirical investigation into the relation between political trust and support for law compliance. *European Journal of Political Research, 50,* 267–291. http://dx.doi.org/10.1111/j.1475-6765.2010.01930.x

Marmot, M. G. (2004). *The status syndrome: How social standing affects our health and longevity*. New York, NY: Times Books/Henry Holt.

Marmot, M. G. (2006). Introduction, In M. G. Marmot & R. G. Wilkinson (Eds.), *Social determinants of health* (2nd ed., pp. 1–5). Oxford, England: Oxford University Press.

Marmot, M. G., Rose, G., Shipley, M., & Hamilton, P. J. S. (1978). Employment grade and coronary heart disease in British civil servants. *Journal of Epidemiology and Community Health, 32*, 244–249. http://dx.doi.org/10.1136/jech.32.4.244

Marmot, M. G., Stansfeld, S., Patel, C., North, F., Head, J., White, I., . . . Davey Smith, G. (1991). Health inequalities among British civil servants: The Whitehall II study. *Lancet, 337*, 1387–1393. http://dx.doi.org/10.1016/0140-6736(91)93068-K

Marmot, M. G., & Wilkinson, R. G. (Eds.). (2006). *Social determinants of health* (2nd ed.). Oxford, England: Oxford University Press.

Marsh, I., & Miller, R. (2012). *Democratic decline and democratic renewal: Political change in Britain, Australia and New Zealand*. Cambridge, England: Cambridge University Press. http://dx.doi.org/10.1017/CBO9781139198691

Marsh, N. S. (1992). Some aspects of the German legal system under national socialism. In C. Varga (Ed.), *Comparative legal cultures* (pp. 566–571). New York: New York University Press. (Original work published 1946)

Marx, K. (1979). The eighteenth brumaire of Louis Bonaparte. In K. Marx & F. Engels, *Collected works of Karl Marx and Frederick Engels* (Vol. 11, pp. 99–197). London, England: Lawrence & Wishart. (Original work published 1852)

Marx, K., & Engels, F. (1967). *The Communist manifesto*. New York, NY: Pantheon. (Original work published 1848)

Maslow, A. H. (1970). *Motivation and personality* (3rd ed.). New York, NY: Harper & Row.

Mattes, R. (1999). Do diverse social identities inhibit nationhood and democracy? Initial considerations from South Africa. In M. Palmberg (Ed.), *National identity and democracy in Africa* (pp. 261–286). Uppsala, Sweden: Nordic Africa Institute.

Mayer, R. (1997). Lenin, the proletariat, and the legitimation of dictatorship. *Journal of Political Ideologies, 2*, 99–115. http://dx.doi.org/10.1080/13569319708420752

McCammon, H. J., Campbell, K. E., Granberg, E. M., & Mowery, H. J. (2001). How movements win: Gendered opportunity structures and U.S. women's suffrage movements, 1866–1919. *American Sociological Review, 66*, 49–70. http://dx.doi.org/10.2307/2657393

McCoy, S. K., & Major, B. (2007). Priming meritocracy and the psychological justification of inequality. *Journal of Experimental Social Psychology, 43*, 341–351. http://dx.doi.org/10.1016/j.jesp.2006.04.009

McCoy, S. K., Wellman, J. D., Cosley, B., Saslow, L., & Epel, E. (2013). Is the belief in meritocracy palliative for members of low status groups? Evidence for a benefit for self-esteem and physical health via perceived control. *European Journal of Social Psychology, 43*, 307–318. http://dx.doi.org/10.1002/ejsp.1959

McCutcheon v. Federal Election Commission, 134 S. Ct. 1434, 188 L. Ed. 2d 468 (2014). Retrieved from http://www2.bloomberglaw.com/public/desktop/document/McCutcheon_v_Fed_Election_Commn_No_12536_2014_BL_89958_US_Apr_02_

McDonald, D. P., & Parks, K. M. (Eds.). (2012). *Managing diversity in the military.* London, England: Routledge.

McNamee, S. J., & Miller, R. K., Jr. (2014). *The meritocracy myth* (3rd ed.). New York, NY: Rowman & Littlefield.

McNollgast. (2006). Conditions for judicial independence. *Journal of Contemporary Legal Issues, 15*, 105–127.

Mehta, P. B. (2013, July 8). Snowden's revelations highlight the moral decline of America. *Financial Times*, p. 11.

Meltzer, A. H., & Richard, S. F. (1981). A rational theory of the size of government. *Journal of Political Economy, 89*, 914–927. http://dx.doi.org/10.1086/261013

Milani, A. (2011). *The Shah.* New York, NY: Palgrave Macmillan.

Miles, E., & Crisp, R. J. (2014). A meta-analytic test of the imagined contact hypothesis. *Group Processes & Intergroup Relations, 17*, 3–26. http://dx.doi.org/10.1177/1368430213510573

Milgram, S. (1974). *Obedience to authority.* New York, NY: Harper & Row.

Mill, J. S. (1975). *On liberty.* New York, NY: Norton. (Original work published 1859)

Miller, C. C. (2008, November 7). How Obama's internet campaign changed politics. *New York Times: Bits.* Retrieved from http://bits.blogs.nytimes.com/2008/11/07/how-obamas-internet-campaign-changed-politics/

Miller, P., & Rose, N. (1995). Production, identity, and democracy. *Theory and Society, 24*, 427–467. http://dx.doi.org/10.1007/BF00993353

Mills, B. J. (Ed.). (2000). *Alternative leadership strategies in the prehistoric Southwest.* Tucson: University of Arizona Press.

Milner, H. V., & Mukherjee, B. (2009). Democratization and economic globalization. *Annual Review of Political Science, 12*, 163–181. http://dx.doi.org/10.1146/annurev.polisci.12.110507.114722

Moghaddam, F. M. (1987). Psychology in the three worlds: As reflected by the crisis in social psychology and the move toward indigenous third-world psychology. *American Psychologist, 42*, 912–920. http://dx.doi.org/10.1037/0003-066X.42.10.912

Moghaddam, F. M. (1992). There can be a just and moral social constructionist psychology, but only in a social world that is homogeneous and/or static. In D. N. Robinson (Ed.), *Social discourse and moral judgment* (pp. 167–179). New York, NY: Academic Press.

Moghaddam, F. M. (1997). *The specialized society: The plight of the individual in an age of individualism.* New York, NY: Praeger.

Moghaddam, F. M. (2002). *The individual and society: A cultural integration*. New York, NY: Worth.

Moghaddam, F. M. (2004). The cycle of rights and duties in intergroup relations: Interobjectivity and perceived justice reassessed. *New Review of Social Psychology, 3*, 125–130.

Moghaddam, F. M. (2006). *From the terrorist's point of view*. Santa Barbara, CA: Praeger.

Moghaddam, F. M. (2008a). *How globalization spurs terrorism: The lopsided benefits of 'one world' and why that fuels violence*. Westport, CT: Praeger.

Moghaddam, F. M. (2008b). *Multiculturalism and intergroup relations: Psychological implications for democracy in global context*. Washington, DC: American Psychological Association. http://dx.doi.org/10.1037/11682-000

Moghaddam, F. M. (2008c). The psychological citizen and the two concepts of social contract: A preliminary analysis. *Political Psychology, 29*, 881–901. http://dx.doi.org/10.1111/j.1467-9221.2008.00671.x

Moghaddam, F. M. (2010). Intersubjectivity, interobjectivity, and the embryonic fallacy in developmental science. *Culture & Psychology, 16*, 465–475. http://dx.doi.org/10.1177/1354067X10380160

Moghaddam, F. M. (2012). The omnicultural imperative. *Culture & Psychology, 18*, 304–330. http://dx.doi.org/10.1177/1354067X12446230

Moghaddam, F. M. (2013). *The psychology of dictatorship*. Washington, DC: American Psychological Association. http://dx.doi.org/10.1037/14138-000

Moghaddam, F. M., & Harré, R. (2015). *Questioning causation: Explorations of causes and consequences across contexts*. Santa Barbara, CA: Praeger.

Moghaddam, F. M., & Stringer, P. (1986). "Trivial" and "important" criteria for social categorization in the minimal group paradigm. *Journal of Social Psychology, 126*, 345–354. http://dx.doi.org/10.1080/00224545.1986.9713595

Moghaddam, F. M., & Taylor, D. M. (1987). The meaning of multiculturalism for visible minority immigrant women. *Canadian Journal of Behavioural Science/Revue canadienne des sciences du comportement, 19*, 121–136. http://dx.doi.org/10.1037/h0080008

Moghaddam, F. M., & Vuksanovic, V. (1990). Attitudes and behavior toward human rights across different contexts: The role of right-wing authoritarianism, political ideology and religiosity. *International Journal of Psychology, 25*, 455–474.

Moller, J., & Skaaning, S. E. (2011). Preface. In J. Moller & S. E. Skaaning (Eds.), *Requisites of democracy: Conceptualization, measurement, and explanation* (pp. xiv–xix). London, England: Routledge.

Montesquieu, C. Baron de (2011). *The spirit of laws* (T. Nugent, Trans.). New York, NY: Cosimo Classics. (Original work published 1750)

Montoya, R. M., Horton, R. S., & Kirchner, J. (2008). Is actual similarity necessary for attraction? A meta-analysis of actual and perceived similarity. *Journal of Social and Personal Relationships, 25*, 889–922. http://dx.doi.org/10.1177/0265407508096700

More, T., Sir. (1965). *Utopia* (P. K. Marshall, Trans.). New York, NY: Washington Square Press. (Original work published 1516)

Morgan, K. (2003). The tyranny of the audience in Plato and Isocrates. In K. Morgan (Ed.), *Popular tyranny* (pp. 181–213). Austin: University of Texas Press.

Moulton, G. E. (Ed.). (1983). *The journals of the Lewis and Clark expedition* (Vol. 6). Lincoln: University of Nebraska Press.

Mueller, U., & Mazur, A. (1996). Facial dominance of West Point cadets as a predictor of later military rank. *Social Forces, 74*, 823–850. http://dx.doi.org/10.1093/sf/74.3.823

Mulgan, R. (2003). *Holding power to account: Accountability in modern democracies.* New York, NY: Palgrave Macmillan. http://dx.doi.org/10.1057/9781403943835

Munro, R. (2000). Judicial psychiatry in China and its political abuses. *Columbian Journal of Asian Law, 14*, 1–125.

Murray, C. (2012). *Coming apart: The state of White America, 1960–2010.* New York, NY: Crown Forum.

Musterd, S. (2005). Social and ethnic segregation in Europe: Levels, causes, and effects. *Journal of Urban Affairs, 27*, 331–348. http://dx.doi.org/10.1111/j.0735-2166.2005.00239.x

Myers, S. (2000). Empathic listening: Reports on the experience of being heard. *Journal of Humanistic Psychology, 40*, 148–173. http://dx.doi.org/10.1177/0022167800402004

Myers, T. A., Maibach, E. W., Roser-Renouf, C., Akerlof, K., & Leiserowitz, A. A. (2012). The relationship between personal experience and belief in the reality of global warming [Letter]. *Nature Climate Change, 3*, 343–347. http://dx.doi.org/10.1038/nclimate1754

Nemeth, C. J., & Ormiston, M. (2007). Creative idea generation: Harmony versus stimulation. *European Journal of Social Psychology, 37*, 524–535. http://dx.doi.org/10.1002/ejsp.373

Nemeth, C. J., Personnaz, B., Personnaz, M., & Goncalo, J. A. (2004). The liberating role of conflict in group creativity: A study in two countries. *European Journal of Social Psychology, 34*, 365–374. http://dx.doi.org/10.1002/ejsp.210

Nevitte, N., Blais, A., Gidengil, E., & Nadeau, R. (2000, August). *Socio-economic status and non-voting: A cross-national comparative analysis.* Paper presented at the 18th World Congress of the International Political Science Association, Quebec, Canada.

Neumann, H. (2010). Identity-building and democracy in the Philippines: National failure and local responses in Mindanao. *Journal of Current Southeast Asian Affairs, 29*, 61–90.

Noam, E. M. (2009). *Media ownership and concentration in America.* New York, NY: Oxford University Press. http://dx.doi.org/10.1093/acprof:oso/9780195188523.001.0001

Norris, P. (2012). *Making democratic governance work: How regimes shape prosperity, welfare, and peace.* New York, NY: Cambridge University Press. http://dx.doi. org/10.1017/CBO9781139061902

Norris, P., & Inglehart, R. F. (2012). Muslim integration into Western cultures: Between origins and destinations. *Political Studies, 60,* 228–251. http://dx.doi. org/10.1111/j.1467-9248.2012.00951.x

Novoa, C., & Moghaddam, F. M. (2014). Policies for managing diversity. In V. Benet-Martinez & Y.-Y. Hong (Eds.), *The Oxford handbook of multicultural identity* (pp. 462–484). New York, NY: Oxford University Press.

Nye, R. A. (1975). *The origin of crowd psychology: Gustave LeBon and the crisis of mass Democracy in the Third Republic.* Beverly Hills: Sage.

Nyhan, B., Reifler, J., & Ubel, P. A. (2013). The hazards of correcting myths about health care reform. *Medical Care, 51,* 127–132. http://dx.doi.org/10.1097/MLR. 0b013e318279486b

Nussbaum, M. C. (2000). *Women and human development.* New York, NY: Cambridge University Press. http://dx.doi.org/10.1017/CBO9780511841286

O'Donnell, G. (2004). The quality of democracy: Why the rule of law matters. *Journal of Democracy, 15,* 32–46. http://dx.doi.org/10.1353/jod.2004.0076

Oishi, S., Kesebir, S., & Diener, E. (2011). Income inequality and happiness. *Psychological Science, 22,* 1095–1100. http://dx.doi.org/10.1177/0956797611417262

Olivola, C. Y., Sussman, A. B., Tsetsos, K., Kang, O. E., & Todorov, A. (2012). Republicans prefer Republican-looking leaders: Political facial stereotypes predict candidate electoral success among right-leaning voters. *Social Psychological and Personality Science, 3,* 605–613. http://dx.doi.org/10.1177/1948550611432770

Olivola, C. Y., & Todorov, A. (2010a). Elected in 100 milliseconds: Appearance-based trait inferences and voting. *Journal of Nonverbal Behavior, 34,* 83–110. http:// dx.doi.org/10.1007/s10919-009-0082-1

Olivola, C. Y., & Todorov, A. (2010b). Fooled by first impressions? Reexamining the diagnostic value of appearance-based inferences. *Journal of Experimental Social Psychology, 46,* 315–324. http://dx.doi.org/10.1016/j.jesp.2009.12.002

Open Society Institute. (2010). *Muslims in Europe: A report on 11 EU cities.* New York, NY: Author.

Oppenheimer, D., & Edwards, M. (2012). *Democracy despite itself: Why a system that shouldn't work at all works so well.* Cambridge, MA: MIT Press.

Orfield, G., & Lee, C. (2005). *Why segregation matters: Poverty and educational inequality.* Cambridge, MA: The Civil Rights Project, Harvard University. Retrieved from http://www.civilrightsproject.ucla.edu/research/k-12-education/integration-and-diversity/why-segregation-matters-poverty-and-educational-inequality/ orfield-why-segregation-matters-2005.pdf

Orwell, G. (1949). *1984.* New York, NY: Signet.

Osbeck, L. M., Moghaddam, F. M., & Perreault, S. (1997). Similarity and attraction among majority and minority groups in a multicultural context. *International*

Journal of Intercultural Relations, 21, 113–123. http://dx.doi.org/10.1016/S0147-1767(96)00016-8

Oyedele, L. O. (2010). Sustaining architects' and engineers' motivation in design firms: An investigation of critical success factors. *Engineering, Construction and Architectural Management, 17*, 180–196. http://dx.doi.org/10.1108/09699981011024687

Overbeck, J. R., & Droutman, V. (2013). One for all: Social power increases self-anchoring of traits, attitudes, and emotions. *Psychological Science, 24*, 1466–1476. http://dx.doi.org/10.1177/0956797612474671

Pakulski, J., & Körösényi, A. (2012). *Toward leader democracy.* London, England: Anthem Press. http://dx.doi.org/10.7135/UPO9781843317715

Pareto, V. (1935). *The mind and society: A treatise in general sociology* (Vol. 1–4). New York, NY: Dover.

Patterson, T. E. (2003). The vanishing voter. *Kettering Foundation Connections, 14*(1), 13–16. Retrieved from https://www.kettering.org/sites/default/files/periodical-article/5_CONSUMMER2003_VanishingVoter.pdf

Pecora, N., Murray, E., & Wartella, A. (Eds.). (2007). *Children and television: Fifty years of research.* Mahwah, NJ: Erlbaum.

Peffley, M., & Rohrschneider, R. (2003). Democratization and political tolerance in seventeen countries: A multi-level model of democratic learning. *Political Research Quarterly, 56*, 243–257. http://dx.doi.org/10.1177/10659129030500301

Pehrson, S., Brown, R., & Zagefka, H. (2009). When does national identification lead to the rejection of immigrants? Cross-sectional and longitudinal evidence for the role of essentialist in-group definitions. *British Journal of Social Psychology, 48*, 61–76. http://dx.doi.org/10.1348/014466608X288827

Peng, K., & Nisbett, R. E. (1999). Culture, dialectics, and reasoning about contradictions. *American Psychologist, 54*, 741–754. http://dx.doi.org/10.1037/0003-066X.54.9.741

Perry, E. J. (2001). Challenging the mandate of heaven: Popular protest in modern China. *Critical Asian Studies, 33*, 163–180. http://dx.doi.org/10.1080/14672710122544

Pettigrew, T. F., & Tropp, L. R. (2006). A meta-analytic test of intergroup contact theory. *Journal of Personality and Social Psychology, 90*, 751–783. http://dx.doi.org/10.1037/0022-3514.90.5.751

Pettigrew, T. F., & Tropp, L. R. (2008). How does intergroup contact reduce prejudice? Meta-analytic tests of three mediators. *European Journal of Social Psychology, 38*, 922–934. http://dx.doi.org/10.1002/ejsp.504

Pettigrew, T. F., & Tropp, L. R. (2013). *When groups meet: The dynamics of intergroup contact.* New York, NY: Psychology Press.

Pettigrew, T. F., Tropp, L. R., Wagner, U., & Christ, O. (2011). Recent advances in intergroup contact theory. *International Journal of Intercultural Relations, 35*, 271–280. http://dx.doi.org/10.1016/j.ijintrel.2011.03.001

Petty, R. E., & Cacioppo, J. T. (1986). *Communication and persuasion: Central and peripheral routes to change.* New York, NY: Springer. http://dx.doi.org/10.1007/978-1-4612-4964-1

Pew Research Center. (2014a, October 31). *The party of nonvoters: Younger, more racially diverse, more financially strapped.* Retrieved from http://www.people-press.org/2014/10/31/the-party-of-nonvoters-2/

Pew Research Center. (2014b, November 13). *Public trust in government: 1958–2014.* Retrieved from http://www.people-press.org/2014/11/13/public-trust-in-government/

Phelps, J. M., Eilertsen, D. E., Türken, S., & Ommundsen, R. (2011). Integrating immigrant minorities: Developing a scale to measure majority members' attitudes toward their own proactive efforts. *Scandinavian Journal of Psychology, 52,* 404–410. http://dx.doi.org/10.1111/j.1467-9450.2011.00876.x

Phillips, D. (2010). Minority ethnic segregation, integration and citizenship: A European perspective. *Journal of Ethnic and Migration Studies, 36,* 209–225. http://dx.doi.org/10.1080/13691830903387337

Phillips-Fein, K. (2009). *Invisible hands: The making of the conservative movement from the New Deal to Reagan.* New York, NY: Norton.

Piaget, J. (1965). *The moral judgment of the child* (M. Gabain, Trans.). New York, NY: Free Press. (Original work published 1932)

Piaget, J. (1970). *Structuralism* (C. Maschler, Trans.). New York, NY: Basic Books.

Piketty, T. (2014). *Capital in the twenty-first century* (A. Goldhammer, Trans.). Cambridge, MA: Belknap Press.

Pinker, S. (2011). *The better angels of our nature: Why violence has declined.* New York, NY: Viking.

Pinkney, R. (2005). *The frontiers of democracy: Challenges in the West, the East and the Third World.* Aldershot, England: Ashgate.

Plato. (1954). *The last days of Socrates* (H. Tredennick, Trans.). Harmondsworth, England: Penguin Books.

Plato. (1987). *The republic* (D. Lee, Trans.). Harmondsworth, England: Penguin Books.

Polleta, F. (2013). Participatory democracy in the New Millennium. *Contemporary Sociology: A Journal of Review, 42,* 40–50.

Polleys, M. S. (2002). One university's response to the anti-leadership vaccine: Developing servant leaders. *Journal of Leadership & Organizational Studies, 8,* 117–130. http://dx.doi.org/10.1177/107179190200800310

Polo, M. (1958). *The travels* (R. Latham, Trans.). London, England: Penguin.

Popper, K. R. (1966). *The open society and its enemies.* Princeton, NJ: Princeton University Press.

Porter, S., & ten Brinke, L. (2009). Dangerous decisions: A theoretical framework for understanding how judges assess credibility in the courtroom. *Legal and Criminological Psychology, 14,* 119–134. http://dx.doi.org/10.1348/135532508X281520

Posner, R. A. (2008). *How judges think*. Cambridge, MA: Harvard University Press.

Przeworski, A. (2009). Conquered or granted? A history of suffrage extensions. *British Journal of Political Science, 39*, 291–321. http://dx.doi.org/10.1017/S0007123408000434

Przeworski, A., & Limongi, F. (1993). Political regimes and economic growth. *Journal of Economic Perspectives, 7*, 51–69. http://dx.doi.org/10.1257/jep.7.3.51

Putnam, R. D. (1993). *Making democracy work: Civic traditions in modern Italy*. Princeton, NJ: Princeton University Press.

Putnam, R. D. (2001). *Bowling alone: The collapse and revival of American community*. New York, NY: Simon & Schuster.

Quoidbach, J., Gilbert, D. T., & Wilson, T. D. (2013). The end of history illusion. *Science, 339*, 96–98. http://dx.doi.org/10.1126/science.1229294

Raff, D. (1988). *A history of Germany from the medieval empire to the present* (B. Little, Trans.). Oxford, England: Berg.

Ramirez, F. O., Soysal, Y., & Shanahan, S. (1997). The changing logic of political citizenship: Cross-national acquisition of women's suffrage rights, 1890–1990. *American Sociological Review, 62*, 735–745. http://dx.doi.org/10.2307/2657357

Rancière, J. (2014). *Hatred of democracy* (S. Corcoran, Trans.). London, England: Verso.

Rawls, J. (1971). *A theory of justice*. Cambridge, MA: Harvard University Press.

Redlawsk, D. P. (2002). Hot cognition or cool consideration? Testing the effects of motivated reasoning on political decision making. *Journal of Politics, 64*, 1021–1044. http://dx.doi.org/10.1111/1468-2508.00161

Redlawsk, D. P., Civettini, A. J. W., & Emmerson, K. M. (2010). The affective tipping point: Do motivated reasoners ever "get it"? *Political Psychology, 31*, 563–593. http://dx.doi.org/10.1111/j.1467-9221.2010.00772.x

Rice, R. E. (Ed.). (2008). *Media ownership: Research and regulation*. Cresskill, NJ: Hampton Press.

Riggs, W. (2010). Open-mindedness. *Metaphilosophy, 41*, 172–188.

Rodrik, D., Subramanian, A., & Trebbi, F. (2004). Institutional rule: The primacy of institutions over geography and integration in economic development. *Journal of Economic Growth, 9*, 131–165. http://dx.doi.org/10.1023/B:JOEG.0000031425.72248.85

Roemer, J. E. (1999). Does democracy engender justice? In I. Shapiro & C. Hacker-Cordón (Eds.), *Democracy's values* (pp. 56–68). Cambridge, England: Cambridge University Press.

Rogers, C. R. (1951). *Client-centered therapy*. Boston, MA: Houghton Mifflin.

Rogers, C. R. (1957). The necessary and sufficient conditions of therapeutic personality change. *Journal of Consulting Psychology, 21*, 95–103. http://dx.doi.org/10.1037/h0045357

Rorty, R. (1997). Justice as a larger loyalty. In R. Bontekoe & M. Stepaniants (Eds.), *Justice and democracy: Cross-cultural perspectives* (pp. 9–22). Honolulu: University of Hawaii Press.

Rosenthal, L., Levy, S. R., Katser, M., & Bazile, C. (in press). Polyculturalism and attitudes toward Muslim Americans. *Peace and Conflict*.

Rule, N. O., & Ambady, N. (2010). First impressions of the face: Predicting success. *Social and Personality Psychology Compass, 4*, 506–516. http://dx.doi.org/10.1111/j.1751-9004.2010.00282.x

Rule, N. O., Moran, J. M., Freeman, J. B., Whitfield-Gabrieli, S., Gabrieli, J. D., & Ambady, N. (2011). Face value: Amygdala response reflects the validity of first impressions. *NeuroImage, 54*, 734–741. http://dx.doi.org/10.1016/j.neuroimage.2010.07.007

Runciman, D. (2008). *Political hypocrisy: The mask of power, from Hobbes to Orwell and beyond*. Princeton, NJ: Princeton University Press.

Runciman, D. (2009). How messy it all is. *London Review of Books, 31*(20), 3–6.

Runciman, D. (2013). *The confidence trap: A history of democracy in crisis from World War I to the present*. Princeton, NJ: Princeton University Press.

Russell, P. H. (2001). Conclusion: Judicial independence in comparative perspective. In P. H. Russell & D. M. O'Brien (Eds.), *Judicial independence in the age of democracy: Critical perspectives from around the world* (pp. 301–307). Charlottesville: University Press of Virginia.

Saltkjel, T., & Malmberg-Heimonen, I. (2014). Social inequalities, social trust and civic participation—The case of Norway. *European Journal of Social Work, 17*, 118–134. http://dx.doi.org/10.1080/13691457.2013.789004

Sarat, A. (2008). Contested terrain: Visions of multiculturalism in an American town. In M. Minow, R. A. Shweder, & H. Markus (Eds.), *Just schools: Pursuing equality in societies of difference* (pp. 101–131). New York, NY: Russell Sage Foundation.

Schlesinger, A. M. (1998). *The disunity of America: Reflections on a multicultural society*. New York, NY: Norton.

Schmidt, V. A. (2009). Re-envisioning the European Union: Identity, democracy, economy. *Journal of Common Market Studies, 47*, 17–42. http://dx.doi.org/10.1111/j.1468-5965.2009.02012.x

Schug, J., Yuki, M., Horikawa, H., & Takemura, K. (2009). Similarity attraction and actually selecting similar others: How cross-societal differences in relational mobility affect interpersonal similarity in Japan and the USA. *Asian Journal of Social Psychology, 12*, 95–103. http://dx.doi.org/10.1111/j.1467-839X.2009.01277.x

Schumpeter, J. A. (2010). *Capitalism, socialism, and democracy*. London, England: Routledge. (Original work published 1942)

Seeley, T. D. (2010). *Honeybee democracy*. Princeton, NJ: Princeton University Press.

Sen, A. K. (1977). "Rational fools": A critique of the behavioral foundations of economic theory. *Philosophy & Public Affairs, 6*, 317–344.

Sen, A. K. (1999). *Development as freedom*. New York, NY: Knopf.

Sen, A., & Drèze, J. (2013). *An uncertain glory: India and its contradictions*. Princeton, NJ: Princeton University Press.

Shaker, P., & Hellman, E. (2008). *Reclaiming education for democracy: Thinking beyond No Child Left Behind*. New York, NY: Routledge.

Shapiro, I., & Hacker-Cordón, C. (1999). Promises and disappointments: Reconsidering democracy's values. In I. Shapiro & C. Hacker-Cordón (Eds.), *Democracy's values* (pp. 1–20). Cambridge, England: Cambridge University Press.

Sharp, E. B. (2012). Citizen participation at the local level. In H. L. Schachter & K. Yang (Eds.), *The state of citizen participation in America* (pp. 101–129). Charlotte, NC: Information Age.

Sherif, M. (1936). *The psychology of social norms*. New York, NY: Harper.

Shore, T., Sy, T., & Strauss, J. (2006). Leader responsiveness, equity sensitivity, and employee attitudes and behavior. *Journal of Business and Psychology, 21*, 227–241. http://dx.doi.org/10.1007/s10869-006-9026-5

Shweder, R. (1991). *Thinking through cultures: Expeditions in cultural psychology*. Cambridge, MA: Harvard University Press.

Sirin, S. R. (2005). Socioeconomic status and academic achievement: A meta-analytic review of research. *Review of Educational Research, 75*, 417–453. http://dx.doi.org/10.3102/00346543075003417

Skinner, B. F. (1962). *Walden two*. New York, NY: Macmillan. (Original work published 1948)

Skinner, B. F. (1971). *Beyond freedom and dignity*. New York, NY: Knopf.

Smith, A. D. (1995). *Nations and nationalism in a global era*. Cambridge, England: Polity Press.

Smith, A., & Porter, D. (Eds.). (2004). *Sport and national identity in the post-war world*. New York, NY: Taylor & Francis.

Sol Hart, P., & Nisbet, E. C. (2012). Boomerang effects in science communication: How motivated reasoning and identity cues amplify opinion polarization about climate mitigation policies. *Communication Research, 39*, 701–723. http://dx.doi.org/10.1177/0093650211416646

Son Hing, L. S., Bobocel, D. R., Zanna, M. P., Garcia, D. M., Gee, S. S., & Orazietti, K. (2011). The merit of meritocracy. *Journal of Personality and Social Psychology, 101*, 433–450. http://dx.doi.org/10.1037/a0024618

Sophocles. (1977). *The Oedipus cycle* (D. Fitts & R. Fitzgerald, Trans.). New York, NY: Harvest/HBJ.

Sophocles. (1994). *Antigone* (H. Lloyd-Jones, Trans.). Cambridge, MA: Harvard University Press. (Original work published 442 BC)

Sparks, P., & Durkin, K. (1987). Moral reasoning and political orientation: The context sensitivity of individual rights and democratic principles. *Journal of Personality and Social Psychology, 52*, 931–936. http://dx.doi.org/10.1037/0022-3514.52.5.931

Spears, L. C. (Ed.). (1998). *Insights on leadership: Service, stewardship, spirit and servant-leadership*. New York, NY: Wiley.

Spencer-Rodgers, J., Williams, M. J., & Peng, K. (2010). Cultural differences in expectations of change and tolerance for contradiction: A decade of empirical research. *Personality and Social Psychology Review, 14,* 296–312. http://dx.doi.org/10.1177/1088868310362982

Stadelmann-Steffen, I., & Freitag, M. (2011). Making civil society work: Models of democracy and their impact on civil engagement. *Nonprofit and Voluntary Sector Quarterly, 40,* 526–551. http://dx.doi.org/10.1177/0899764010362114

Stavrositu, C. D. (2014). Does TV viewing cultivate meritocratic beliefs? Implications for life satisfaction. *Mass Communication & Society, 17,* 148–171. http://dx.doi.org/10.1080/15205436.2013.816741

Steffensmeier, D., & Britt, C. L. (2001). Judges' race and judicial decision making: Do Black judges sentence differently? *Social Science Quarterly, 82,* 749–764. http://dx.doi.org/10.1111/0038-4941.00057

Stepan, A., & Linz, J. J. (2013). Democratization theory and the Arab Spring. *Journal of Democracy, 24,* 15–30. http://dx.doi.org/10.1353/jod.2013.0032

Stiglitz, J. E. (2012). *The price of inequality.* New York, NY: Norton.

Stockemer, D., LaMontagne, B., & Scruggs, L. (2013). Bribes and ballots: The impact of corruption on voter turnout in democracies. *International Political Science Review, 34,* 74–90. http://dx.doi.org/10.1177/0192512111419824

Sullivan, J. L., & Transue, J. E. (1999). The psychological underpinnings of democracy: A selective review of research on political tolerance, interpersonal trust, and social capital. *Annual Review of Psychology, 50,* 625–650. http://dx.doi.org/10.1146/annurev.psych.50.1.625

Sunshine, J., & Tyler, T. R. (2003). The role of procedural justice and legitimacy in shaping public support for policing. *Law & Society Review, 37,* 513–548. http://dx.doi.org/10.1111/1540-5893.3703002

Sveiby, K. E. (2011). Collective leadership with power symmetry: Lessons from Aboriginal prehistory. *Leadership, 7,* 385–414. http://dx.doi.org/10.1177/1742715011416892

Szasz, T. S. (1961). *The myth of mental illness.* New York, NY: Delta Books.

Taber, C. S., & Lodge, M. (2006). Motivated skepticism in the evaluation of political beliefs. *American Journal of Political Science, 50,* 755–769. http://dx.doi.org/10.1111/j.1540-5907.2006.00214.x

Tajfel, H. (1978). Social categorization, social identity and social comparison. In H. Tajfel (Ed.), *Differentiation between social groups* (pp. 61–76). London, England: Academic Press.

Tajfel, H., Billig, M. G., Bundy, R. P., & Flament, C. (1971). Social categorization and intergroup behavior. *European Journal of Social Psychology, 1,* 149–178. http://dx.doi.org/10.1002/ejsp.2420010202

Tajfel, H., & Turner, J. C. (1979). An integrative theory of intergroup conflict. In W. G. Austen & S. Worchel (Eds.), *The social psychology of intergroup relations* (pp. 33–47). Monterey, CA: Brooks/Cole.

Talbot, I. (2009). *Pakistan: A modern history*. London, England: Hurst.

Tamanaha, B. Z. (2004). *On the rule of law: History, politics, theory*. Cambridge, England: Cambridge University Press. http://dx.doi.org/10.1017/CBO9780511812378

Taylor, D. M., & Moghaddam, F. M. (1994). *Theories of intergroup relations: International social psychological perspectives* (2nd ed.). Westport, CT: Praeger.

Taylor, F. W. (1911). *Principles of scientific management*. New York, NY: Harper & Row.

Tee, E. Y. J., Paulsen, N., & Ashkanasy, N. M. (2013). Revisiting followership through a social identity perspective: The role of collective follower emotion and action. *Leadership Quarterly, 24*, 902–918. http://dx.doi.org/10.1016/j.leaqua.2013.10.002

ten Dam, G., & Volman, M. (2004). Critical thinking as a citizenship competence: Teaching strategies. *Learning and Instruction, 14*, 359–379. http://dx.doi.org/10.1016/j.learninstruc.2004.01.005

Teixeira, R. A. (1992). *The disappearing American voter*. Washington, DC: Brookings Institute.

Thibaut, J., & Walker, L. (1975). *Procedural justice*. Hillsdale, NJ: Erlbaum.

Thomas, P. N. (2004). Agendas for research and strategies for intervention. In P. N. Thomas & Z. Nain (Eds.), *Who owns the media? Global trends and local resistances* (pp. 293–305). London, England: Zed Books.

Thompson, D. F. (2011). Representing future generations: Political presentism and democratic trusteeship. In M. Matravers & L. H. Meyer (Eds.), *Democracy, equality, and justice* (pp. 17–35). London, England: Routledge.

Thoreau, H. D. (2008). *Walden, civil disobedience and other writings* (3rd ed.; W. J. Rossi, Ed.). New York, NY: Norton.

Tiede, L. B. (2006). Judicial independence: Often cited, rarely understood. *Journal of Contemporary Legal Issues, 15*, 129–161.

Todorov, A., Mandisodza, A. N., Goren, A., & Hall, C. C. (2005). Inferences of competence from faces predict election outcomes. *Science, 308*, 1623–1626. http://dx.doi.org/10.1126/science.1110589

Tonry, M. (2010). The social, psychological, and political causes of racial disparities in the American criminal justice system. *Crime and Justice, 39*, 273–312. http://dx.doi.org/10.1086/653045

Tropp, L. R., & Pettigrew, T. F. (2005). Relationships between intergroup contact and prejudice among minority and majority status groups. *Psychological Science, 16*, 951–957. http://dx.doi.org/10.1111/j.1467-9280.2005.01643.x

Trudeau, P. E. (1992). Statement by the Prime Minister in the House of Commons, October 8, 1971. In *Multiculturalism in Canada: The challenge of diversity* (pp. 281–283). Scarborough, Ontario, Canada: Nelson Canada. (Original work published 1971)

Turner, J. C. (2005). Explaining the nature of power: A three-process theory. *European Journal of Social Psychology, 35,* 1–22. http://dx.doi.org/10.1002/ejsp.244

Tversky, A., & Kahneman, D. (1974). Judgment under uncertainty: Heuristics and biases. *Science, 185,* 1124–1131. http://dx.doi.org/10.1126/science.185.4157.1124

Tyler, T. R. (1987). Procedural justice research. *Social Justice Research, 1,* 41–65. http://dx.doi.org/10.1007/BF01049383

United Nations. (1948). *Universal declaration of human rights.* Retrieved from http://www.un.org/en/documents/udhr/

United Nations. (2011). *United Nations rule of law indicators: Implementation guide and project tools.* New York, NY: Author.

Uslaner, E. (2002). *The moral foundations of trust.* New York, NY: Cambridge University Press.

van Dick, R., Tissington, P. A., & Hertel, G. (2009). Do many hands make light work? How to overcome social loafing and gain motivation in work teams. *European Business Review, 21,* 233–245. http://dx.doi.org/10.1108/09555340910956621

Varga, C. (Ed.). (1992a). *Comparative legal cultures.* New York: New York University Press.

Varga, C. (1992b). Lenin and the revolutionary law-making. In C. Varga (Ed.), *Comparative legal cultures* (pp. 515–527). New York: New York University Press. (Original work published 1982)

Vicente, P. C., & Wantchekon, L. (2009). Clientelism and vote buying: Lessons from field experiments in African elections. *Oxford Review of Economic Policy, 25,* 292–305. http://dx.doi.org/10.1093/oxrep/grp018

Vidmar, N. (2011). The psychology of trial judging. *Current Directions in Psychological Science, 20,* 58–62.

Villa-Vicencio, C. (2009). *Walk with us and listen: Political reconciliation in Africa.* Washington, DC: Georgetown University Press.

Vygotsky, L. S. (1978). *Thought and language.* Cambridge, MA: MIT Press.

Wachs, T. D., & Kohnstamm, G. A. (Eds.). (2001). *Temperament and context.* Mahwah, NJ: Erlbaum.

Wagner, U., Becker, J. C., Christ, O., Pettigrew, T. F., & Schmidt, P. (2012). A longitudinal test of the relation between German nationalism, patriotism, and outgroup derogation. *European Sociological Review, 28,* 319–332. http://dx.doi.org/10.1093/esr/jcq066

Wantchekon, L. (2003). Clientelism and voting behavior. *World Politics, 55,* 399–422. http://dx.doi.org/10.1353/wp.2003.0018

Warren, M. E. (1993). Can participatory democracy produce better selves? Psychological dimensions of Habermass's discursive model of democracy. *Political Psychology, 14,* 209–234. http://dx.doi.org/10.2307/3791409

Wegner, D. M. (2002). *The illusion of conscious will.* Cambridge, MA: MIT Press.

Wegner, D. M. (2005). Précis of the illusion of conscious will. *Behavioral and Brain Sciences, 27,* 649–659.

Weldon, S. A. (2006). The institutional context of tolerance for ethnic minorities: A comparative, multilevel analysis of Western Europe. *American Journal of Political Science, 50,* 331–349. http://dx.doi.org/10.1111/j.1540-5907.2006.00187.x

Wenzel, M., Okimoto, T. G., Feather, N. T., & Platow, M. J. (2008). Retributive and restorative justice. *Law and Human Behavior, 32,* 375–389. http://dx.doi.org/10.1007/s10979-007-9116-6

Westheimer, J., & Kahne, J. (2004). What kind of citizen? The politics of educating for democracy. *American Educational Research Journal, 41,* 237–269. http://dx.doi.org/10.3102/00028312041002237

Whitman, W. (1955). *Leaves of grass.* New York, NY: New American Library. (Original work published 1855)

Whitson, J. A., Liljenquist, K. A., Galinsky, A. D., Magee, J. C., Gruenfeld, D. H., & Cadena, B. (2013). The blind leading: Power reduces awareness of constraints. *Journal of Experimental Social Psychology, 49,* 579–582. http://dx.doi.org/10.1016/j.jesp.2012.10.009

Wilder, D. A., & Allen, V. L. (1978). Group membership and preference for information about others. *Personality and Social Psychology Bulletin, 4,* 106–110. http://dx.doi.org/10.1177/014616727800400122

Wiley, S., Deaux, K., & Hagelskamp, C. (2012). Born in the USA: How immigrant generation shapes meritocracy and its relation to ethnic identity and collective action. *Cultural Diversity and Ethnic Minority Psychology, 18,* 171–180. http://dx.doi.org/10.1037/a0027661

Wilkinson, R., & Pickett, K. (2009). *The spirit level: Why more equal societies almost always do better.* London, England: Allen Lane.

Wilkinson, R. G. (2005). *The impact of inequality: How to make sick societies healthier.* New York, NY: New Press.

Williams, K. D., & Karau, S. J. (1991). Social loafing and social compensation: The effects of expectations of co-worker performance. *Journal of Personality and Social Psychology, 61,* 570–581. http://dx.doi.org/10.1037/0022-3514.61.4.570

Wolff, R. (2012). *Democracy at work: A cure for capitalism.* Chicago, IL: Haymarket Books.

Wolff, R. P. (1970). *In defense of anarchism.* New York, NY: Harper Torchbooks.

Womack, J. (1968). *Zapata and the Mexican revolution.* New York, NY: Knopf.

Woo-Cumings, M. (1994). The "new authoritarianism" in East Asia. *Current History, 93,* 413–416.

Worchel, S. (1999). *Written in blood: Ethnic identity and the struggle for human harmony.* New York, NY: Worth.

Worthington, I. (2013). *Demosthenes of Athens and the fall of classical Greece.* New York, NY: Oxford University Press.

Wright, S. C., Aron, A., McLaughkin-Volpe, T., & Ropp, S. A. (1997). The extended contact effect: Knowledge of cross-group friendships and prejudice. *Journal of Personality and Social Psychology, 73*, 73–90.

Wright, S. C., Taylor, D. M., & Moghaddam, F. M. (1990). Responding to membership in a disadvantaged group: From acceptance to collective protest. *Journal of Personality and Social Psychology, 58*, 994–1003. http://dx.doi.org/10.1037/0022-3514.58.6.994

Wright, T. (Ed.). (2000). *The British political process: An introduction.* London, England: Routledge. http://dx.doi.org/10.4324/9780203408599

Wu, B., & Zheng, Y. (2008, February). *Expansion of higher education in China: Challenges and implications* (Briefing Series, Issue No. 36). Nottingham, England: University of Nottingham.

Wu, D. (2008). *William Hazlitt: The first modern man.* Oxford, England: Oxford University Press.

Wu, D. (Ed.). (2012). *Romanticism: An anthology* (4th ed.). Oxford, England: Wiley-Blackwell.

Young, M. D. (1994). *The rise of the meritocracy.* New Brunswick, NJ: Transaction. (Original work published 1958)

Zaret, D. (2000). *Origins of democratic culture.* Princeton, NJ: Princeton University Press.

Zavedei, B. (1956). *Democracy and dictatorship: Their social psychology.* New York, NY: Grove Press.

Zenasni, F., Besancon, M., & Lubart, T. (2008). Creativity and tolerance of ambiguity: An empirical study. *Journal of Creative Behavior, 42*, 61–73. http://dx.doi.org/10.1002/j.2162-6057.2008.tb01080.x

Zimbardo, P. (1972). Pathology of imprisonment. *Transactional/Society*, 4–8 (a).

Zimbardo, P. (2007). *The Lucifer effect: Understanding how good people turn evil.* New York, NY: Random House.

Zizek, S. (1991). *For they know not what they do.* London, England: Verso.

INDEX

239

Cooperation, 93–94

Cooter, R., 141

Coriolanus (Shakespeare), 151

Corruption, 104–107, 115, 162

Crick, B., 89

Crime and Punishment (Dostoevsky), 62–63

Critical questioning, 52

Critical thinking, 117–118

Cromwell, Oliver, 28

Cuba
    additive globalization in, 32
    censorship in, 119, 120
    collectivism in, 174
    support for workers' rights in, 143

Cultural context
    for social loafing, 172
    for treatment of minorities, 121–123

Cultural context of democracy, 23–44
    and globalization, 31–34, 36–39
    in Great Britain, 26–29
    in Iran, 39–43
    and social identity, 34–38
    in Switzerland, 29–31
    in United States, 23–25

Danziger, S., 147

Darwin, Charles, 64

Deaton, A., 189, 190

Deaux, K., 169

Decision making
    about morality and fairness, 6
    biases in, 84
    by democratic citizens, 53
    in groups, 106
    in independent judiciary, 141–148
    by voters and politicians, 16

Declaration of Independence, 58, 182

Deficit model of science, 157

Democracy(-ies), 3–20. *See also* Actualized democracy; Cultural context of democracy
    capitalist, 9, 17–18, 37, 97, 102
    context for, 21–22
    defined, 14–16
    direct, 14, 30–31
    divergent vs. convergent forms of, 32–34, 54
    emergence of contemporary, 7–11

    idealist vs. realist approaches to, 16–18
    psychology of, 4–7
    questioning the workings of, 11–14
    representative, 14, 30–31
    strong form of, 177

Democracy circle, 57–66
    and actualization of democracy, 63–65
    and attitudes vs. state practices in support of democracy, 59–61
    and collective–individual integration, 62–63
    components of, 10–11, 65–66
    and step-by-step vs. all-at-once adoption of democracy, 28, 57–59

Democracy–dictatorship continuum, 8–9, 19–20

Democratic actualization, 193–201. *See also* Actualized democracy
    challenges with, 196–197
    collective psychological journey to, 55
    in contemporary societies, 193–194
    and democracy circle, 63–65
    goal of, 197–198
    indicators of increasing, 194–196
    limitations on, 191–192
    principles of, 197–200

Democratic citizens, 45–54
    in ancient Greece, 46–48
    characteristics of, 10
    convictions/beliefs of, 50–54
    diversity for, 37, 53
    educating, 162–163
    and Stanley Milgram's obedience studies, 45–46
    psychological skills of, 58–59, 66
    values/activities of, 48–50
    views of political participation by, 185

Democratic dictatorships, 153

Descriptive meritocracy, 166–167, 169–171

Dewey, John, 162

Diamond, Jared M., 81–82

Diamond, L. J., 198–199

Dictatorship(s)
    antidemocratic sentiment in, 60
    charismatic leaders in support of, 55–56

on democracy–dictatorship
continuum, 8–9, 19–20
democratic, 153
educational system in, 160–162
in Iran, 39–43
movement between democracy and,
13–14, 61
temporary, 44
violence in, 161
Direct democracy, 14, 30–31
Discrimination, 170–171, 192
Distinctiveness, of identity, 77
Distributive justice, 72, 180–182
Divergent democracy, 32–34, 54
Diversity
democratic citizens' view of, 37, 53
policies for managing, 123, 130,
134–136
and psychology of democracy, 6
and sense of self, 194
Divine right, 96
Dodd, M. D., 156
Donne, John, 54
Dostoevsky, F., 62
Double-democracy, 31
Druckman, J. N., 151
Duelfer, Charles, 156
Duties, 96–97

East Asians, 50
Easterlin, Richard, 188
Economic incentives, 73
Economic inequalities, 17–18
Education system
critical thinking in, 117–118
and democratic actualization, 4,
160–163, 200
inequalities in, 133
minority groups' participation in, 130
Edwards, M., *xi–xii*
Egypt
Arab Spring in, 38
motivations of leaders in, 78
movement toward less openness in,
47, 61
Muslim Brotherhood in, 13
power transfers in, 197
Eliot, George, 97–98
Elite, entrenched, 100–102
Ellickson, R. C., 88

Embryonic fallacy, 64
Emotions, political candidates' appeals
to, 150
Empathic listening, 116–117
Empowerment, 118
England. *See also* Great Britain; United
Kingdom
influence of, on Third World,
139–140
middle class in, 98
removal of leaders in, 94
responsiveness of leaders in, 68
social mobility in, 102
Englich, B., 147
English Defense League, 12
English Parliament, 68
English Revolution, 27
Entrenched elite, 100–102
Equality, political, 198–199
Equality of opportunity, 185–187
Equal rights movements, 170
Equity theory, 180–181
Esposito, John, 43
Ethics, personal, 79–81
Ethnic revivals, 130
Ethnocentrism, 5, 12, 52
European Union. *See also* Western
Europe; *specific countries*
collective identity threat in, 36–37
democratic actualization in, 193
questioning of democracy in, 12
race relations in, 192
Switzerland in, 29
treatment of Muslims in, 124
Experiences, for democratic citizens,
53–54
Exploitation, 122, 140
Expression, freedom of. *See* Freedom of
expression
Extended contact, 127

Fairness
decision making about, 6
in international context, 86–90
and procedural justice, 72, 182–184
False consciousness, 77, 111–112, 125,
170
False meritocracy, 166–171
Farrelly, C., 182
The Federalist Papers, 138–139

Justice, 48, 177–192
and democracy, 177–179
distributive, 72, 180–182
as equality of opportunity, 185–187
as happiness, 187–189
and power, 140
procedural, 72–75, 182–185
and psychology of democracy, 5–6
restorative, 185
retributive, 185
rule of law and, 140
and servant leadership, 72
and social identity, 73–75
subjective, 180
and trust, 178–179, 189–190
varieties of, 179–185
Justification
for group-based inequalities,
111–112
for leadership, 96, 98–103

Kahne, J., 160
Kahneman, D., 83, 84, 155, 189, 190
Kamp, A., 125
Kansas, voting in, 125
Kant, Immanuel, 145
Keane, J., 62
Kennedy, John F., 105
Khamenei, Ali, 42
Khomeini, Ruhollah
corruption under, 104
dictatorship established by, 42, 65,
118
in Iran–Iraq war, 113, 114
legal system under, 86
tolerance of minority groups under,
123
violation of logical social contract
by, 95–96
on women's right to vote, 39
King, Martin Luther, Jr., 80
King Lear (Shakespeare), 70
Kohlberg, L., 53, 141–142
Kohlberg model of moral development,
141–142, 144–145
Kraus, P. A., 134
Kruglanski, A. W., 50
Kuklinski, J. H., 156
Kurdish independence movement,
130

Laboring, social, 7, 173–174
Labor unions, 143
Ladner, A., 30
Laing, R. D., 85
Laitin, D. D., 124
Lalonde, R. N., 126
Lamiell, J. T., 126
LaMontagne, B., 183
Languages, official, 133
Laos, 34
Latin America, 197
LaVaque-Manty, M., 167
Law. *See also* Rule of law
black-letter, 180
civil, 88
common law, 88
formal, 5, 79–81
interpretations of, 88
socialist, 88
Laypersons, moral decision making by,
146–148
Leaders
accountability of, 103–107
charismatic, 55–56, 72
cooperation with, 93–94
motivations of, 70–71
personality of, 107
relationship of followers and, 75,
96–98
removability of. *See* Removability of
leaders
responsiveness of. *See*
Responsiveness of leaders
in support of dictatorship, 55–56
Leadership
in actualized democracies, 5
in democracy circle, 65
in identity construction, 75–77
justifications for, 96, 98–103
prodemocracy, 56, 61
servant, 71–75
Learning
democratic citizens' view of, 52–53
of official languages, 133
Legal pluralism, 87–88
Legal uniformity, 87–88
Leighley, J. E., 154
Leiserowitz, A. A., 157
Lenin, Vladimir, 44, 86
Leonardo da Vinci, 64

as motivation of leaders, 70–71
and responsiveness of leaders, 68
Prejudice, 128
Prescriptive meritocracy, 166–167, 170
Priestly, Joseph, 112, 114
Priming, 132
The Prince (Machiavelli), 93–94
Principled decision making, 53
Procedural justice, 72–75, 182–185
Prodemocracy leadership, 56, 61
Progress, measuring, 7, 185
Psychoanalytic theory, 83–84
Psychological skills, of democratic
citizens, 58–59, 66
Psychology of democracy, 4–7
Putin, Vladimir, 13, 107, 160
Putnam, R. D., 184, 190

Questioning, 11–14
Quirk, P. J., 156

Race, discrimination based on, 171, 192
Racial profiling, 83–84
Ramirez, F. O., 58
Rancière, J., 151
Randazzo, K. A., 148
Randomness, of social mobility, 103
Rationality
assumption of, 82–84
of social contract, 95–96
Rationality–affect–motivation triangle,
158
Rational voters, 149, 151, 155–158
Rawls, J., 95, 145, 185
Reagan, Ronald, 85, 138, 143
Realist approaches
to examining societies, 16–18
to responsiveness of leaders, 67–68
Reasoning, motivated, 156–158, 163
Redlawsk, D. P., 158
Reifler, J., 157
Relative deprivation theory, 181
Relativism, 89–90, 106–107, 135
Religion, leadership justification with,
98–99
Religiosity, 132
Religious conflicts, in Switzerland, 30
Religious fundamentalism, 12–13,
39, 89–90. *See also* Islamic
fundamentalism

Religious taxes, 40–41
Removability of leaders, 93–108
and accountability, 104–107
and justifications for leadership,
98–103
prior to modern democracies, 93–94
and the social contract, 94–98
Representative democracy, 14, 30–31
Representative heuristic, 147
The Republic (Plato), 79–80, 94, 99
Republican Guards, 140
Resource inequalities
and democratic actualization, 198
in divergent democracies, 54
and happiness, 187–188
and health, 186–187
increases in, 195
and trust, 190
Respect, 131–132
Responsibility, personal, 129, 167
Responsiveness of leaders, 67–78
in early societies, 69–70
and leadership's role in identity
construction, 75–77
in monarchies, 93–94
and motivations of leaders, 70–71
realist vs. idealist approach to, 67–68
and servant leadership, 71–75
Restorative justice, 185
Retributive justice, 185
Revolution in the British Isles, 28
Revolutions
changes made after, 191–192
and logical social contract, 96
manipulations of social comparisons
in, 181
use of legal system for ideological
goals after, 86
Reza Shah, 39
Richard, S. F., 153–155
Richard III (Shakespeare), 70
Rights. *See also* Human rights; Minority
rights
in social relationships, 97–98
voting, 152–154
Risala, 40
Roberts, John G., 115, 120
Rodrik, D., 81
Roemer, John E., 177
Rogers, C. R., 116

ABOUT THE AUTHOR

Fathali M. Moghaddam, PhD, is a professor of psychology at Georgetown University, and editor-in-chief of *Peace and Conflict: Journal of Peace Psychology*. He is also director of the interdisciplinary program in cognitive science at Georgetown. Dr. Moghaddam was born in Iran, educated from an early age in England, and worked for the United Nations and McGill University before joining Georgetown University in 1990. His research focus includes the psychological changes required to move from dictatorship to democracy, a topic he studied for 5 years in postrevolution Iran, when he returned there in 1979. His most recent books include *Psychology for the Third Millennium* (2012, with Rom Harré), *The Psychology of Friendship and Enmity* (two volumes, 2013, with Rom Harré), and *The Psychology of Dictatorship* (2013), which received an honorable mention from the American Publishers Awards for Professional and Scholarly Excellence PROSE Awards. He currently is editing the two-volume *Encyclopedia of Political Behavior*.